BROTHERS in VALOR

BROTHERS
in VALOR

BATTLEFIELD STORIES OF THE
89 AFRICAN AMERICANS AWARDED
THE MEDAL OF HONOR

ROBERT F. JEFFERSON JR.

LYONS
PRESS

GUILFORD, CONNECTICUT

For Mario Spencer, Sofia, Gabriella, Logan, and my growing number of nieces and nephews. To much is given, much is expected.

An imprint of Globe Pequot, the trade division of
The Rowman & Littlefield Publishing Group, Inc.
4501 Forbes Blvd., Ste. 200
Lanham, MD 20706
www.rowman.com

Distributed by NATIONAL BOOK NETWORK

British Library Cataloguing in Publication Information available

Library of Congress Cataloging-in-Publication Data

Names: Jefferson, Robert F., 1963- author.
Title: Brothers in valor : battlefield stories of the 89 African Americans
   awarded the Medal of Honor / Robert F. Jefferson Jr.
Description: Guilford, Connecticut : Lyons Press, [2019] | Includes
   bibliographical references and index.
Identifiers: LCCN 2018022647 (print) | LCCN 2018035127 (ebook) | ISBN
   9781493031740 (hardback : alk. paper) | ISBN 9781493031757 (e-book)
Subjects: LCSH: African American soldiers—Biography. | United States—Armed
   Forces—African Americans—Biography. | Medal of Honor—Biography.
Classification: LCC E185.63 (ebook) | LCC E185.63 .J44 2019 (print) | DDC
   355.0092/396073 [B]—dc23
LC record available at https://lccn.loc.gov/2018022647

ISBN 9781493060832 (paperback)

∞™ The paper used in this publication meets the minimum requirements of American National Standard for Information Sciences—Permanence of Paper for Printed Library Materials, ANSI/NISO Z39.48-1992.

CONTENTS

Foreword

Definitions of honor and service are always changing, perhaps never more so than in our world today. We face a wide range of enemies, arguably more complex than those confronted by the heroes we meet in *Brothers in Valor: Battlefield Stories of the 89 African Americans Awarded the Medal of Honor*. Yet the lessons we can learn from this volume are profound and timeless.

African Americans have served in the US military with great distinction throughout our nation's history, defending American freedom. Here, Robert Jefferson introduces us to the remarkable black soldiers who have been recognized with the military's highest award. Each soldier played a part in shaping the very definition of courage during the fiercest moments in our military past. Their acts of valor have forever marked the American portrait, and provide us with a rich source of inspiration.

The quest for honor among African Americans in the military has been deeply intertwined with race relations. The soldiers vividly portrayed in these accounts showed just as much courage in their daily lives as they did on the battlefield. Jefferson's narrative reveals how these men resisted segregation and discrimination in both the military and in society as they pursued their dreams of equality. He also offers a detailed exploration of ever-changing military policy and presidential politics, and the roles they played in defining honor through the years.

In one such account, Jefferson describes a White House ceremony in 1966 where President Lyndon Baines Johnson declared that the Medal of Honor was "bestowed for courage demonstrated not in blindly overlooking danger, but in meeting it with eyes clearly open." This is the powerful message the author conveys throughout *Brothers in Valor*, and something I truly believe in.

In 1966 I was earning my pilot's wings, after which I flew more than a hundred combat missions as a member of the 557th Tactical Fighter Squadron at Cam Ranh Bay, Vietnam. I was always conscious of the presence of danger during the Vietnam War, and certainly developed my ideas about bravery and service during my time as a fighter pilot. After my combat duty, I earned a master's and a PhD in aerospace engineering, and in 1979, I was chosen to become a NASA astronaut. I continued to hone my understanding of service while participating in several space shuttle flights, becoming the first African American in space in 1983, as a mission specialist on the Orbiter *Challenger*. It's been a privilege to serve my country, and I'm proud to share my story with others, including African-American children who aspire to be scientists, engineers, and astronauts.

I share Robert Jefferson's belief that courage and service should be revered. In this book, he honors a group of soldiers who embody these qualities, providing a comprehensive and inspiring history of how they not only served their country, but also paved the way for all who seek equality and freedom. Just as important, he makes us consider our own impact on the world around us. How can we translate bravery into action in the future? Hopefully, with our eyes wide open.

—Col. Guion S. Bluford Jr., PhD, US Air Force (Ret.),
NASA astronaut (Ret.) May 2018

Introduction

Entering the Pantheon of Heroes

UNCOVERING WAR AND HONORING AFRICAN-AMERICAN SOLDIERS

For conspicuous gallantry and intrepidity at the risk of life, above and beyond the call of duty, in action involving actual conflict with an opposing armed force.

—Senate Committee on Veterans' Affairs, Medal of Honor Recipients, 1863

Before his death in 1906, noted essayist and poet luminary Paul Laurence Dunbar penned "The Colored Soldiers," a literary paean commemorating the gallant exploits of men who risked all for a nation that seemed to be in the throes of historical forgetfulness. In his poetry, Dunbar captured the heroic sacrifice made by African-American GIs. These heroes rushed to the nation's colors to protect and defend a fledgling democracy that repeatedly teetered throughout history. For Dunbar, this dirge of poetic magic reflected his own military service, as well as the personal and political struggle for citizenship.

Born in Dayton, Ohio, in 1872, Dunbar was the son of former slaves and a direct descendant to the cause of freedom. He grew up in a household where his father, Joshua Dunbar, told him endless stories of how he had escaped from the bonds of slavery in Kentucky and had promptly headed north, where he joined the famed Massachusetts 55th Regiment during the Civil War. Afterward, Joshua moved to Dayton, Ohio, where he not only taught himself to read and write, but also elevated his family to middle-class status in the city.[1] Remaining forever alert to the important contributions that blacks made militarily toward safeguarding the nation, Dunbar spent his adult life illuminating his father's accomplishments, and the bravery of his father's comrades in the face of fierce foreign and domestic enemy fire.

In "The Colored Soldiers," Dunbar aptly captures the selfless bravery that blacks acted upon during moments of war where they would, knowingly or not, live to enjoy the medals and adulation commemorating their deeds during the fiercest battles of the Civil War:

Ah, they rallied to the standard
To uphold it by their might;
None were stronger in the labors,
None were braver in the fight.
From the blazing breach of Wagner
To the plains of Olustee,
They were foremost in the fight
Of the battles of the free.

And their deeds shall find a record
In the registry of Fame;
For their blood has cleansed completely
Every blot of Slavery's shame.
So all honor and all glory
To those noble sons of Ham—
The gallant colored soldiers
Who fought for Uncle Sam![2]

Thirty years later, W. E. B. Du Bois, preeminent scholar-activist-intellectual of the twentieth century, punctuated Dunbar's assessment of black grace under fire during the Civil War. In 1935, Du Bois published his tour de force, *Black Reconstruction in America*, in which he commented on black Americans who took up arms in defense of freedom and democracy during the Civil War. Du Bois rendered a stinging indictment of the nation's insistence upon questioning the fitness and valor of African Americans on the battlefield, and questions as to whether or not they should even be acknowledged as first-class citizens. At the outset of the Civil War, the venerable historian stated that among Northern military officials, pundits, and abolitionists, "nothing else made Negro citizenship possible in the United States. Nothing else made Negro citizenship conceivable but the record of the Negro soldier as a fighter." This would be a titanic mountain for African Americans to scale. In order to be recognized as citizens, black men had to first confront the dominant ideology that excluded them from the very definition of "men." But Du Bois also offered a nuanced portrait of black Americans: "The Negro is a man, a soldier, a hero," he emphasized.[3]

Du Bois's invocation serves as the basis for the eighty-nine African-American servicemen who appear in *Brothers in Valor*. Writers have celebrated the courageous actions of African Americans on the battlefield as a living testament to their strength of character and devotion to US military might. From Fort Wagner to Los Animas Canyon; from Tayabacao to the Argonne Forest; and from Sommocolonia to Chipo-ri and Phu Cuong, they have underscored the sacrifices that black GIs have made to their country, even though the nation often expressed deeply ambivalent, if not hostile, attitudes about their suitability as fighting soldiers. Where these heroes came from, their entry into the armed forces, their outlook regarding American democracy, the historical public memory of who they were, and the degree to which their brave actions have become enmeshed in the national identity and consciousness are just as important as the heroic deeds they performed in the heat of battle.[4]

Yet, a fuller understanding of the heroic actions performed by African-American servicemen will remain in a social and political vacuum unless we historicize the concept of honor and how the meaning of the word has changed for blacks since the Civil War. "Honor" and its evolving meaning in the United States have influenced the policies that the country adopted to reward acts of valor performed by black soldiers, sailors, and marines, and how the selection process mirrored American attitudes toward race relations. In many ways, the creation and evolution of the nation's highest award for gallantry was as arduous as the enduring dilemma of race in American society itself. In the heady days of the American Revolutionary War, the Continental Congress formalized the meritorious process by ordering special medals be struck for generals George Washington, Horatio Gates, and Daniel Morgan, for their distinguished action during the conflict. However, the formal medal-bestowing process languished until 1847, when Congress passed legislation that expanded the United States Army during the Mexican-American War. Attached to the legislation was a rider that authorized the issuing of a Certificate of Merit to privates who distinguished themselves in peacetime and in war. But by the beginning of the 1860s, the Certificate of Merit had faded from public view and would later be reintroduced in 1876 following the Battle of the Little Bighorn.

In the opening stages of the Civil War, members of Congress held a series of discussions about ways in which Official Washington could recognize acts of bravery performed by soldiers, sailors, and marines during the fighting. Following the lead of Iowa senator James W. Grimes, the Senate Naval Committee introduced a bill that would present a token of appreciation to petty officers, seamen, landsmen, and marines who distinguished themselves during the hostilities. Passed by both Houses of Congress and approved by President Abraham Lincoln on December of 1861, the Medal of Honor was created for the navy.

Around the same time, Senator Henry Wilson of Massachusetts introduced a resolution that created a similar award for the army. Signed into law on July 12, 1862, the measure called for the Medal of Honor to be awarded "to such noncommissioned officers and privates as shall most distinguish themselves by their gallantry in action and other soldier-like qualities during the present insurrection." Within months, Secretary of War Edwin Stanton began to bestow medals upon soldiers and sailors who performed acts of bravery during the battles of 1863. However, here is the rub: The awards were largely reserved for officers and enlisted men serving in the regular armed forces, thus excluding the deeds of US citizens who performed acts of valor as volunteers.[5]

Over the past century and a half since the Medal of Honor's creation, only 3,500 servicemen and -women have been recognized with this distinction. Of that population, 89 of these heroes are African-American, 59 are Hispanic-American, 33 are Asian-American, and 32 are Native American. As will be seen in the pages of this book, the Civil War and the destruction of slavery gave new meaning to honor—and citizenship—as a fierce struggle ensued over the historical memory and the ideas for which the war had been fought.

As Dunbar and Du Bois effectively remind us, blacks may have had the same ethic of honor, but their perspective was undermined and diverged widely from their white counterparts. With this in mind, *Brothers in Valor* illustrates the complicated relationship of race and valor throughout history.[6]

Du Bois's evolving ideas about honor and race may be aptly applied to the life history of Medal of Honor recipients like Milton Olive III. Similar to MOH recipients who previously served in the American military, Olive answered the nation's call to duty, but would not be present for the acknowledgment of his deeds. Born in Chicago, Illinois, in 1946, he moved to Lexington, Mississippi, to live with his grandparents after his mother died in childbirth. He grew up in a proud and strongly race-conscious family. His great-uncle, Ben Olive, was an architect and laid the foundation for the Holmes County Bank and the Asia Church, two of the first establishments founded by blacks in the region after Reconstruction. His father, Milton Olive Jr., became an influential figure in Chicago's educational and business community during the 1950s. A precocious youth, Milton Olive attended Saints Junior College after graduating from high school, with the sincere hope of developing his skills as a budding singer and still photographer. His father recalled, "My son, my only child, bore a heavy cross because he always aspired to do something more with his life."

In 1964, Olive enlisted in the army and went to Fort Knox, Kentucky, for basic training before going on to attend paratroop school at Fort Benning. Upon graduation, Olive was assigned to a company in the famed 503rd Infantry Regiment, one of the most elite airborne units in the military. Olive and elements of the 503rd were deployed as a part of the 173rd Airborne Brigade to Vietnam, and engaged in several combat operations in the jungles of Phu Cuong, an area heavily infested with Vietcong. One day, the Chicago native and members of his platoon found themselves pinned down by continuous enemy fire, but were able to rally against Vietcong units, forcing them to flee their positions. But as Olive and other platoon members advanced throughout the jungle, a grenade was tossed in their direction. Without thinking of his well-being, concerned only about his fellow soldiers, Olive picked up the grenade and fell on it, absorbing the full blast of its discharge with his body.[7] His heroism and selfless act that fateful day not only earned him the gratitude of the rescued soldiers, but the respect and admiration of a grateful nation, as well.

On April 21, 1966, President Lyndon B. Johnson appeared on the White House steps to bestow the country's highest medal for bravery upon Chicago's fallen native son, stating,

The Medal of Honor is awarded for acts of heroism above and beyond the call of duty. It is bestowed for courage demonstrated not in blindly overlooking danger, but in meeting it with eyes clearly open. That is what Private Olive did. Men like Milton Olive die for honor. In dying, Private Milton Olive taught those of us who remain how we ought to live. He is the eighth Negro American to receive this Nation's highest award. Fortunately, it will be more difficult for future presidents to say how many Negroes have received the Medal of Honor. For unlike the other seven, Private Olive's military records have never carried the color of his skin or racial origin, only the testimony that he was a good and loyal citizen of the United States of America.[8]

Not long afterward, the image of the martyred soldier and his place among the pantheon of heroes became enshrined in the nation's historical memory. In 1966, Olive's parents gave an interview that was published in Chicago's *Daily Defender* and other newspapers, and televised by the National Broadcasting Company. In 1979, the City of Chicago dedicated a park along Michigan Avenue in his name. In addition, Olive's act of bravery was consecrated when Olive–Harvey Junior College was named after him. Such gestures are hardly isolated to the Windy City. During the last fifty years, a steady number of monuments and historical markers have been erected at public schools and on military installations throughout the country, immortalizing the bravery of young servicemen, the latest constructed at Fort Benning, Georgia, home of the US Army's Infantry and Airborne Training Schools.

It's hardly surprising that the bravery of men like Milton Olive—along with the politics of historical memory surrounding their valor—corresponded with the torturous path the country took toward recognizing blacks as citizens, with all the rights accorded by the Constitution. The military has long been seen as an evocative barometer of the values and mores of the American landscape, but has also been at the forefront of change in society.[9] This book is a history of the heroic deeds that black Medal of Honor recipients performed on the fields of battle during American wars, from Fort Wagner to Vietnam, and how the nation has struggled to commemorate them through presidential decree and public memory. Definitions of honor in battle were historically defined and reshaped through the policies underpinning the awarding of the Congressional Medal of Honor and other forms of memory, such as presidential politics, military policy, monument building, and commercial usage of their achievement. Special emphasis will be placed on the role played by the voices and recollections of the soldiers, along with their families and friends as custodians of memory, long after the fallen veterans departed the fields of fire.

Despite their involvement in American wars, the incessant battles between black attempts to create a shared sense of bravery on the battlefield and public historical debates over the very meaning of honor would continue into the waning years of the twentieth century. The tenor and tenacity of the black American campaign to define honor ultimately convinced Congress and Presidents George Herbert Walker Bush and William Jefferson Clinton to recast the meaning of valor and citizenship for a changing American society.

Yet even as new policies are being devised for preparing a new generation of Americans for what they will face on twenty-first-century battlefields, the army—and American society—is also deeply engaged in evaluating how to determine who should receive the nation's highest decoration for bravery. The time-tested attributes of personal sacrifice, selfless love for family, and loyalty to one's country continue to hold weight in the minds of the nation's policymakers, citizens, and GIs who stand in the ranks of its military. Notions of valor will serve as a crucible through which these values will be measured.

As Gen. Colin Powell, the nation's first black chairman of the Joint Chiefs of Staff, stated on the last day that he donned the nation's uniform: "In the years that I had worn it, I had benefited beyond my wildest hopes from all that is good in this country, and I had overcome its lingering faults. I had found something to do with my life that was honorable and useful, that I could do well, and that I loved doing."[10]

For General Powell and other long-distance runners in the struggle for equality, the quest for honor has and will continue to play an indelible role in the national portrait.

Three Medals Of Honor, Battle Of New Market Heights, September 29, 1864, 2013
(oil on canvas), Troiani, Don (b. 1949)

CHAPTER 1

"For Honor, Duty, and Liberty"

HEROES OF THE CIVIL WAR, 1862-1865

"The Colored man will fight,—not as a tool, but as an American patriot. He will fight most desperately because he will be fighting against his enemy, slavery, and because he feels that among the leading claims he has to your feelings as fellow-countrymen, is, that in the page of facts connected with the battles for liberty which his country has fought, his valor—the valor of black men—*challenges comparison.*"

—*"'The Colored Man Will Fight' (1861)," in* The American Mosaic: The African American Experience, ABC-CLIO

The paths that black Medal of Honor recipients took to the battlefields of the Civil War were just as diverse as the colors of the unit flags they swore to uphold. Many of them came of age sometime between the years that marked the *Dred Scott v. Sanford* Supreme Court decision of 1857 and the presidential election of 1860. The Supreme Court's ruling spelled trouble for all blacks, for it meant that they fell outside the bounds of United States citizenship and possessed no legal rights in federal courts. For many free blacks, the federal case concomitant with the presidential election that followed three years later intensified African-American calls for solidarity and resistance to the institution of slavery. Between 1857 and 1860, thousands of black men, women, and children rallied against the federal ruling across the North, and revered John Brown's raid at Harpers Ferry. By the time the Southern states had seceded from the Union and Confederate forces opened fire on Fort Sumter, hundreds of young black men were discussing their status in the war effort.

By the beginning of 1862, African-American soldiers faced more than just the Confederate Army on the field. Employment in the Union Army also meant overcoming white commanders' misgivings about the conduct and character of black soldiers in uniform. Black soldiers were paid less than their white contemporaries. Many white officers of the Northern

United States Colored Troops (USCT) harbored deeply held racist prejudices against black soldiers.[1] Loaded down with the long-standing baggage of class distinction, gender, background, generation, region, and upbringing, stereotypes and innuendoes played a large role in their thinking about the capabilities of black troops. In many ways, their attitudes paralleled their white Southern adversaries and Union commanders, like Maj. Gen. William Tecumseh Sherman, who preferred to place black soldiers in rear-guard assignments. "I won't trust niggers to fight yet," Sherman told his brother John, the sitting senator from Ohio.

As historian William Dobak points out, Sherman may have had other reasons for distrusting newly deployed troops on the battlefield.[2] During the Battle of Bull Run in July 1861, the venerated general had witnessed the disadvantages of rushing new recruits into combat. He had also discovered that draftees were especially prone to contracting measles, mumps, diphtheria, and other maladies present in camp areas. But his racist proclivities may have shaped his perceptions of the battlefield capabilities of black soldiers more than anything else. "I like niggers well enough as niggers, but when fools and idiots try and make niggers better than ourselves, I have an opinion. A large proportion of our fighting men would not tolerate blacks in the front line, for white soldiers and volunteers will not be placed on a par with the negro," he observed.[3]

The question of using blacks as soldiers weighed heavily on the minds of government leaders throughout the spring and summer of 1862. The battle casualties of the Union Army began to climb in the wake of the Battle at Shiloh, during the Seven Days' Battles outside of Richmond, and in the Battle of Antietam. As the initial enthusiasm for the fighting began to wane, many Northern Republicans began to seriously consider arming slaves and freed blacks. However, Lincoln advised his Cabinet members that a Union victory was essential before he could issue such a decree. So when the Union Army finally won a victory at the Battle of Antietam on September 17, the president issued a proclamation five days later. It not only contained the momentous clause, forever freeing all slaves in the rebellious states, but also permitted those newly freed to actively enlist in the Union Army. Six months later, the War Department issued General Order 143, expediting the recruitment of African Americans to fight for the army.[4] With that, the stage was set for the acts of bravery performed by black soldiers who would later earn the Medal of Honor in the Civil War.

For most of the MOH recipients who entered the Union Army at the time, the battle flags representing their respective units came to epitomize the characteristics of valor and bravery more than anything else. In March 1863, Sgt. Milton Holland and the men of the 5th United States Colored Troops attended a flag presentation at Camp Delaware where John Mercer Langston administered an oath they would never forget. As Holland recalled, "Our company C—the color company—took the flag made by the kind citizens of Athens, and we pledged that we would ever be true to the flag; though it may be tattered or torn by hard service, it should never be disgraced."

Later that spring, the men of the 54th Massachusetts left Camp Meigs, boarding railcars heading for Boston. As soon as they reached the city, companies of the unit passed through the downtown streets before arriving at the Boston Commons, where the Massachusetts governor presented them with four flags. In addition to the American flag, they received the regimental colors featuring a banner with the state emblem of the Goddess of Liberty. While handing the colors to the 54th Massachusetts commander, Governor John Andrew told the men, "From the beginning of this rebellion to the present day, that banner has never been surrendered to the foe; fifty-three regiments have marched from the Bay State, but we have yet to learn that they ever surrendered that noble banner. Hold on to the staff; if every thread is blown away, your glory will be the same."[5]

Given the numerous examples of distinguished action exhibited by black MOH recipients later in the war, Governor Andrew's exhortation accurately points to the tremendous importance the colors would play in their performances on the battlefield. The flag, along with the dress blue uniforms and Enfield rifled muskets, celebrated an identity that enlarged black claims to freedom and equality while negating the inferences of slavery and black inferiority that proliferated throughout white-dominated society at the time. While the flag itself was not meant as a direct political statement, the

> We pledged that we would ever be true to the flag; though it may be tattered or torn by hard service, it should never be disgraced.

social context in which it was presented and the meaning that was attached to it rendered it so. For many of the MOH recipients and their uniformed contemporaries, the flag, whether federal, regimental, or otherwise, symbolized honor, duty, and country—the vivid symbol of American patriotism and loyalty.

"BOYS, THE OLD FLAG NEVER TOUCHED THE GROUND"

William H. Carney and the Battle of Fort Wagner, South Carolina, July 18, 1863

William H. Carney, born a slave in 1840, was taught to read and write by a minister at an early age. His father, William Sr., and mother, Ann Dean, had worked as slaves in the Hampton Roads Region of Norfolk, Virginia, for decades prior to the Civil War. During the late 1850s, the couple moved toward freedom, using the Underground Railroad to successfully escape through Maryland, Pennsylvania, and New York before eventually ending up in New Bedford, Massachusetts, Frederick Douglass's hometown. Like Douglass, Carney and his father worked as seamen and performed odd jobs there prior to the Civil

War. They were encouraged by the fiery antislavery movement found in the pages of Douglass's *Monthly*, advocating for the Union cause.

During the spring of 1861, William Carney established a friendship with a pastor of a local church and began studying to become a minister. After the first shots were fired at Fort Sumter, the twenty-one-year-old flocked to the colors. He was told his services were not required. At that moment, Carney linked God's call to the altar to the cause of black freedom. As he recalled, "When the country called for all *persons*, I decided I could best serve my God by serving my country and my oppressed brothers. The sequel is short—I enlisted for the war."[6]

> "I decided I could best serve my God by serving my country and my oppressed brothers."

In January of 1863, Carney gained his chance following the Emancipation Proclamation. With the passage of the measure, Governor John Andrew of Massachusetts received permission from the War Department to create a regiment of free Northern blacks that would be commanded by twenty-five-year-old abolitionist Robert Gould Shaw. Designated as the 54th Massachusetts, the unit holds the distinction of being the first Northern black regiment to fight in the Civil War. Over the course of the next few months, more than one thousand free blacks from Boston and other Northern cities enlisted. By April, Carney stood among the first twenty-five volunteers recruited from New Bedford. After training at Camp Meigs in Readville, a neighborhood in Boston, the 54th marched to the city proper, where hundreds of onlookers watched them march off to war.

Less than three months later, on July 18, they received orders to lead an attack on Fort Wagner, South Carolina, as the leading element of a Union assault. Fort Wagner held strategic value for Union Army and Navy commanders. As a major enemy stronghold, it rested at a strategic point in Charleston Harbor. Composed of palmetto logs and sandbags, the beachhead fortification was capable of withstanding the fiercest naval bombardment and could house over one thousand garrison troops.

Carney and the men of the 54th were eager to join the battle. The moment to strike a blow against slavery and free their brothers and sisters in bondage was finally within their reach. But their euphoria proved to be short-lived. Intense enemy shelling from the walled fortification stymied their initial approach, making each advance more costly as crucial minutes stretched into hours. In the face of a withering barrage of enemy fire, Private Carney dropped his rifle and seized the regimental colors when Sgt. John Wall, the unit's regimental flag bearer, was wounded. Carrying the flag, Carney continued to march forward to the fort's entrance as his comrades fell around him. Despite being severely wounded in the chest, right arm, and in each leg, Carney never dropped the flag. When a soldier with another regiment offered to carry the colors, he responded, "No one but a member of my regiment should carry them." His fellow soldiers cheered, and Carney could be overheard saying to them, "Boys, the old flag never touched the ground."

While the flag may have signified the exact location of the front line on the battlefield, black troops like William Carney also saw the rectangular piece of fabric as a symbol of African-American determination to seize their freedom from the vestiges of bondage that had held them for centuries. To give an inch of ground was to relinquish their present and future claims to citizenship.

Although the assault on Fort Wagner was deemed a failure, news about the outstanding performance of William Carney left an indelible mark in the minds of his contemporaries. For his performance on the battlefield, the New Bedford native was promoted to sergeant. In a letter home to the *New Bedford Mercury*, Cpl. James Gooding trumpeted the 54th's actions during the offensive, but he also recognized Carney's conduct in battle:

The men of the 54th behaved gallantly on the occasion—so the Generals say. The color bearer of the State colors was killed on the parapet. Colonel Shaw seized the staff when the standard bearer fell, and in less than a minute after, the Colonel fell himself. When the men saw their gallant leader fall, they made a gallant effort to get him out, but they were either shot down, or reeled in the ditch below. One man succeeded in getting hold of the State color staff, but the color was completely torn to pieces. It is not for us to blow our horn, but when a regiment of white men gave us three cheers as we were passing them, it shows that we did our duty as men should.[7]

For his heroic performance, William Carney was accorded the nation's highest military medal, the Congressional Medal of Honor. But while he was the first African-American soldier to receive the award, he would have to wait nearly four decades to receive public recognition of his deed.[8]

RESCUING THE REGIMENTAL COLORS "WITHOUT A SCRATCH"

Christian A. Fleetwood and the Ordeal at Chaffin's Farm, Virginia, September 29, 1864

Born in Baltimore, Maryland, in 1840 to Charles and Anna Fleetwood, both free persons, Christian Fleetwood received a public education from the Maryland State Colonization Society and attended the all-black Ashmun Institute (later named Lincoln University) in Pennsylvania. Fleetwood was a budding singer, musician, and choirmaster in the church, and was known for engaging in spirited discussion on topics ranging from religion and politics to physics and literature.[9] Prior to the Civil War, he published editorials for the Episcopal Church's *Christian Recorder*, and founded and published the *Lyceum Observer*, known by many observers as the region's first black-owned and -operated newspaper.[10]

But public espousal of freedom and citizenship was not enough for the young Baltimore resident. When the Civil War broke out in 1861, Fleetwood and thousands of other black volunteers from Maryland rushed to sign up for the army, determined "to assist in abolishing slavery and to save the country from ruin."[11] However, as he and others quickly discovered, to their chagrin, President Abraham Lincoln and the War Department were not ready for blacks to help save the country. As Fleetwood bitterly recounted years later, "The North came slowly and reluctantly to recognize the Negro as a factor for the good in the war. 'This is a white man's war' met the Negroes at every step of [their] first efforts to gain admission to the armies of the Union."[12]

Nearly two years later, Fleetwood got his wish when Congress passed the Second Confiscation and Militia Act in July of 1862. While the first confiscation measure issued in 1861 only seized property (including slaves) that the Confederates used to execute the war effort, the second congressional act authorized the president to enroll "persons of African descent" for war service. The measure was of great significance to Fleetwood and other young black men, for it allowed free Northern blacks to enter the army as soldiers.

In August of 1863, the Maryland native ventured to nearby Camp Birney, where he entered the ranks of Company G of the United States Colored Troops' 4th Regiment as a sergeant major. Fleetwood and his compatriots participated in some of the fiercest fighting of the Civil War. In late September of 1864, Fleetwood distinguished himself in the face of enemy fire during the Battle of Chaffin's Farm, located southeast of Richmond. Fleetwood earned the Medal of Honor for saving the regimental colors "without a scratch" after the color-bearer and most of the company had been killed or wounded, delivering a pivotal victory for the Union Army.

But other soldiers lauded the Baltimore native's actions under fire in a somewhat different way. Maj. Augustus Boernstein honored the performance of the men who served with the 4th United States Colored Troops (USCT) at New Market Heights, specifically mentioning the distinguished actions taken by black noncommissioned and enlisted men in his unit. "Sergeant Major Fleetwood and Corporal Veale have always been good, obedient, faithful soldiers. Sergeant Fleetwood is a highly educated gentleman and is one of the many instances of what the African race is capable of being brought to by patient persistent effort," Boernstein exclaimed. For their efforts, Fleetwood and nearly two hundred other black soldiers received medals for gallantry in battle.[13]

Years later, the battle-tested noncommissioned officer placed his own value on his service that day: "Before the colors could touch the ground, Corporal Charles Veale, of Company D, seized the blue flag, and I, the American flag, which had been presented to us by the patriotic women of our home in Baltimore."[14]

"LED THE MEN GALLANTLY THROUGH THE DAY"

The Leadership of Milton Holland at Chaffin's Farm, Virginia, September 29, 1864

Milton Holland was born in 1844 on a farm near Carthage, Texas. Like William Carney, Holland and his two brothers were slaves, until fate intervened. Their owner, Bird Holland, was a longtime state official and former secretary of state who harbored serious misgivings about the institution of slavery. He believed in self-improvement through education, so acting on this idea, he freed the Holland brothers in the late 1850s, before sending them to Athens County, Ohio, where they attended Albany Enterprise Academy. There, young Milton Holland debated with his peers about the issues affecting his brothers in bondage while taking classes in history, literature, civics, and economics.

In 1861, seventeen-year-old Milton attempted to enlist, but was turned away based on his race. Undeterred, he accepted entrance into the quartermaster corps and worked as a servant with Col. Nelson H. Van Vorhes, an officer with several of the Ohio regiments. Later Milton was mustered into the army in June of 1863.[15] Milton Holland, along with three hundred other men from the Buckeye State, traveled to Massachusetts to join an Ohio regiment of the USCT. Holland and his comrades had no sooner arrived at Camp Delaware than they received disappointing news. The War Department had reneged on Massachusetts governor John Andrew's promise to provide the volunteers with the same pay and clothing as their white counterparts. When the men of the 5th Ohio Regiment threatened to leave the camp, demanding the pay due them, Holland persuaded the group to remain in camp.

John Mercer Langston, an influential Ohio educator and a prominent recruiter of black troops during the period, actually visited the camp during the dispute. He was so moved by the selfless efforts made by Holland and the men during the crisis that he wrote years later, "They were decided and manly at once in their course. Such was the conduct of the men coming to camp, and their reputation for considerate behavior, aptness and attention to drill, and soldierly advancement, that all over the camp, young colored men were moved to the emulation of their example." Holland was promoted for his inspiring leadership and charisma to the rank of sergeant, a position he would hold with great distinction the following year.

Milton Holland's true test of leadership and heroism came in 1864 at the Battle of Chaffin's Farm. Marked by the yawning open fields that lay south of the Confederate capital, Chaffin's Farm was part of an elaborate system of enemy defenses that surrounded Richmond. In the eyes of Union strategists, capture of the Confederate railroad supply lines in the area would greatly hamper Lee's ability to reinforce his army in the Shenandoah Valley. In late September a contingent of the USCT, commanded by Maj. Gen. David Bell Birney, was ordered to lead an attack against a Confederate line of defense along the New Market Road. Unknown to Holland and other advancing soldiers, battle-tested Texas veterans led by Brig. Gen. John Gregg were among the infantrymen defending the heights. They were accompanied by the 3rd Richmond Howitzers and the 1st Rockbridge Artillery, and these units were reinforced by a well-trained cavalry brigade. When USCT soldiers moved up to the Confederate line, they drew heavy fire from well-fortified enemy pits. The incessant enemy shelling and the screams of wounded soldiers punctuated the smoke-covered battlefield. As the commanders and junior officers fell with severe wounds and the unit stood on the brink of collapse, seasoned black troops like Texas's own Milton Holland stepped into their fallen leaders' roles, barking orders and commanding the remaining troops forward.

Milton Holland's true test of leadership and heroism came in 1864 at the Battle of Chaffin's Farm.

As the fog cleared that morning, many of the men of the USCT were heartened by the leadership abilities shown by Holland and the victory they had won. As Milton Holland noted in a letter to the *Athens* (OH) *Messenger* at the time: "To our great surprise, we found that the boasted Southern chivalry had fled. They could not see the nigger part as the man on the white horse presented it. I have never heard anything to equal it before or since; for a while whole batteries discharged their contents into the Rebel ranks at once. The result was a complete success."

Black heroism in rural Virginia led to a turning point in white opinion regarding whether African Americans could be effective combat soldiers. On October 11, Gen. Benjamin Butler addressed the soldiers of the Army of the James and praised their efforts during the successful campaign: "All these gallant colored soldiers were left in command, all of their company officers being killed and wounded, and led them gallantly and meritoriously through the day."

But their victory came at a tremendous cost. Of the 3,291 Union troops killed at New Market Heights, 1,773 were black soldiers, constituting more than 50 percent of all battlefield casualties. For his gallantry, Holland received the award for valor in April of 1865.

"FOR GOD'S SAKE, SMITH, SAVE THE FLAG"

Andrew Jackson Smith and the Battle of Honey Hill, South Carolina, November 30, 1864

Andrew Jackson Smith was born in Lyon County, Kentucky, in September of 1843. The child of a slave woman and a wealthy slave owner, Smith was introduced to the hardships of involuntary servitude at an early age, working as a ferryman carrying people and commerce across the Cumberland River. Little did the nineteen-year-old realize at the time, but the outbreak of war would alter his life in several important ways.

Days after the Battle of Fort Sumter, his father (and owner) left and enlisted in the Confederate Army, where he found himself in the midst of some of the fiercest fighting during the opening stages of the war. After spending a short period of time away from the family, his father returned home and announced that he was taking Smith with him to serve with the Confederates. Determined to take his fate into his own hands, Smith and another slave walked twenty-five miles northwest to Paducah, Kentucky, where they presented themselves to the 41st Illinois. Shortly afterward, Smith became a manservant to the unit's regimental officer, a role he maintained until the Emancipation Proclamation of 1863.[16]

Smith's first taste of war came as the collapse of Atlanta and other areas of the Deep South left the Confederacy in shambles. Conducted by Maj. Gen. William Tecumseh Sherman, the scorched-earth style of the Savannah Campaign represented a new form of warfare, setting the bar of valor higher than before. For Smith and other men with the 54th and the 55th Massachusetts Infantry, the Battle of Honey Hill, South Carolina, would prove to be most costly.

Under the command of Col. Alfred S. Hartwell, transports carrying the all-black force steamed up the Broad River, heading to Boyd's Neck on the night of November 28. The units had just spent an extended period of time performing garrison duties at Hilton Head, South Carolina. Their orders were to cut off enemy access to the Charleston and Savannah Railroad as a way of facilitating Sherman's march to the sea. Nothing went as planned. The troops ran headlong into a dense fog that slowed them down to a mere crawl. In the cornfield-dotted area, the troops were further slowed by poorly detailed operational maps and unreliable guides.

On the morning of November 30, elements of the 55th launched an attack at Honey Hill against Confederate troops composed of militia and Regular Army units. Union forces battled the enemy and the elements as they fought valiantly for nearly seven hours. The thickly wooded area made it next to impossible for Federal troops to see the heavily armed enemy earthworks until they literally stood right in front of them. The skirmish between the two combatants raged on until Union forces decided to withdraw later that evening. As night descended on the battlefield, nearly 140 men had been killed, and 108 wounded. Among those killed were eight commissioned officers; a Vincennes, Indiana, resident named John Posey; and the commander of the 55th, Colonel Hartwell, who was wounded after being trampled by his dying horse.[17]

Yet the high rate of casualties and the steadily rising number of wounded men did not overshadow the acts of valor performed by the men that day. When flag-bearer Robert King was struck down by an enemy shell, Cpl. Andrew Jackson Smith heard his commander give the order, "For God's sake, Smith, save the flag!" After watching King's lifeless body fall near the parapet, the twenty-two-year-old former boatman felt himself move forward. "When King was killed, I caught him with one hand and the flag with the other," Smith described years later. "I brought the National flag from the field of Honey Hill. Beside me was Comrade John H. Patterson, who carried the State flag. When his arm was broken by a bullet, I carried both flags."

"When King was killed, I caught him with one hand and the flag with the other."

Smith's moment of glory at Honey Hill would be shrouded in the fog of war and largely forgotten by the public. While his performance earned him a promotion to sergeant and color-bearer, some of his comrades in arms failed to legitimize his test of courage while under fire. Official recognition of his battlefield exploits in the form of the Medal of Honor would not take place until nearly a century and a half later.[18]

"STAYING AT HIS STATION
IN THE LINE OF DUTY"

John H. Lawson and the Battle of Mobile Bay, August 5, 1864

Black sailors serving with the Union Navy during the Civil War faced different challenges on the open sea from those that foot soldiers experienced. But unlike their armed contemporaries who stood in the ranks, their tests of valor often revolved around their abilities to load guns, tug shell whips of full powder boxes to the gun decks, and quickly troubleshoot disastrous problems in the face of seemingly hopeless situations.

Among the lesser-known heroes who displayed their talents on the water during the summer of 1863 was African-American landsman John Lawson, at the Battle of Mobile Bay. A native of Philadelphia, Pennsylvania, Lawson served with sailors working aboard Rear Admiral Farragut's flagship USS *Hartford* during successive attacks against Fort Morgan.

In August, the ship advanced too quickly and ran headlong into Confederate gunboats. Lawson and several other sailors were thrown violently against the side of the USS *Hartford* when it was struck by an enemy shell. Lawson was knocked unconscious and thrown into the hold. After regaining consciousness, Lawson's attention was drawn to the severe shrapnel wounds in his leg. Although he could barely stand, this did not deter the young sailor. He soon regained his composure and remained at his workstation, tugging powder box after powder box onto the berth deck during the fighting. For his selfless effort, Lawson, along with several other landsmen, was awarded the Medal of Honor years later.[19]

"A NEW BIRTH OF FREEDOM"

Black Medal of Honor Recipients after the Civil War

Black leaders and members of the press used MOH recipients like John Lawson, Christian A. Fleetwood, and other African Americans to draw national attention to black demands for freedom and equality. Throughout October of 1864, the *Cleveland Daily Leader*, Boston's *Liberator*, and Columbus's *Daily Ohio Statesman* carried stories on the performance of the United States Colored Troops at Chaffin's Farm. At the front, Philadelphia *Press* correspondent Thomas Morris Chester filed colorful dispatches about the heroic activities of noncommissioned officers like Christian Fleetwood and Milton Holland at Chaffin's Farm. Chester claimed that the regiment "covered itself with glory, and wiped out effectually the imputation against the fighting qualities of the colored troops."

How did the newly decorated African-American heroes feel about their postwar prospects? For that matter, how comfortable were they with being treated as representatives of their race and exemplars of liberation for blacks everywhere? How, and to what degree, were they cognizant of their role as living reminders of humiliation and defeat for Southern whites, and as moving targets for white reprisal? While black MOH recipients received the same recognition as their white counterparts, the legacy of their valor in combat did not automatically grant them honor and respect in the collective memory of the white public.

As the war drew to a close, members of the United States Colored Troops and volunteers from the 54th Massachusetts entered Richmond in the crisp winter air filled with pride and hope. Elsewhere, as Confederate president Jefferson Davis and members of his cabinet withdrew from the city for points south, black soldiers with the 9th USCT marched through the streets to the deafening cheers of spectators and well-wishers. The soldiers strode under the Stars and Stripes past the seemingly endless onlookers who lined the battle-stricken pathways. Many of them had been born and raised during the horrors of slavery, had reached adulthood in the uncertain years of the 1850s, and had rushed to the Federal colors after the Emancipation Proclamation. They had participated in the suicidal assault on Fort Wagner, the Union Army's debacle at the Crater, and the heroic charge at New Market Heights and Fort Fisher. With the surrender of Richmond, they were buoyed by the Union victory and ecstatic about returning to hearth and kin. Most of all, black soldiers saw themselves fulfilling the roles they had originally imagined that military service would provide them: They were liberators of slaves, and protectors of their families. Combat performance on the battleground was the measuring stick for the freedom and equality they had earned, and that they now planned to use to challenge notions of race and citizenship.

> As the war drew to a close, members of the United States Colored Troops and volunteers from the 54th Massachusetts entered Richmond in the crisp winter air filled with pride and hope.

But their combat performance also allowed the soldiers to validate and refine their ideas about honor and manhood. As the 54th's acting commander, Luis Emilio, later recalled, "The courage and fidelity of the blacks, so unmistakably demonstrated during the Civil War, assures to us, in the event of future need, a class to recruit from now more available, intelligent, educated, and self-reliant, and more patriotic, devoted, and self-sacrificing, if such were possible, than thirty years ago."[20] Appointed commander after Col. Robert Gould Shaw was killed in action during the assault on Fort Wagner, Emilio had witnessed the gallantry of black soldiers firsthand through the final months of the war. His recollections proved insightful after the war when the nation's historical memory of black soldiers' valiant service in the Civil War began to fade.

For most black Medal of Honor recipients, the road home included mustering out of the service, getting paid, saying farewell to comrades, and contemplating reunions with loved ones. But they also knew that the battle for first-class equality and citizenship was just beginning.

Throughout September of 1865, large crowds assembled in Boston to greet the men of the 54th and 55th Massachusetts Regiments. The soldiers had just been mustered out of the service, receiving their final pay near Charleston before being discharged at Gallops Island, located near Boston Harbor. As the train pulled into the station, a celebrated drill club performed a series of maneuvers while marching to the music of the New Bedford Brass Band. The men assembled into formation along Commercial Wharf and marched to Boston Common. There they listened to speeches by Massachusetts senators Charles Sumner and Henry Wilson before being disbanded by their unit commander. Shortly afterward, the black veterans boarded trains heading for their different points of destination.[21]

Among the soldiers returning home that day was Andrew Jackson Smith. After the Battle of Honey Hill, Smith stayed in Boston for a short time before leaving for Kentucky to visit his mother and three sisters. Like so many other black volunteers, Smith wished to pick up a new life, only to discover that it would not be easy. "I saw all of my former playmates, many of whom were ex–Confederate soldiers. I then saw my former owner, who came to me and gave me good advice. He told me that he was as poor as I."[22]

Other returning MOH recipients expressed the desire to return to civilian life as soon as possible. Some, like Aaron Anderson, Robert Blake, Joachim Pease, and Charles Veale, disappeared from the historical record after they were mustered out of the USCT and the navy in 1865 and 1866. James Lawson left the navy in December of 1864 and returned to Philadelphia, where he landed work as a barber and a night watchman for a local firehouse. After being honorably discharged in June of 1864, William Carney returned home to New Bedford, married Susannah Williams, and worked as a streetlight repairman. Carney had a restless spirit, however, and left Massachusetts in 1866, in search of better opportunities. After spending nearly two years in California, he returned to New Bedford and eventually was hired by the local post office.

Some men found the military to their liking and wished to parlay their service in the USCT and their acts of valor into new opportunities in the Regular Army. After serving with the 4th USCT, 1st Sgt. Christian Fleetwood offered his services in the spring of 1865, in hopes of landing a coveted position as a company officer. The Baltimore native had witnessed the carnage of war firsthand. In the wake of his brilliant action at Chaffin's Farm, Fleetwood was recognized by his fellow enlisted men not only as one of the most capable soldiers in the army, but also as a man of character and integrity.

But Fleetwood faced a personal dilemma: Prior to his unit's participation in the Union siege on Petersburg the previous year, a bishop in Kentucky had offered him a position as rector of an Episcopal church. He considered the offer, but, believing that a commission in the army would allow him to do much more for African Americans everywhere, he declined. Fleetwood's aspirations for rank and respect were short-lived. Not only did his superiors turn down his application for a Regular Army officer's commission, but they also denied his request to leave at the end of his enlistment. Disillusioned with the army, Fleetwood harshly criticized its treatment of black troops, and wrote an angry letter from the front (see appendix).

Undaunted, Fleetwood finished out the war and continued to serve in the District of Columbia's National Guard, commanding the unit at the rank of major until the end of the century. Although he never relinquished his quest to command troops on the battlefield, the venerable war hero would feel the sting of the American military's racial discrimination for the rest of his life. He would never forget the bittersweet lessons of bravery and betrayal he had learned during the Civil War. Fleetwood wrote about the military legacy of black soldiers in American wars for the 1895 Cotton States and International Exposition: "After each war, of 1776, of 1812, and of 1861, history repeats itself in the absolute effacement of the gallant deeds done for the country by its brave black defenders and in their relegation to outer darkness."[23]

More than fifty years after the Civil War, sympathetic white officers like Benjamin Butler, George Sherman, Luis Emilio, Charles Fox, and Burt Wilder used their own personal diaries and letters, along with official correspondence left by Union and Confederate officials, to write histories of their regiments in which they consecrated the heroic activities of Christian Fleetwood, William Carney, and Andrew Jackson Smith to public memory. Soon, local, regional, and even national veterans' organizations joined their cause.

In 1866, Dr. Benjamin Stephenson and a coterie of Civil War veterans met in Decatur, Illinois, and formed the Grand Army of the Republic. The GAR promoted the role of black soldiers who served in the Civil War, and supported black voting rights throughout the 1870s and 1880s. In April of 1890, surviving Civil War veterans gathered in Boston to organize the Medal of Honor Legion to attract greater public attention to individuals whose acts of bravery on the battlefield had not been recognized by Congress. Formed as a local society, members of the Legion nationalized their organization during the twenty-fourth annual encampment of the Grand Army of the Republic.

Throughout the 1890s, the MOH Legion members assembled to discuss the well-being of their comrades. After marching through the streets of the nation's capital, thousands of veterans representing GAR posts from all over the country would gather for dinner and to hear speeches by civic leaders, elected officials, and businesspeople. Most of all, they reinvigorated remembrances and rekindled sentiments of long-lost brotherhood. Among the ex-servicemen groups that attended the reunion were associations of naval veterans, the Cavalry of the Army of the Potomac, former prisoners of war, Sons of Veterans, survivors of the US Colored Troops, and Medal of Honor recipients.[24]

> They reinvigorated remembrances and rekindled sentiments of long-lost brotherhood.

Among those active with the GAR who stood among living Medal of Honor Legionnaires were Milton Holland and Christian Fleetwood. During the 1890s, both men had firmly established themselves as astute businessmen, rising to prominence in their local communities. Holland became chief of the checking division in the US Treasury Department before his death in 1910. He had also created the Alpha Life Insurance, Real Estate, and Banking Company, where Fleetwood served as secretary and cashier. For his part, Fleetwood's long-standing interest in the military led to his appointment as drill instructor of the Washington Colored High School Cadet Corps.

There, he established a unique *esprit de corps* and a tradition of excellence among several generations of young men, many of whom would become commissioned officers at Fort Des Moines, Iowa, in 1917.[25]

The battlefield acts of valor performed by Milton Holland, Christian Fleetwood, and other black heroes were hardly atypical, and did not occur in a vacuum. Among those whose Civil War exploits are not described in this narrative are Bruce Anderson, William Barnes, Powhatan Beaty, Robert Blake, James H. Bronson, Wilson Brown, Clement Dees, Decatur Dorsey, James Gardner, James Harris, Alfred B. Hilton, Miles James, Alexander Kelly, James Mifflin, Joachim Pease, Robert Pinn, Edward Ratcliff, and Charles Veale. Their bravery and sense of honor set a lofty standard for their heirs to attain that would take generations to realize.

Meanwhile, a new storm was brewing in the waning years of the nineteenth century—one that would involve the thoughts and energies of a new cadre of black Medal of Honor recipients. They would develop their own understanding of valor in battle, but this consciousness would also encourage new ideas about citizenship and rights.

CHAPTER 2

Frontier Honor

HEROES OF THE INDIAN WARS, 1867–1897

Few people realize the hardships and privations endured by these soldiers during the 1860s and 1870s. Their service and sacrifices have rarely been appreciated; only the mountains and plains of the Great West know the story of their devotion to duty; and many a hero sleeps in an unknown grave, where his only requiem is sung by the tall sycamores and cottonwoods that border some nameless stream.[1]

—*George W. Ford, First Sergeant, Tenth Cavalry, 1924*

At the turn of the century, many resplendent images of black Medal of Honor recipients in their formal wear were captured for posterity. In 1900, Thomas Calloway organized an exhibit for the Paris Exposition designed to educate the international public about African-American life, education, and literature. Housed in the Palace of Social Economy and earning one of the Exposition's gold medals for excellence, the images, charts, and graphs were multidimensional in scope and panoramic in focus, covering the social and economic progress of African Americans since the Civil War.

Among the displays was a three-volume collection of photographs compiled by a precocious young sociologist named William Edward Burghardt Du Bois. Du Bois was about to embark on a defining journey, well on his way to being recognized as one of the foremost intellectuals of the twentieth century. He had just published his epic study, *The Philadelphia Negro*, and was starting to write the engaging yet haunting semiautobiographical *The Souls of Black Folk*. Soon after the venerable scholar had arrived in Georgia

Black soldier, Indian war period, Infantry, Co. D with shoulder knots, holding noncom sword, wearing aiguelette, crossed rifles with "D" on kepi, white gloves plus three service stripes (i.e., fifteen years service)

and assumed his professorship at Atlanta University, he witnessed the ghastly April 1899 lynching of farmer Sam Hose. Desperately trying to make sense of the epidemic of mob violence being meted out against blacks across the country, Du Bois aimed to use his collection of photographs to challenge racist discourse and perceptions of black criminality, as well as present African-American middle-class respectability to a wider audience.

Among the 360 prints that Du Bois compiled were single and collective portraits taken of living soldiers and sailors who had received the nation's highest award for valor, from the Civil War through the Spanish-American War. The Civil War MOH recipients included Powhatan Beaty, William Carney, Christian Fleetwood, James Gardner, James Harris, Thomas Hawkins, Milton Holland, Alexander Kelly, John Lawson, and Robert Pinn.

Du Bois's photographic essay also contained dignified images of four of the eighteen African-American soldiers who received the Medal of Honor for valiant service during the Indian Wars of the western United States: John Denny, Isaiah Mays, Thomas Shaw, and Brent Woods. The service records of MOH recipients Dennis Bell, Fitz Lee, and William Thompkins from the Spanish-American War were also included among the exhibit items.

The promising young scholar-activist considered these soldiers members of a talented tenth of a new generation of African Americans, and the photographs represented how they wished to be perceived by people at home and abroad. Du Bois claimed, "Not the least contribution to history is the case given to Negro Medal of Honor men in the army and the navy—from the man who 'seized the colors after two color-bearers had been shot down and bore them nobly through the fight' to the black men who 'voluntarily went ashore in the face of the enemy and aided in the rescue of their wounded comrades.'"[2]

As part of his exhibit, Du Bois described the African-American military experience in the Trans-Mississippi West during the late nineteenth century. For many black regulars, the West was a world marked by dust and drought, one in which loyalty to and protection of one's troops was critical to the black military experience. It was a place where one's reputation as a person rested upon being known by all for strength, ferocity, and toughness. Indeed, having good character and ensuring that "your word is your bond" were necessary accoutrements of this value system. The environment and its rough-and-tumble characteristics were as invaluable as the stripes of rank one earned while serving in the West itself.

THE HEROISM OF EMANUEL STANCE

Those who donned the nation's uniform faced a different set of problems in the Trans-Mississippi West. The Mexican border along the lower Rio Grande called for greater troop presence to stave off a French invasion of Mexico and to forestall the creation of a European government. Throughout the Trans-Mississippi West, Regular Army units were stationed at nearly 260 military posts, part of a vast constellation of departments and districts running from Arizona to Oregon and from Montana to Texas.

Meanwhile, the growing presence of settlers in the Great Plains after the Civil War forced the army to provide additional regiments and companies to guard against the increasing possibility of Indian hostility in the region. Only three regiments of cavalry, the 3rd, 7th, and 10th, and four regiments of infantry were assigned to the Department of Missouri—an area that covered all of Kansas, Missouri, Indian Territory, and the Territory of New Mexico. As Maj. Gen. Philip H. Sheridan observed during the late 1860s, "Part of this section of country—western Kansas, particularly—had been frequently disturbed and harassed during two or three years past, the savages every now and then massacring an isolated family, boldly attacking the surveying and constructing parties of the

Kansas-Pacific railroad, sweeping down on emigrant trains, plundering and burning stage-stations and the like along the Smoky Hill route to Denver and the Arkansas route to New Mexico."[3]

Where military district commanders like Philip Sheridan perceived danger, others—such as future MOH recipient, Emanuel Stance—saw a new life and unexplored vistas of opportunity. Born in 1843, Stance grew up in East Carroll Parish, Louisiana, and toiled as a sharecropper. At nineteen, he went to the closest recruiting station he could find and traveled to Lake Providence, Louisiana, where he joined Company F of the 9th Cavalry. Shortly afterward, he and a group of fifty fellow recruits withstood six months of basic training at New Orleans before they were transferred to Carrollton, Louisiana, in February of 1867. Standing just over five feet tall and possessing a rather unassuming personality, Stance's ability to read and write and his talents as a natural leader of men were immediately recognized by his superiors. He advanced from private to corporal to sergeant in a matter of months, and earned a two-month leave of absence. In the spring of 1867, Stance and his Company F counterparts, along with other elements of the 9th Cavalry, were ordered to San Antonio, Texas, to practice field instruction. Within two months, the cavalry regiment had reached full strength, with nearly one thousand enlisted men and a steadily growing number of officers.

It was in San Antonio that Stance and the men underwent their baptism by fire. Among their assigned duties were putting down Native American uprisings, policing and protecting American settlers and railroad crews, guarding stage and mail routes in western Texas, and building roads and military installations. However, they also spent much of their time performing garrison and fatigue duty (nonmilitary labor, like digging or cleaning). After being transferred west to Fort Davis, Stance and Company F spent much of the next two and a half years helping open the Western territory that stretched from Fort Clark through El Paso, and from the Rio Grande to the Concho.[4]

On May 20, 1870, Stance, with a small party of men from Company F, received orders from their company commander to leave Fort McKavett and advance twenty miles north toward Kickapoo Springs. Apache Indians had abducted Phillip Bruckmeier's two step-children from Loyal Valley, and it had been four days since they had seen the children. The detachment of men had barely made it halfway to their destination when they spotted a group of approximately twenty Indians driving a team of horses.

Stance took command of the situation, quickly organizing the men into a lined, mounted formation and charging the confused enemy forces until they had captured nine of their horses. After pursuing the Indian party into the hills, Stance and his men abandoned the attack and bivouacked for the night. They had decided to return to Fort McKavett the following morning. The next day, the patrol decamped and proceeded toward the post. A group of Indians stood in their way, intent on capturing a herd of government horses. The Indians flanked left and Stance directed his comrades against the advancing Indians. Stance managed to stave off the enemy advance, forcing them to flee, and sustaining minimal injuries to his men and horses in the process.

> "The gallantry displayed by the Sergeant and his party, as well as the good judgement used on both occasions, deserves much praise."

Capt. Henry Carroll, Stance's commanding officer, heard this story and recommended the diminutive noncommissioned officer for the Medal of Honor. Of Stance's activities under fire, Carroll said, "The gallantry displayed by the Sergeant and his party, as well as the good judgement used on both occasions, deserves much praise. As this is the fourth and fifth encounter that Sergeant Stance has had with Indians within the past two years, on all of which occasions he has been mentioned for good behavior by his immediate commanding officer, it is a pleasure to commend him to higher authority."

On June 28, 1870, Stance received the nation's highest honor for valor, becoming the first black regular in the post–Civil War era to garner such attention. In a letter acknowledging receipt of the award, Stance mused, "I will cherish the gift as a thing of priceless value and endeavor by my future conduct to merit the high honor conferred upon me."[5]

THE HEROISM OF CLINTON GREAVES

In late January 1877, a small group of six troopers with the 9th Cavalry, along with three Navajo scouts, moved out from Fort Bayard. They had received orders to search for Indian raiders who had been active in an area located about thirty-five miles east of Fort Cummings. The soldiers aimed to suppress future attacks by hostile Chiricahua Apaches, who posed a potential threat to the New Mexico border. The arid conditions surrounding the San Carlos reservation located just northeast of the Gila River, where the Apaches resided, proved to be virtually uninhabitable. Indian raiding parties roamed through the territory in search of food and more desirable terrain. The situation intensified as more army troops poured into the area to suppress the hostile Indian forces.

Placed under the command of Lt. Henry Wright, the detachment had barely left the military installation and was approaching an area near the Florida Mountains when they discovered an encampment of nearly fifty hostile Indians. The troop was outnumbered. Wright and his men calmly approached the Apache council, hoping to negotiate peaceful terms. It was not to be. As Apache warriors surrounded them, troopers began laying down a suppressive line of fire.

When the shooting devolved to close-quarter, hand-to-hand combat, Cpl. Clinton Greaves, a native of Prince George's County, Maryland, found himself at the epicenter of the fighting. Using his empty carbine as a club, he beat off the band of attacking Apaches. By taking such bold action, the five-foot-seven-inch noncommissioned officer created an opening that allowed his comrades to escape the nightmare. In this brief half hour of fighting, Greaves and the detachment of soldiers managed to kill five Indians and capture several rifles and eleven horses in the process.

For his efforts, Clinton Greaves would receive the Medal of Honor on June 26, 1879. While the actions taken by Lieutenant Wright and his men during the conflict with the Apaches received immediate attention from the Fort Bayard post commandant, official recognition of Greaves's loyalty and devotion to his comrades at the front that day would have to wait until months later.[6]

Greaves was no stranger to adversity. Born in 1855 in Madison County, Virginia, he moved to Maryland's Prince George's County, where he worked for a short time as a day laborer. At the age of twenty-two, he enlisted in the army and was assigned to the 9th Cavalry, while the unit was stationed at Fort Bayard. On the heels of his heroic encounter in the Florida Mountains, Greaves had reenlisted in the army and worked as a blacksmith with H Troop at Fort Stanton, New Mexico, where he managed to maintain an unblemished record as a first-rate soldier.

> Greaves was no stranger to adversity.

When Wright requested that Greaves receive a Certificate of Merit along with the Medal of Honor for his heroism in southwestern Mexico, his recommendation became ensnarled in technicalities that were commonplace in the nineteenth-century peacetime army. In Wright's view, even though Greaves protected the provisions that sustained the men in his detachment, according to the rules, the fact that the intrepid corporal was a noncommissioned officer disqualified him for the certificate. Only after Gen. William Tecumseh Sherman interceded on his behalf did Greaves receive the War Department's official acknowledgment of his gallant deed.

Despite these obstacles, Greaves's loyalty to the 9th Cavalry and his devotion to his unit remained unwavering. He would spend twenty years on active duty before retiring from the army in 1893. After moving to Ohio, he worked as a civilian employee with the quartermaster department at Columbus Barracks until his death, in 1906.[7]

HEROES ON THE BORDER

Pompey Factor and other Seminole-Negro Indian Scout Medal of Honor Recipients in Southern Texas

Throughout the 1870s, Seminole-Negro Indians were recruited by the US Army to serve as scouts along the Texas border. Approximately fifty-three of the recruits descended from African Americans who had fled the harsh conditions of slavery in antebellum Florida. They had married among Seminole Indians for protection against being recaptured by marauding slave catchers. After being forced to move westward by the US government during the late 1830s and early 1840s, the majority of their families settled on the Mexican side of the Rio Grande District.

By the end of the Civil War, a series of costly skirmishes with Native American tribes had taken place on the Texas frontier. Maj. Zenas Bliss of the 25th Cavalry realized he needed residents with local knowledge to best patrol the borders. In March of 1870, Bliss invited a group of Black Seminoles to return to the United States to serve as scouts. In return for their service, the US government agreed to provide them with cavalryman's pay, provisions for their families, and grants of land. In less than three months, many of these families had accepted the offer and crossed the border into Texas. In August, the first group of scouts traveled to Fort Duncan.[8]

Among the first Black Seminole scouts who appeared at the Texas installation that month was Pompey Factor. Born in Arkansas, he was a product of the forced removal of Seminoles to the Indian Territory during the 1840s. Standing five-foot-eight with black hair and eyes, Factor was twenty-one years old and at the height of his physical powers when he enlisted at Fort Duncan. He and ten other newly recruited scouts received Sharp's carbines at the fort, but they had to furnish their own horses. Factor and his fellow scouts were noted for their skill as exceptional hunters and fearless fighters. Their commanding officers also praised them for their ability to fluently speak, interpret, and translate languages commonly spoken by indigenous populations that lived on the Texas–Mexico border.

Kentucky-born ex-slave and 9th Cavalry member Jacob Wilks had a clear image of Black Seminole scouts like Factor who served on the frontier: "Many of these were part Indian. They all spoke Spanish; only a few of them, the Texas ex-slaves, spoke any English, and were conceded to be the best body of scouts, trailers, and Indian fighters ever engaged along the border." Their heroics would be shared in family lore for more than a century.

During the spring of 1875, Factor found himself summoned to glory at the Eagle's Nest Crossing of the Pecos River. On April 16, he, two fellow Black Seminole scouts, and 1st Lt. John Bullis of the 24th Infantry rode out of Fort Clark, heading toward the lower Pecos River. Accompanying an element of the 25th Infantry en route from Fort Stockton, their mission was to ride one hundred miles northwest to investigate a large party of Comanche who had allegedly stolen seventy-five horses. The Comanche had encamped along the banks of the lower Pecos River where it emptied into the Rio Grande. After spending nearly a week with soldiers of the 25th in pursuit of the elusive party, Bullis decided on April 22 to strike out southwest toward the Pecos. After discovering signs of a group of Indians near Johnson's Run, a dry arroyo on the east side of the river, Factor and his party continued southwest until they reached the mouth of Howard's Creek. There they enjoyed a rare opportunity to rest and water and feed their horses before picking up the trail west toward the Rio Grande a few hours later.

On the morning of April 25, the scouting party had marched twenty miles south down the Rio Grande and crossed the Pecos when they stumbled upon a fresh set of horse tracks heading northwest, toward Eagle's Nest Crossing. As Bullis filed in his report, "The trail was quite large and came from the direction of the settlements and was made, I judge, by seventy-five head or more, of horses." The spirited junior officer and his scouts promptly pursued the new trail for nearly an hour before running almost headlong into the raiding party and the stolen horses. Undetected, the reconnaissance team dismounted and exchanged a volley of fire with the enemy combatants, killing three Comanche and capturing their herd of horses twice, before being forced to withdraw.

During the skirmish, Pvt. Pompey Factor and two other scouts distinguished themselves in action. Their commanding officer had lost his horse and was now on foot, standing directly in the path of the onrushing Indians. The scouts laid down supportive fire to their left and right flank while riding through the Comanche party. At the same time, one of them raced through the enemy, pulling Bullis up onto his horse and out of harm's way. Shortly afterward, the men returned to Fort Clark virtually unscathed, having successfully confronted enemy forces and accomplished the mission at hand. Of the hair-raising moment and the willingness of the men to risk life and limb on his behalf that day, Bullis commented a day later, "They are brave and trustworthy, and are each worthy of a medal." On May 28, 1875, Factor and his fellow scouts received the Medal of Honor for their "gallantry in action."[9]

The Seminole-Negro Indian scouts continued to serve with the US Army on the southwest Texas–northern Mexico frontier. Most of them probably had the same experiences with frontier honor as Pompey Factor—a brief moment in the sun as a famous Indian War hero, followed by racial resentment harbored by indigenous populations living on the border.

Factor served intermittently in the army throughout the 1870s before deserting military service for Mexico in 1877, where he rode for two years with Col. Pedro Avincular

Valdez, a famous Mexican Indian fighter. In May of 1879, Factor returned to Fort Clark, Texas, where the army restored him to active duty as a scout, but garnished the previous wages he had earned during his absence as punishment for his indiscretion. While his reasons for deserting remain unclear, it is conceivable that interethnic strife and violence meted out against Black Seminole scouts who served on the Texas border may have been root causes for his defection. Factor remained at Fort Clark until he was mustered out of the army in November of 1880, at the ripe old age of thirty. But he continued to wage war against what he perceived as personal affronts to his reputation.

As a case in point, Factor eventually moved to south Texas where he engaged in subsistence farming in Brackettville, Texas, and Muzquiz, Mexico. During the period, he and his descendants filed a petition with the US government in 1926, demanding compensation for his military service and status as a Medal of Honor recipient. After his death in 1928, Factor's reputation as a nineteenth-century hero was shrouded in ignominy, including the fact that he was laid to rest in an unmarked grave that failed to meet the standards of honor.

His application for government recognition did bear fruit several generations later. In 1991, descendants of the Seminole-Negro Indian scouts traveled to a rural tribal cemetery outside of Brackettville and looked on with pride as the army paid homage to the memory of Factor and his fellow scouts, Isaac Paine, Adam Payne, and John Ward, by placing Medal of Honor headstones over their grave sites.[10]

Benjamin Brown   Isaiah Mays

BLACK HEROISM ON WESTERN STAGECOACHES

Benjamin Brown and Isaiah Mays and the Wham Robbery of 1889

During the late 1880s, African-American soldiers were stationed in the Far Southwest at Forts Grant, Thomas, Bowie, and Apache. They performed myriad duties ranging from digging holes, planting poles, and stringing telegraph wire to renovating military posts, surveying, mapping, and building new roads, and locating sources of water for newly arrived settlers. Some of the most important assignments given to black units garrisoned at these posts involved preventing whites from venturing onto reservations in the Indian Territory, as well as providing an armed presence for stagecoaches, trains, wagons, railroad crews, surveying parties, and paymasters who traveled between military outposts in the region. The latter engaged and taxed the energies of even the most committed and dedicated members of the Buffalo Soldier units. According to one historian, "Because Indian Territory was off limits to white settlers and travelers, the garrisons were more isolated than usual from civilization. The army had to build its own access roads to the posts, and what travel did occur in Indian Territory was restricted to official business with the army garrisons or Indian agencies." Members of the 24th Infantry faced a combustible mix of violence, lawlessness, political instability, latent anger toward Official Washington, and religious intolerance that combined with white animosity toward the presence of armed black troops.[11]

This was the volatile environment that shaped the acts of courage performed by Sgt. Benjamin Brown and Cpl. Isaiah Mays on the morning of May 11, 1889. A day earlier, the two men had been ordered to travel from Fort Grant to a nearby railroad depot where they were to accompany veteran paymaster Maj. Joseph Wham and his clerk, William Gibbon, along with a party of ten young privates, on a mission to Fort Thomas. The War Department had asked Wham and other paymasters to travel throughout the Department of Arizona to pay all troops listed among the April muster who served at Camp Carlos and Forts Bowie, Thomas, and Apache.

While traveling along the Fort Grant–Fort Thomas Road, the men were tasked with guarding a strongbox containing exactly $28,348.10, composed largely of gold and silver coins weighing approximately 250 pounds. The precious cargo was carried aboard an ambulance driven by a team of twelve army mules and supported by an open wagon driven by Brown, Mays, and seven other soldiers from the 24th Infantry.

Brown, a native who hailed from Spotsylvania County, Virginia, was one of the longest-serving soldiers of the group, having been in the army for eight years after enlisting at Harrisburg, Pennsylvania, in 1881. While relatively young, Brown's reputation as a proficient soldier had earned him a series of promotions, from corporal to sergeant, and he was attracting the attention of his counterparts as an expert marksman. By the end of the 1890s, he would become a permanent fixture at rifle competitions held throughout the Department of Arizona. Born as a slave in Carter's Bridge, Virginia, Isaiah Mays's experience was also marked by an extended period of time in the Indian Territory of Arizona. The thirty-one-year-old had just risen to the rank of corporal before being assigned to this detail.

Much of the forty-two-mile trek from Fort Grant to Fort Thomas proved to be uneventful. As the men moved past Bonita, a small civilian community close to Fort Grant, as well as several prominent ranches in the territory, they encountered few obstacles. After passing Eureka Springs and making the climb through Eagle Pass to Cedar Springs, the soldiers changed teams, and Brown moved to sit alongside the paymaster's driver. Fort Thomas was within sight. As the men rode through the last leg of the journey, they were probably eagerly awaiting the soft bedding of the barracks, some welcome victuals, and the chance to swap a few stories with their compatriots. But around 1:00 p.m. that day, the progress they had made seemed to be all for naught.

The men had driven five miles down a sharp cut of rock into a dry streambed called the Cottonwood Wash when Major Wham's wagon came to a stuttering halt. The paymaster, his vision obstructed by the inside of the covered wagon, asked his team of drivers about the source of the team's trouble. Brown replied, "A boulder is in the road, sir." As the highest-ranking noncommissioned officer with the party, Brown quickly organized the soldiers to dislodge the rock from the road.[12]

As the men worked to remove the roadblock, they heard a series of gunshots ringing out from rocky formations above their positions. Pvt. George Short, a 24th infantryman with the escort party, later recalled, "There was a volley fired and at the same time, a voice said, 'Git out, you black sons of bitches.'" In that instant, the army detail found themselves subjected to several fierce rounds of gunfire coming from highwaymen armed with Winchester rifles, fiercely determined to take the payroll from them.

With enemy bullets raining down on them, the escort party used the covered ambulances and fallen mules as defensive cover before regrouping behind a rocky ledge located nearby. During the holdup, Sergeant Brown used his revolver to answer the challenge laid down by the gang, firing upon them as they crouched behind cedar trees located above them. Brown continued discharging his weapon, laying down suppressive fire despite sustaining gunshot wounds to his left side. The wounded sharpshooter then ordered Private Short to give him his carbine, which Brown used to fire on the highwaymen. He continued shooting from a prone position until he received a bullet slug in his left forearm, totally incapacitating him. Meanwhile, Corporal Mays also fired on the robbers, emptying his revolver. Despite their valiant efforts, the bandits managed to obtain the payroll. Mays eventually ordered a retreat for the detail before "walking and crawling two miles to a nearby ranch in order to get help."[13]

After the two-hour gun battle, an ambulance carrying members of the escort party made the twelve-mile journey to Fort Thomas. Eight members of the detail were severely wounded, and the army payroll belonging to the US government was now in the hands of the outlaw highwaymen. Nonetheless, the performances of Sergeant Brown and Corporal Mays during the ordeal impressed Major Wham to such an extent that he recommended them for Medals of Honor in September of 1889. Their "gallantry and meritorious action" was on full display during the skirmish, and Wham emphasized this point in his letter: "I was a soldier in Grant's world regiment during the entire war; it was justly proud of its record of sixteen battles and of the reflected glory of its old Colonel, the 'Great Commander,'" he stated. "[B]ut I never witnessed better courage or better fighting than [what was] shown by these colored soldiers, on May 11, 1889, as the bullet marks on the robbers' positions to-day abundantly attest."[14]

Wham's request advanced slowly up the chain of command, through the Headquarters Department of Arizona, earning the approval of Col. Zenas Bliss, the 24th Infantry's commanding officer, and landing on the desk of the Secretary of War in Washington.[15]

> They heard a series of gunshots ringing out from rocky formations above their positions.

Before Wham's endorsement arrived in the nation's capital, a robust debate had ensued among Department of Arizona officers that reflected the wide range of interpretation within the late nineteenth-century army over military action in the Trans-Mississippi West. Some white officers like Joseph Wham recognized that the role of the Regular Army was moving beyond one of primarily protecting settlements from indigenous Indian populations. But policymakers stubbornly held on to their views about what constituted "distinguished action" on the battlefield. Nowhere were these differing views more evident than during the processing and awarding of Medals of Honor to the two standout heroes of the paymaster robbery.

After investigating the Wham robbery, the Department of Arizona's acting inspector general disagreed with the paymaster's recommendation, stating that the actions taken by Brown and Mays failed to pass the bar of "distinction on the field of battle" as specified by army regulations 175 and 176. "The fact remains that the robbers drove them away from the funds they were detailed to protect," he stated.[16] Major General Schofield, the army's senior officer at the time, concurred, arguing that "these cases do not seem to be of that class properly designated as 'extraordinary' or 'most distinguished.'"[17] Schofield's views failed to carry the day, however. Upon further investigation, Secretary of War Redfield Proctor overruled the dissenting views and awarded medals to the two men on February 19, 1890.[18]

FRONTIER HONOR AND THE BUFFALO SOLDIERS

Like their white counterparts, black Medal of Honor recipients in the post–Civil War army did not always follow the rules of frontier honor. Occasionally, their sense of manhood and character produced acts of rebellion, causing them to brush up against army standards—not to mention the military justice system that existed in the segregated army. The monotony of garrison duty in Indian Territory meant endless bouts of boredom, booze, and belligerency for restless black troopers. And frequently, disciplinary problems—both major and minor—arose, involving recruits and noncommissioned officers alike.

This was certainly the case for black MOH recipients during this period. Even while displaying extraordinary leadership skills on the Texas frontier, Emanuel Stance frequently violated army regulations, resulting in numerous garrison court-martial proceedings stemming from charges of "conduct prejudicial to good order and discipline" throughout the 1870s and early 1880s. Each time, he was fined, his rank was reduced, and he forfeited his pay and benefits.

Some MOH recipients found that their feelings about the army had profoundly changed after they were recognized for bravery. After receiving his medal, Cpl. Isaiah Mays reenlisted in 1891, only to reverse course and seek a discharge a year later. Ten years in the Far Southwest had apparently provided him with a strong desire to quit frontier life and return to his home state of Virginia. Mays registered his increasing frustration with his inability to support family members and his deeply felt yearning to leave military service: "My reasons for wanting my discharge is that my parents are old and they are not able to take care of themselves. I want to be with them so that I can properly support them."

After the Secretary of War denied his request, Mays staged his own acts of rebellion, suggesting that his commanding officer's rejection of his discharge was motivated by racial prejudice. As a consequence for his actions, he was reassigned to Fort Bayard, New Mexico, reduced in rank, and forced to relinquish pay in the process. In 1893, he got his chance to leave military service. He chose to remain in the Southwest, working as a miner in Arizona until his death in 1925.

Others devised more drastic strategies to bid farewell to military life. In April of 1891, Cpl. William O. Wilson—recognized by fellow soldiers within his battalion for his heroic actions during the 9th Cavalry's Pine Ridge Campaign against the Sioux just a few months earlier—decided to leave his military outpost. He headed for southern Nebraska, without authorization from his superior officers.[19]

And sometimes, the same personal attributes and behavior that distinguished these men as tough and fearless fighters also predisposed them to volatile confrontations with other soldiers.

Intemperate action followed by charges of insubordination punctuated the career of 1st Sgt. John Denny after he won the Medal of Honor for service against the Apaches in 1879. During the spring of 1891, Denny came to blows with his fellow 9th cavalryman Lawrence Galloway after the enlisted man cheated him of three dollars and seventy-five cents. After Galloway called him a liar, the decorated noncommissioned officer angrily retorted, "You damned bastard—I'll knock your goddamned head off!" At the court-martial that followed, Denny defended his actions by pointing to his exemplary military record: "I have always endeavored to perform my duties as a soldier. During any period while serving as a noncommissioned officer, I have taken every precaution practicable to preserve discipline."[20]

> Others devised more drastic strategies to bid farewell to military life.

Often such skirmishes ended in tragedy. Known by many as a hot-tempered heavy drinker, Emanuel Stance came to blows with many enlisted men before meeting his untimely demise at the hands of his own troops on Christmas morning of 1887.

After receiving his discharge from the 24th Infantry in 1875, Adam Payne found himself facing a warrant for his arrest when he stabbed a fellow soldier during a dance held near Brownsville, Texas. Not long afterward, Payne—whom his fellow servicemen had dubbed "Bad Man"—suffered a similar fate when a local deputy sheriff decided to act as judge, jury, and executioner in the case. Without bothering to arrest Payne, the law enforcement officer simply unloaded his double-barreled shotgun into the back of the former Black Seminole scout, killing him instantly.[21]

Meanwhile, Clinton Greaves, the hero of the Florida Mountains mission, spent nearly twenty years with the 9th Cavalry before he was transferred to Columbus Barracks, Ohio, in 1888. He worked there for five years before retiring from the army in 1893. While living in Ohio, he worked for the quartermaster department until he passed away in 1906, at the age of fifty-one. His wife, Bertha Williams, survived him by several decades, laboring as a domestic worker before dying in 1936. While Greaves was laid to rest in Columbus, Ohio, his likeness has been immortalized by a statue located at Fort Bayard, New Mexico.[22]

The Medal of Honor was the highlight in the careers of soldiers like Thomas Boyne, Thomas Shaw, Augustus Walley, Moses Williams, William Othello Wilson, and Brent Woods. Although little information exists about what happened to them after their moments of glory, the legacy of their service in the American West and their devotion to duty resonated in the memory of generations of African Americans at the end of the nineteenth century.

By the close of the 1890s, Elizabethtown, North Carolina, native William McBryar stood unwittingly between two worlds. Like most of his fellow Buffalo Soldiers, McBryar had witnessed firsthand the widespread changes occurring throughout the country. America's industrial growth and increased presence on the global stage spelled a new set of challenges regarding race and gender for him and the twenty-two other MOH recipients who had served in the Indian-fighting army just after the Civil War. Beginning in the late

1870s and well into the 1880s, Jim Crow segregation, coupled with an epidemic of race pogroms and lynchings, had structured their lives from cradle to grave. And by the 1890s, McBryar and many other blacks were excluded from industrial jobs in the South, as more than 80 percent were relegated to domestic and day-laboring occupations in the region. In the North and major parts of the Midwest, job conditions for working-class blacks struck a similar dour note.

But here is where most of the similarities come to an end. In an era during which most African-American soldiers served as enlisted men and noncommissioned officers, McBryar stood worlds apart. Born in 1861 prior to the Civil War, he joined the army in 1887. Three years later, he was awarded the Medal of Honor for his "coolness, bravery, and good marksmanship" against the Apaches in southern Arizona as a sergeant with the 10th Cavalry's K Company. When the United States became embroiled in the imperial wars against the Spanish regime in Cuba and in the insurgency in the Philippines, in 1898, McBryar rallied to the nation's colors, serving admirably with the 25th Infantry in Santiago, Cuba. As a result of his gallantry during the campaign, he reported to Fort Thomas, Kentucky, where he earned a commission as a lieutenant with the 8th Volunteer Infantry.

Despite these accolades, McBryar craved a regular commission in the army. While serving as a junior officer with the 49th Volunteer Infantry in the Philippines, he frequently sought the aid of several senior officers in an effort to realize this dream—to no avail. Even though he eagerly volunteered his services during both World Wars, misfortune and age, combined with expanded Jim Crowism, frustrated his attempts at every turn.

After leaving the army in 1905, the eighty-year-old retired soldier moved to Philadelphia, Pennsylvania, where he worked as a public school teacher until his death from cerebral thrombosis on March 8, 1941. A week later, he was interred in Arlington National Cemetery, thus becoming a permanent fixture in the collective memory of his Medal of Honor brethren and fellow soldiers. It would take several generations of black patriots serving their country in battle during the next century to realize his dream.[23]

Among those whose battlefield exploits during the Indian Wars are not described in this narrative are George Jordan and Henry Johnson.

US African-American troops of 10th US Cavalry sharpen sabres in Cuba, Spanish-American War, 1898 (b/w photo), American Photographer (19th century)

CHAPTER 3

"Honor to the Race"

BLACK LOYALISTS AND THE AMERICAN WARS FOR EMPIRE IN CUBA AND THE PHILIPPINES, 1898–1917

Our people can now see that the coolness and bravery that characterized our fathers in the [18]60s have been handed down to their sons of the [18]90s. If any one doubts the fitness of a colored soldier for active field service, when the cry of musketry, the booming of cannon, and bursting of shells seem to make the earth tremble, ask the regimental commanders of the Twenty-fourth and Twenty-fifth infantries and Ninth and Tenth Cavalry. Ask Generals Lawton, Kent, and Wheeler, of whose divisions these regiments form a part.

—M. W. Saddler, 25th Infantry, 1898

While serving on a diplomatic mission as a US military attaché to Hispaniola in 1906, Maj. Charles Young wrote a treatise in which he linked his perceptions of valor and courage to African-American empowering strategies in the new century. In a book titled *Military Morale of Nations and Races*, Young claimed that "military virtues can be cultivated," and he appealed to "countrymen of all race extractions to foster and encourage the things that keep alive civic and military courage, patriotism, and the vigor, strength, and sturdiness of American manhood, upon which virile virtues depend so largely our national life and the honor and dignity among nations of our common country—our Motherland, America."[1]

In many ways, Young's racial interpretation of national military prowess may be seen as a directive for the acts of heroism performed by the regular cavalry and infantry units. This is most notably true for black Medal of Honor winners in the war against Spain in 1898, and during the rebellion in the Philippines in 1899. It points toward the ways in which black troops in the Spanish-American War used their guns to fight for dignity and honor on the battlefield, even though they were contending with the federally sanctioned indignities of a racially segregated army and constant harassment from white citizens.

As we have previously seen, since the Civil War, African Americans perceived military service and the donning of the nation's uniform as a badge of honor, promoting an antiracist image and a strong, masculine sense of self. Writing about African-American military exploits in Cuba at the time, 25th Infantry chaplain Theophilus G. Steward expressed his hope "that the reader will be inspired to a more profound respect for the brave and skilled black men who passed through that severe baptism of fire and suffering, contributing their full share to their country's honor."

As the century drew to a close, the country faced pressing challenges both abroad and at home. By the time federal policymakers and pundits began to discuss the explosion of the USS *Maine* in Havana Harbor and America's role in world affairs, black Americans were raising their voices, pointing out the painful contradictions between US professions of world leadership and the rising tide of violence at home. Coming from various points on the political spectrum, many African-American pro-war and anti-imperial advocates frequently used terms like *protection*, *duty*, and *honor* to compare the country's skirmish with Spain over control of Cuba with the plight of black Americans at home. And by doing so, they enveloped the racially charged international conflict between the two colonial powers squarely in the context of the black struggle for equality in the United States.

In the months leading up to the American declaration of war, some members of the black press argued that the United States should not intervene in the Spanish-Cuban War to safeguard the rights of Cuban residents until Southerners obeyed the laws of the land. "Let Uncle Sam keep hands off of other countries till he has learned to govern his own," asserted the Kansas City *American Citizen*. "Human life at home is at a low ebb now and should be protected before reaching out to protect others," the newspaper contended. The *Washington Bee* echoed this sentiment: "The United States may play the coward in the [USS] *Maine* explosion by the Cubans, but whether it does or not the American negro must look to his own interest and protection. A government that claims to be unable to protect its own citizens against mob law and political violence will certainly not ask the negroes to take up arms against a foreign government."

Around the same time, Ida B. Wells-Barnett traveled with a Chicago delegation of Illinois congressmen to the White House to meet with President William McKinley, and described the issue for the president in the following manner: "For nearly twenty years, lynching crimes, which stand side by side with Armenian and Cuban outrages, have been committed and permitted by this Christian nation. Postmaster [Frazier] Baker's case was a federal matter, pure and simple. He died at his post of duty in defense of his country's honor, as truly as ever a soldier on the field of battle. We refuse to believe this country, so powerful to defend its citizens abroad, is unable to defend its citizens at home."[2]

> "We refuse to believe this country, so powerful to defend its citizens abroad, is unable to defend its citizens at home."

But other black pundits saw the war and black loyalty somewhat differently, viewing the group's participation in the military conflict as a chance to test and prove their loyalty, to assert their manhood, and to gain public respect. The *Iowa Bystander* expressed its belief that "the present war will help the colored man in America, that is, his real worth will be more respected; his help is needed; his loyalty will establish a friendlier feeling in the South between the two races, his bravery and patriotism in the hour of need, may serve as a lesson to their southern brothers as to what loyalty, true and equal manhood is, and we hope will hereafter be more willing to grant equal justice and freedom to their neighbors and citizens."

Immediately following on the heels of the congressional declaration of war against Spain, the *Indianapolis Freeman* stated, "As in other cities the Negro is discussing his attitude toward the government in case of war—shall he go to war and fight for his country's flag? Yes, for every reason of true patriotism. It is a blessing in disguise for the Negro. He will if for no other reason be possessed of arms, which in the South, in face of threatened mob violence, he is not allowed to have. He will become trained and disciplined [. . .] he will get honor. He will have an opportunity of proving to the world his real bravery, worth, and manhood."[3]

In time, the words uttered by black civil rights advocates like Ida Wells-Barnett and the black press framed the experiences of Medal of Honor recipients William Thompkins, George Wanton, Dennis Bell, Fitz Lee, Edward Baker, and Robert Penn, who served admirably during the Spanish-American War. More than 75 percent of the soldiers who earned the nation's highest honor for valor did so while assigned to the celebrated 10th Cavalry; the sole exception—Robert Penn—served as a sailor on board the USS *Iowa* off the coast of Santiago. All of them, however, interpreted bravery and honor through lenses forged from their immediate pasts. For the most part, they were born and bred along the Eastern Seaboard and in the Great Plains region of the United States during the years following the Civil War, and had eagerly enlisted for military service out of concern for their own personal well-being and for the collective advancement of black people. Almost to a man, most served with the Regular Army in the Trans-Mississippi West, and spent some time in the South before venturing on to Cuba and the Philippines.

"He will have an opportunity of proving to the world his real bravery, worth, and manhood."

In short, military service and the American imperial project provided them with a framework for understanding manhood and respectability both at home and abroad. As MOH recipient Edward L. Baker reflected, several years after serving in the war against Spain:

The great Napoleon is credited with the following assertion: that there were only two professions open to a gentleman—statecraft and the profession of Arms; in other words, the grandest known to the world is the profession of Arms. When a man satisfies the recruiting officer of his ability to enter the service, he is given a chance to convince himself as to whether or not he desires to accept the profession. His future, however, is, in a great measure, what he makes it. No one is indifferent to his obligations as a man and his duties as soldier. Certificates of merit, for distinguished service; medal of honor for distinguished gallantry in action and prizes for excellence in any target practice; [these] are manly pursuits and enviable acquisitions, but are in reach of us all.[4]

As the black regulars advanced through their training, they ran headlong into an old adversary. Throughout their training they faced pernicious Jim Crow laws and white racial antagonism that dogged their steps at nearly every turn. Despite the increasing presence of racial hostility, however, black troops, along with six white regiments, traveled to Tampa, where on June 14, 1898, they marched up the gangplanks of the *Miami, Alamo, Comal, Concho, City of Washington*, and *Leona*, bound for Cuba. As the transport ships dropped anchor off the coastline of Santiago, several contingents of black regulars stood poised for action on the Cuban mainland.[5]

After rowing ashore, three columns of Regular Army and volunteers established an American operations base at Daiquiri and Siboney before trudging west toward lightly fortified enemy defenses near Santiago. Led by Maj. Gen. William R. Shafter, their objective was to land on Cuba's southern shore and march west toward Santiago, to capture the city and its harbor. But a contingent of the 10th Cavalry's mission received an assignment to deliver food and ammunition to the Cuban insurgents who were operating in the western areas of the front. Among these troops were cavalry privates Dennis Bell from Washington, DC, Fitz Lee from Dinwiddie County, Virginia, and Paterson, New Jersey, natives William Thompkins and George Wanton. Little did they realize that within weeks, they would receive their first, bittersweet taste of war and a call to glory.

Dennis Bell

Fitz Lee

"SERVICE OF A HAZARDOUS NATURE"

Dennis Bell, Fitz Lee, William Thompkins, and George Wanton
and the Rescue Mission at Tayabacao, Cuba

On the night of June 30, Tunas, an area near the port of Cienfuegos, became the site of chaos. A small party of Cuban army regulars and fifty Americans led by Gen. Jose Manuel Nunez waded ashore in hopes of replenishing the food supplies and ammunition of a detachment of Cuban forces actively engaged in attacking a heavily defended enemy fort located in the area. After landing at the mouth of the San Juan River, however, the landing party found that reinforcing their comrades in arms required more than good fortune. As soon as the black regulars conquered the rough surf and reached a densely jungled area near Tayabacao, enemy artillery forced them to retreat back to the coastline. The invading soldiers fled to a nearby beachhead where they discovered that several of their landing boats had been damaged beyond repair by Spanish artillery fire. The party of regulars was forced to leave their wounded comrades exposed to fire from the heavily fortified

William Thompkins

George Wanton

blockhouse. One officer who witnessed the nightmarish assault stated, "Had I known the fate that awaited them, I would not have permitted my men to run so great a risk as the undertaking exposed them to."

After learning about the unfolding events, the American command aboard the transport ship *Florida* launched a series of attempts to rescue the stranded survivors of the failed attack. Led by 9th Infantry captain George P. Ahern, a group of American regulars volunteered for a relief expedition aimed at rescuing the men left behind. Among the contingent of rescuers who immediately stepped forward for the covert operation were sergeants William Thompkins and George Wanton, and privates Dennis Bell and Fitz Lee of the 10th Cavalry. With the exception of Bell, all of the troopers served with M Company, and each soldier was no stranger to extreme danger. All had served a stint of duty in the Trans-Mississippi West with the Indian-fighting army prior to the turn of the twentieth century. George Wanton was somewhat the exception to the rule: Like William Thompkins, he was born and raised in Paterson, New Jersey, but Wanton had entered the 10th Cavalry in 1889 after serving more than four years in the US Navy. For these GIs, rescuing the captured soldiers was a way to salvage what was left of the ill-fated invasion—not to mention the fact that each man considered the self-styled "filibusters" as "intimate friends of the wounded," and simply wanted to bring the soldiers back home.[6]

Using nightfall to conceal their clandestine movement, the four men descended from the *Florida* and quietly rowed their boats ashore. The element of surprise proved short-lived for the quartet, however. Upon arriving at the shoreline where the wounded men had fallen, the party fell prey to a hail of enemy fire from a Spanish detachment. Unflinchingly calm, Wanton, Thompkins, and the rest of the volunteers shot the sentries who guarded the prison stockade and freed the captured soldiers. By the early-morning hours of July 1, they had successfully returned to the troop transport ship.

In the weeks that followed, their courageous acts of bravery drew praise from their superior officers. In the words of Troop M's first sergeant James Williams, "It seemed as if this little band of heroes were doomed to find

> Congress conferred the Medal of Honor upon the four members of the 10th Cavalry four months later.

a watery grave on the coast of Cuba. But clearing themselves from the sandbar, they proceeded in capturing stores and munitions of war, winning to themselves the admiration of the Commander-in-Chief of the Cuban forces." For their efforts, Lieutenant Johnson recommended the squad of heroes for the nation's highest award for bravery in February of 1899. After receiving commendations from their superior officers, Congress conferred the Medal of Honor upon the four members of the 10th Cavalry four months later.[7]

"BLACK HEROES IN ARMS"

Edward Baker and the Valorous Conduct of the 10th Cavalry at Santiago

Meanwhile, the July offensive in the Province of Santiago posed a new set of challenges for American invading forces and created new moments of bravery for Medal of Honor recipients. Spanish defenders led by General Vara converted the houses on the low-lying hills of the heights of San Juan and Kettle Hills into a heavily armed fortress. Located just northeast of the village, the area was reinforced by a large blockhouse encircled by barbed-wire entanglements, rifle pits, and trenches. This strategic position provided the outer line of defense for the portals of Santiago.

The climate proved to be just as ominous as the fortified enemy positions. A week earlier, a detachment of newly arrived black troopers from the 10th had landed on the southeastern tip of Cuba near Santiago and marched westward toward El Caney. After advancing north toward the enemy stronghold, the men had to fight their way through the dense undergrowth. The jungle-like vegetation was so thick they could barely march single file. Overall, the troops fell thirty to forty minutes off the pace of their attack because of the steep and rugged slopes. What's more, the searing Cuba heat and humidity weaved an ominous spell of exhaustion among the men and reduced the blanket rolls and the blue woolen and flannel uniforms they wore into mud-drenched pools of sweat. The terrain and climate were such that Edward Glass, an officer with the 10th Cavalry,

> "The vapor from wet clothing rose with the sun, so that you could scarcely recognize a man ten feet away."

observed, "Deployment was difficult owing to the high grass and vegetation. There was difficulty in maintaining any kind of skirmish line." As he and his fellow troopers marched toward the enemy fortifications, Edward Baker noted that "the vapor from wet clothing rose with the sun, so that you could scarcely recognize a man ten feet away."[8]

A veteran noncommissioned officer with the 10th Cavalry, Edward Baker earned the Medal of Honor during the assault on San Juan Hill. Originally from Laramie County, Wyoming, Baker was familiar with the privations and hardships that accompanied inclement weather and impassable terrain, having become acquainted with frontier life at an early age. Born in 1865, he grew up in a multiethnic household, with an African-American mother and a French father. His parents were pioneers who survived the harsh summers and winters while traveling through the Rocky Mountain region during the waning days of the American Civil War. In fact, Baker's first recollections of life on the Great Plains stem from an early childhood spent aboard a freight wagon crossing the Dakota Territory. While living in eastern Wyoming, Baker learned to ride horseback and rope cattle by the tender age of thirteen. Desiring something more out of life, he left the high plains frontier and enlisted in the army in July of 1882. He reported to active duty at Fort Riley, Kansas, and was assigned to the 9th Cavalry Regiment. He served with the celebrated unit for nearly ten years before reporting to Santa Fe, New Mexico, where he was reassigned to the 10th Cavalry.

While serving with the troops at the southwestern military outpost, Baker discovered that military service appealed strongly to his sense of self. His fluent language skills in Russian, Spanish, Chinese, and French, and his considerable abilities as a talented trumpeter and horseman, earned him a sterling reputation among his peers as a professional soldier of the highest order. After being reassigned to the 10th Cavalry's Troop B, Baker was promoted from a lowly private to regimental quartermaster sergeant. His troop commander may have said it best when he wrote: "I have always found Sergeant Major Baker zealous, efficient and faithful in the performance of every duty. He is a fine type of the true American soldier and is a credit to the enlisted force of the United States Army."

By the time he and his fellow troopers reached the bivouac site just below the heights surrounding the city of Santiago, Baker had concluded that black cavalrymen were essential to the fighting, and that the war in Cuba offered them a chance to present themselves as skilled soldiers, and as black men. "Our daring horsemen were all that was needed to make the situation complete," he stated. "Without participation of cavalry, the ideal warrior disappears from the scene, and the battle and picture of war is robbed of its most attractive feature."[9]

Edward Baker was not the only soldier whose post–Indian War years in the Southwest predated his call to duty at El Caney and San Juan Hill. There were several other Buffalo Soldiers who had previously received congressional recognition for bravery in battle. As a sergeant in Company K, William McBryar had developed a reputation as a skilled marksman while in battle against the Apache Indians in the Arizona Territory in 1890. By the time Troop K had arrived in Cuba, the thirty-seven-year-old Elizabethtown, North Carolina, veteran had been with the unit for nearly ten years.

Meanwhile, the 10th's first sergeant and fellow MOH recipient Augustus Walley had been on active duty for nearly thirty years, and was ten years removed from receiving the nation's highest award for his heroic acts of bravery against hostile Indians at Cuchillo Negro Mountains, New Mexico. When the unit landed at Daiquiri, officers and enlisted men credited the Baltimore, Maryland, noncommissioned officer with providing steady leadership for the squadrons of the regular cavalry regiment.[10]

Once the troopers of the 10th moved into position against the entrenchments at El Caney, they were joined by fellow 9th cavalrymen, along with the 24th and 25th Infantry Regiments. But they also found themselves reacquainted once again with the all-white elements of the 1st US Volunteer Cavalry. Composed of volunteers from Arizona, New Mexico, Oklahoma, and Texas, the unit was organized by former assistant secretary of the navy Theodore Roosevelt and commanded by Col. Leonard Wood. The American volunteers were supplemented by other troops coming from New York, Massachusetts, North Carolina, and an assortment of Cuban forces. Altogether, fifteen thousand soldiers participated in the assault, making up the regiments of one of former Confederate general Joseph Wheeler's advancing brigades.

Just a week earlier, the men of the 1st Volunteer Cavalry had witnessed the heroics of the black troopers firsthand. On June 24, an advancing column of men with the 1st had staged an ambush against the enemy stronghold at Las Guasimas. However, the smokeless fire from the Spanish guns and the thick vegetation had stymied their advance at every turn. With exploding shells and whizzing enemy bullets around them, eight men lay dead and eighteen were wounded along the slopes of the rugged hill. The situation was so dire that Theodore Roosevelt, the officer who commanded the unit for much of that day, later recalled, "The Spaniards who had been holding the trenches and the line of hills had fallen back upon their supports, and we were under a very heavy fire both from rifles and great guns. At the point where we were, the grass-covered hill-crest was gently rounded, giving poor cover, and I made my men lie down on the hither slope."

Just as it appeared that the unit's assault had reached a point of confusion and all was lost, a column of the 10th Cavalry rushed forward. American commanders had initially placed the all-black unit in reserve on one of the roads that led to the outpost. But when the Rough Riders began to display elements of disarray, the 10th quickly moved into position, exposing itself to deadly enemy fire for a sufficient period of time until the 1st Volunteers could reestablish themselves. In particular, Augustus Walley distinguished himself under fire. In the heat of the fighting, Walley carried a badly wounded American soldier to safety despite facing an endless stream of volleys from Spanish riflemen. The selfless heroism that Walley and other Buffalo Soldiers exhibited in the face of enemy fire that day captured the attention of their fellow officers. John J. Pershing, a quartermaster officer who served with the all-black unit, observed that day: "The Tenth Cavalry, having charged up the hill, scarcely firing a shot and being nearest the Rough Riders, opened a disastrous enfilading fire upon the Spanish right, thus relieving the Rough Riders from the volleys that were being poured into them from that part of the Spanish line."[11]

On the morning of July 1, the dismounted companies of the 10th Cavalry once again faced the horrors of war. As part of a cavalry division, black regulars with the 10th Cavalry forded the San Juan River and advanced north toward the city of Santiago. Their mission was to accompany the 1st US Volunteer Cavalry as the all-white unit stormed the Spanish fortifications at El Caney to rout the enemy and capture the city. But as members of the Rough Riders quickly realized, the advance up San Juan and Kettle Hills tested their mettle in more ways than one. There, approximately eight hundred Spanish Regular Troops stood poised to defend the heavily armed outpost. As the dismounted troopers awaited their orders to press the attack, enemy sharpshooters used modern Mauser rifles to rain bullets down on them, causing numerous casualties in the process.

In some ways, the American attack strategy was hampered by the sheer limitations of its own weaponry and tactics. While US regulars like William McBryar, Augustus Walley, and Edward Baker were armed with M-1898 Krag-Jorgensen bolt-action rifles, most of the American cavalry volunteers shouldered single-shot Springfield rifles that belched black powder into the air when they were fired. As the fighting progressed, thick clouds of black powder emanating from the Springfield rifles hampered the sight of the assaulting units, making them easy targets for the Spanish while rendering all approaches by American forces along the slopes of San Juan and Kettle Hills nearly impassable.

In addition, the long lines of communication made it extremely difficult for commanders to relay their orders to the troops on the battlefield. Spanish sharpshooters zeroed in on the reconnoitering balloons that were deployed by a company of the Signal Corps, causing greater damage to approaching American troops. And to make matters worse, American troops launched the offensive forward, using the antiquated Civil War tactics of straight-line advancement, sustaining even greater losses at the hands of the Spanish enemy. Correspondent Richard Harding Davis recalled, "[M]en gasped on their backs, like fishes in the bottom of a boat, their heads burning inside and out, their limbs too heavy to move. They had been rushed here and there, wet with sweat and wet with fording the streams, under a sun that would have made moving a fan an effort, and they lay prostrate, gasping at the hot air, with faces aflame, and their tongues sticking out, and their eyes rolling." Edward Baker later reflected, "The whole of Santiago seemed to be decorated with hospital flags."[12]

Faced with a virtual fog of war and mounting losses, troops with the 1st Volunteer moved about in confusion on the hills leading up to the blockhouse. Once again, American troops found themselves bombarded by the enemy on all sides and stood on the brink of disintegration. As the minutes stretched into hours on the battlefield, Americans ultimately took possession of the summit— but at a tremendous price. More than 200 Americans lay dead, and 1,180 were wounded during the fighting.

> "The whole of Santiago seemed to be decorated with hospital flags."

As the fighting on San Juan Hill commenced, the 1st Cavalry and Theodore Roosevelt's Rough Riders advanced northward, toward the summit of Kettle Hill. Once he had reached the crest of the hill, the bespectacled 1st Volunteer commander discovered that he was not alone. On the southern top portion of the hill rested some of the dismounted Buffalo Soldiers of the 10th Cavalry. During the fighting, Sgt. George Berry of the 10th Cavalry had taken on the burden of carrying the 10th and the 3rd Cavalry's battle flags. He could be heard shouting to his comrades, "Dress on the colors, boys, dress on the colors." While ascending the hill, Horace B. Bivins, a noncommissioned officer with the unit, remembered, "I was sixty hours under heavy fire; four of our gunners were wounded. I got hit myself while sighting my Hotchkiss gun. I was stunned for five minutes but forgot that I had been hit. Bravery was displayed by all of the colored regiments. The officers and reporters of other powers said they had heard of the colored man's fighting qualities, but did not think they could do such work as they had witnessed in the sixty hours' battle."

Kenneth Robinson, a Rough Rider who suffered extensive wounds during the charge up San Juan Hill that day, concurred, stating, "Without any regard to my own regiment, the whitest men in this fight have been the black ones." The officers of the 10th suffered tremendous losses. Jules Ord, one of the commanders with the unit, was killed in action, and D Troop Commander John Bigelow Jr. was shot as the cavalry units reached the half-way point on the hill. Undaunted, Bigelow told his subordinates, "Men, don't stop to bother with me; just keep up the charge until you get to the top of the hill."

Indeed, of the contributions that the 9th and 10th made to the American attack that day, John J. Pershing later claimed, "We officers of the Tenth Cavalry could have taken our black heroes in our arms. They had again fought their way into our affections, as they here had fought their way into the hearts of the American people."[13]

Among the "Black Heroes in Arms" that Pershing may have had in mind was Edward Baker. At daybreak on July 1, Baker and his unit received orders to proceed north of the blockhouse at El Caney and take up a position to the left of the 1st US Cavalry. However, as they approached the meandering San Juan River, they were greeted by a hail of bullets from Spanish enemy combatants that Baker described in his diary as "the Dons." After obeying orders given by Lt. Col. Theodore Baldwin to drop their field packs and seek cover, the veteran noncommissioned officer and his men found themselves in the middle of a fierce firefight as enemy forces used the hot-air balloons deployed by the Signal Corps to pinpoint and fire bullets down on the unit.

The situation became even more dire when one of the enemy shells exploded near Baker and the men, crippling Baldwin's horse and wounding the commanding officer in the process. While crouching in the underbrush to avoid the incoming volleys of fire, Baker heard what he later remembered as a groan coming from wounded private Lewis Marshall, who was flailing about in the river. Without thinking twice, he swam out to rescue his fallen comrade. He managed to drag the drowning enlisted man to safety, despite being exposed to vicious enemy shelling. Shortly afterward, Baker took the wounded soldier to unit headquarters where he was treated by the unit surgeon. While participating in the successful assault on San Juan Heights later that day, Baker himself would unknowingly sustain shrapnel wounds to his arm and left side. Less than four years later, the soft-spoken and unassuming sergeant major gained immortality when he received the nation's preeminent medal for valor. Lt. Col. Theodore Baldwin commended Baker's selfless act of bravery, saying, "There is no man more worthy of a medal than he, and I do not hesitate to recommend him for one."[14]

FROM GLORY TO SLANDER
AND DISBANDMENT

By the time the smoke had cleared over Santiago, the sweet sounds of victory rang out for cavalrymen Fitz Lee, George Wanton, Dennis Bell, William Thompkins, and other members of the Fifth Army Corps. During the waning summer months of 1898, the Spanish Army gave Gen. William Shafter what he wanted as twenty-three thousand Spanish troops laid down their arms. By the end of September, eastern Cuba had fallen into American hands, and diplomatic operations moved steadily from an uneasy truce toward peace negotiations between the United States and Spain in Paris. By the beginning of 1899, the cessation of hostilities between the two nations would become reality as the Senate ratified the treaty that gave Cuba her independence and ceded control over Puerto Rico, Guam, and the Philippines to the United States.

As summer faded into the fall of 1898, however, other black regulars with the 10th Cavalry—along with a detachment of the 1st US Volunteer Cavalry, who had survived the battles of Las Guasimas, El Caney, and San Juan Heights—proceeded from Cuba to Georgia before landing at the Montauk Point, New York, port of entry. After arriving at the Long Island camp, they were quarantined with most of the troops returning from the war. There they received the lion's share of praise from the press, military commanders, and the black public.

The *New York World* stated:

Over against this scene of the cowboy and the college graduate, the New York man about town and the Arizona "Bad Man"—united in one coherent war machine, set the picture of the Tenth United States Cavalry—the famous colored regiment. Their marksmanship was magnificent. Their courage was superb. The Rough Riders and the black regiment. In those two commands is an epitome of almost our whole national character.

In the *North American Review*, a nationally syndicated magazine, journalist Stephen Bonsal wrote, "The Spanish War afforded the negro regulars their first opportunity to show their metal [*sic*] as trained troops upon the theatre of actual war."

The image of brave black soldiers was becoming deeply enmeshed in the collective consciousness of white soldiers. As one Southerner who fought at San Juan Hill later recalled, "I am not a negro lover. My father fought with Mosby's Rangers and I was born in the South, but the negroes saved that fight." And while they were temporarily stationed at Montauk Point, a few of the men with the 10th looked on as the Rough Riders were mustered out of the service. Col. Theodore Roosevelt himself was among those in attendance. During the service, Roosevelt specifically pointed out the courageous acts performed by black soldiers with the 9th and 10th Cavalry, describing them as "an excellent breed of Yankees." He claimed, "I speak the sentiments of every officer and every trooper here when I say that there is a tie between those two cavalry regiments and ours which we trust will never be broken."

Roosevelt then asked the officers who were present if they could have his men and the black troopers in the audience come up single file so that he could shake hands with them. For black soldiers who proceeded up to the dais that day, the gesture was freighted with irony. Little did they realize at the time that the intrinsic bonds of trust, fidelity, and honor that Roosevelt wished to establish with them would be severed irreparably less than a year later.[15]

On the other hand, the black press framed the bravery of the troopers in the Santiago de Cuba campaign in the context of their fitness for leadership positions in the Regular Army. An editorial titled "Brave as the Bravest" in the Omaha, Nebraska, *Afro-American Sentinel* proclaimed, "All honor to the black troopers of the gallant Tenth! All honor to the Black Regiment! Theirs was a double duty: to sustain the reputation of the American arms and to make another plea by valor, heroism on the field for fair play and justice, to be officered by their own men and to receive the advancement ungrudgingly given to others in the service!"

> "All honor to the black troopers of the gallant Tenth! All honor to the Black Regiment!"

Similarly, the Fort Scott, Kansas, *Fair Play* opined, "The colored man with an abiding confidence in his white brother's high sense of justice has gone into the regular army with white officers, believing that when he had shown his worth as a private that he would be rewarded by being appointed to the commissioned offices. Whether this confidence has been misplaced remains to be seen."[16]

In some respects, Edward Baker himself personified their hopes and despair. After sustaining a myriad of injuries in Cuba, Baker was sent home, where he spent some time convalescing at the Montauk Point camp. Besides the shrapnel and gunshot wounds that he sustained during the fighting, Baker's condition was compounded by acute bouts of dysentery, along with a severe case of rheumatism. Ordered to Long Island, New York, he spent a period of time receiving treatment while being quarantined with other returning troops. There, he remained until he received orders to report to Fort Assiniboine, where he was reunited with his family.

But the ambition to lead troops on the battlefield still burned within the veteran Buffalo Soldier. On August 2, 1898, Edward Baker was appointed first lieutenant with the all-black 10th Infantry of the US Volunteers. Not long afterward, Baker, along with other "Immune" regiments, were assigned to Camp Haskell near Macon, Georgia, for five months, between 1898 and 1899, where they anxiously awaited deployment to Puerto Rico.[17] The 10th Infantry never received the call from Official Washington, however, and was mustered out of the service. For his part, Baker was reassigned to Fort Sam Houston, Texas, where he rejoined the 10th Cavalry at his previous rank of sergeant major.

Frustrated by this sequence of events, for months Baker chafed under this lack of opportunity to obtain an officer commission. Fate intervened in March of 1899, when the chief trumpeter was once again offered a volunteer commission, this time as a captain with the 49th US Infantry. After a series of reappointments and reassignments, Baker saw his fortunes rise dramatically as he and the all-volunteer regiment received orders to sail to the Philippine Islands, where they would begin a duty assignment as a detachment of the Philippine Scouts. Almost immediately upon his arrival in the Pacific Rim area, he received word from his commanding officer that he had been accorded the Congressional Medal of Honor for heroism at San Juan Heights. While stationed on Luzon, he served as an intermediary of disputes between indigenous civil and religious authorities in the northern region of the Philippine Islands.

But Baker and other black soldiers became increasingly disillusioned with the contradictory nature of American encounters with Filipinos in the aftermath of the Spanish-American War. Once the United States was ceded dominion over the Philippine Islands in December of 1898, large groups of black troops were deployed against guerrilla forces in an attempt to stem the Filipino drive for independence. Their positioning in the independence movement produced a wide range of questions regarding the existing status of African Americans back at home. They could not help but notice that many of the same epithets white Americans used to describe Filipinos were similar to those used to describe them, including "niggers," "black devils," and "gugus." Why would they allow themselves to be used as instruments of conquest against similar darker brethren in the name of American empire? For Baker and his fellow soldiers, the dilemma of taking up the "White Man's Burden" abroad while being denied the rights of citizenship at home must have been all too readily apparent.

William Simms, a 49th Infantry volunteer serviceman on a patrolling mission near Luzon at the time, observed, "I was struck by a question a little Filipino boy asked me, which ran about this way: 'Why does the American Negro come to fight us when we are much a friend to him and have not done anything to him? He is all the same to me and me all the same as you. Why don't you fight those people in America who burn Negroes, that make a beast of you?'"

Historians Frank Schubert and Michael Robinson skillfully summed up the predicament African-American volunteers faced while serving on the islands: "Black soldiers discovered that 'Old Glory' and Jim Crow arrived simultaneously in the Philippines."[18]

> "Black soldiers discovered that 'Old Glory' and Jim Crow arrived simultaneously in the Philippines."

For Baker, the ambivalent feelings that black troops experienced while participating in the American imperial project manifested in his quest to obtain a commission in the Regular Army. While serving for nearly seven years on the islands, the seasoned black

officer frequently found himself feeling overburdened by the increasing levels of respon-
sibility that his superiors heaped on him, and frustrated by the painstaking, yet thankless,
hours of garrison duty that he assumed as a company commander with the unit. By the end
of the first decade of the new century, Baker's flagging energies soon became a matter of
official inquiry.

During the spring of 1908, Baker applied for promotion only to have a board of review-
ing officers find his leadership capabilities wanting, his attention to detail lacking, and his
diligence to close-order drill rather deficient. After determining that "Lieutenant Baker
appears to the board to be much older than his years indicate," board members concluded
that he would not be promoted or recommissioned at the end of his current appointment.
Despite numerous attempts to restore his reputation, the forty-three-year-old officer
resigned his commission with the Philippine Scouts in 1909. Less than five years later,
the retired quartermaster sergeant passed away at San Francisco's Letterman General
Hospital, succumbing to peritonitis and falling short of his dreams of leading Regular
Army troops into action.[19]

Echoing Baker's plight, a Jim Crow sequence of events reflected a similar downward
spiral in white public perception of black soldiers' conduct. In April of 1899, Theodore
Roosevelt, a longtime supporter of the 9th and 10th Cavalry, expressed misgivings
about the conduct of black soldiers under fire. In an interview with *Scribner's Magazine*,
Roosevelt recounted that during the Battle of San Juan Hill, "the colored soldiers began
to get a little uneasy and to drift to the rear, either helping wounded men, or saying that
they wished to find their own regiments. [. . .] This I could not allow," Roosevelt recalled,
"as it was depleting my line, so I jumped up, and walking a few yards to the rear, drew my
revolver, calling out to them that I should shoot the first man who, on any presence whatever, went to the rear."

While Roosevelt's reasons for revising history remain unclear, and his account would
not go unchallenged, its impact had a dampening effect on public perception of black
regulars during this period, and afterward. In southwest Texas, long-standing white anx-
ieties over the army's stationing of black troops in the Southwest exploded into racial
violence as members of the 25th Infantry squared off against white townspeople in nearby

Brownsville. While it was unclear to military authorities what sparked the conflagration, or who fired the first shots, Roosevelt, the sitting president, seized upon the most negative attributes of black soldiers. As a result, three companies of the famed unit received dishonorable discharges from the army and were barred from seeking future employment with the federal government. By the beginning of the second decade of the twentieth century, the uptick in racism that was reflected in racial conflict between black servicemen and white residents in places like Brownsville and the actions taken by the military in its aftermath had cast serious doubt on the status of blacks in the US military. As noted historian Marvin Fletcher noted, "By 1917 the first golden age of the black soldier had ended."[20]

Meanwhile, the so-called golden age for veteran cavalrymen Dennis Bell, William Thompkins, Fitz Lee, and George Wanton came in the form of Congressional Medals of Honor in late June of 1899. But the war's end spelled different paths of destiny for each soldier. Dennis Bell and William Thompkins received their medals while they served with the occupational forces at Manzanillo, Cuba, parting ways shortly afterward. Bell went on to Texas and the Philippines, where he served until returning home to Washington, DC, where he left the army in 1906. Thompkins continued his military service, assigned first to the Philippine Islands between 1901 and 1907, and then placed on the retired list at Schofield Barracks, Hawaii, in 1914, at the rank of first sergeant. Thompkins's advancement up the noncommissioned ranks was not always smooth, as trouble seemed to follow the veteran soldier throughout the latter stages of his enlistment. While stationed at Subic Bay, Thompkins and a detachment of men with the 25th Infantry became embroiled in an incident involving the accidental shooting of a Zambales villager who happened to be fishing on a river nearby. After a thorough investigation, the army absolved the party of all wrongdoing, but reprimanded them for carelessness.[21]

Some 10th Cavalry soldiers left the Cuba campaign as proud and committed to their principles of loyalty and honor as ever, although their personal struggles and hardships were as diverse as the paths they took home. While convalescing at Fort Bliss, Texas, Fitz Lee received his medal. At that point, he had been with the decorated all-black unit for nearly ten years. But the young 10th Cavalry trooper was now at a crossroads in his career.

The debilitating illnesses and battle injuries Lee had sustained during the fighting had apparently taken their toll, for he received a disability discharge just days after receiving his award. With waves of pain radiating throughout his body, the beleaguered former enlisted man moved on to Leavenworth City, where longtime acquaintances provided him with food and shelter while he received medical treatment. Lee's moment of glory failed to provide him with a source of livelihood; penniless, he remained dependent on friends until he died on September 14, 1899, less than two years after his service in Cuba. Lee was so poor that a local undertaker had to supply suitable clothing for his remains.

Less is known about the career of Spanish-American War MOH recipient Robert Penn. During the conflict, the City Point, Virginia, native served as a sailor, performing his duty off the coast of Cuba. Two weeks after the epic Battle of San Juan Hill, the USS *Iowa* was trolling off the coast of Santiago when a manhole gasket in its boiler area suddenly exploded. As scalding hot water escaped from the boiler room, Fireman 1st Class Robert Penn risked his own safety by balancing on a plank in order to extinguish the coal fire that engulfed the area. On December 14, 1898, Penn's selfless act of bravery earned him the Medal of Honor and the distinction of being the only black sailor decorated during the War with Spain. Penn's subsequent military service and his life after the Spanish-American War remain hazy, and the legacy of the decorated sailor's heroism has receded from public consciousness.[22]

Unlike Robert Penn, other black MOH recipients followed more definitive paths of action following the end of the war. When he received his award, George Wanton had not yet realized that the idea of a military career would grow on him—so much so that when the former corporal with the 10th Cavalry returned to his hometown of Paterson, New Jersey, he reenlisted in the army, even though he had sworn to family and friends that he would never do so again. While assigned to various troop organizations within the celebrated cavalry outfit, Wanton saw extensive duty in the Southwest, including at Fort Huachuca, Arizona, where he and other troopers participated in the Punitive Expedition along the Mexican border against Pancho Villa. Wanton retired in 1925 after being promoted to the rank of master-sergeant. His 10th Cavalry commanding officer proudly proclaimed, "He is an excellent soldier and is a man of high character." Wanton's actions in Cuba created a legacy of service and honor that was also recognized by his peers. He became an active member of the American Legion, Spanish War Veterans, and the Retired Servicemen's Association. In November of 1921, the veteran soldier was invited to Washington, DC, where he served as an honorary pallbearer at the burial of the Unknown Soldier in the Memorial Amphitheater at Arlington National Cemetery.

In 1930, Wanton's ideals and principles were on full display when he appeared at a luncheon in Boston to honor the president of the United States and other previous Medal of Honor recipients.[23] Most of the young people in the audience probably knew next to nothing about the travails that Wanton and other black recipients had endured during the American wars for empire, just as Wanton and his comrades knew very little about William Carney, Christian Fleetwood, and the men of

"He is an excellent soldier and is a man of high character."

valor from the Civil War era, or the Indian War heroes of the post-Reconstruction years of the 1870s and the 1880s.

This new generation of heroes found themselves standing on the threshold of world-wide catastrophe forged on the ashes of the past, where bravery would be redefined once again. In order to fully understand the demands inherent in this historic turn of events, we must move from the years of the emerging American empire to the rise of the modern US military, and explore the making of black heroes during American involvement in World War I.

While most of the heroes in the Spanish-American War receive ample space in this section, Robert Penn's profile is noticeably shorter due to the fact that we know so little about his service and postwar life after his act of gallantry.

Heroes of 369th (old 15th) New York (African American) Infantry, first of Colonel Hayward's command, return to this country, ready to debark at Hoboken, New Jersey. These men covered themselves with glory on the battlefields of France and not a man was captured by the Huns. Soldier in center is wearing a helmet that he took from one of the Huns.

CHAPTER 4

Carrying the Banner of Hope

HEROES FROM THE WAR TO END ALL WARS, 1917–1918

An opinion held in common by practically all officers is that the negro is a rank coward in the dark. His fear of the unknown and unseen will prevent him from ever operating as an individual scout with success. His lack of veracity causes unsatisfactory reports to be rendered, particularly on patrol duty. World War Experience implies that the negro may not stand grilling combat with heavy losses.

—*Army War College Study, 1925*

The World War I experiences of heroes like Freddie Stowers and other Medal of Honor aspirants were forged between the turn of the twentieth century, the 1912 election of Woodrow Wilson, and initial American responses to the exploding guns of war in Europe. During the first decade of the twentieth century, black people experienced a tectonic shift in the political landscape. Since Reconstruction, black voters had supported the Republican Party and its presidential candidates. But the epidemic of black lynchings in Atlanta, Georgia, and Springfield, Illinois, and Theodore Roosevelt's discharge en masse of 167 black soldiers with the 25th Infantry in the wake of the Brownsville, Texas, incident in 1906, produced feelings of disbelief and dismay among many members of the black community.

As the decade progressed, the foreboding sentiments expressed by black leaders turned to disgust as President William Howard Taft tacitly acquiesced to the overt "lily-white" policies devised by Southern whites to eliminate an African-American presence at polling places in the region. By 1912, black disillusionment with the "Party of Lincoln" was rife, as black voters in both the North and the South openly contemplated voting for Woodrow Wilson, the Democratic Party presidential candidate. A Southern-born Democrat, Wilson's pledge to treat blacks justly influenced many black leaders.[1]

Unfortunately, Wilson's first administration did not fulfill his promise, codifying Jim Crow segregation and personally approving the overtly racist film, *The Birth of a Nation* (see appendix). Much to the dismay of black leaders, extralegal violence, racial tension, and conflict increased in many areas throughout the country. Expressing the view that many blacks held of Wilson and the racial climate that existed during the period, noted historian Rayford Logan observed, "I was in my last year of high school in Washington when Wilson was elected. Negroes showed grave concern, especially when some newly elected Southerners publicly declared that they had come to Washington to 'fight niggers and likker.'"[2]

Blacks did not stand idly by and watch while their claims to democracy and equality were under assault. Between 1908 and 1917, a host of leaders and organizations sprang into being. Unhappy with the accommodationist approach of Booker T. Washington and galvanized by the 1908 Springfield Race Riot, W. E. B. Du Bois, Oswald Garrison Villard, and Moorfield Storey organized the National Association for the Advancement of Colored People in 1909. Over a seven-year period, its chapters led boycotts calling for a public ban of the showing of *The Birth of a Nation*, court challenges to the Oklahoma "grandfather clause" that violated the Fifteenth Amendment, as well as crusades against lynching and racial violence. Norfolk, Virginia, resident Addie W. Hunton and Washington, DC, natives Josephine Bruce and Mary Church Terrell worked diligently to combat racism and sexism as members of the National Association of Colored Women. Formed in the fall of 1913, the National Equal Rights League, led by William Monroe Trotter and Ida B. Wells-Barnett, formed a delegation that called on President Wilson, demanding that he abolish racial segregation in Washington, DC.

Achievement in battle served as another concrete way for African Americans to fight for equality and uplift the race. Military service not only provided an image of black men that debunked many of the racial stereotypes, but it also promoted the promise of black political participation both before and during the period. Through the promise of military service, African-American men could redefine their sense of honor and independence in relation to a racially divided American society.

James Weldon Johnson was an editorialist for the *New York Age*, and he and his brother wrote "Lift Every Voice and Sing," recognized by many as the "Negro National

Anthem." Although he often expressed his disgust for Wilson and his segregationist policies, he intuitively understood the importance of black military service in relation to social
conventions of manhood and citizenship. Writing in the wake of the exploding guns of
August and Wilson's reelection, Johnson opined, "If they don't take these colored men
and give them the right to bear arms and fight as equal citizens, they have got to send to
the trenches, perhaps to die, a white man for each Negro they refuse."[3]

Like W. E. B. Du Bois, some believed that the Great War provided blacks the opportunity to "close ranks." Du Bois wrote, "Let us, while this war lasts, forget our special
grievances and close ranks shoulder to shoulder with our own white fellow citizens and the
allied nations that are fighting for democracy. We make no ordinary sacrifice, but we make
it gladly and willingly with our eyes lifted to the hills."[4]

But soon black leaders like Johnson and Du Bois had to face reality. A few days after
President Wilson's war message, army planners had begun to consider expanding black
troops in the armed forces by inducting large numbers of men in each of the divisional
training areas. Nearly seventy-five thousand soldiers would be drawn from among the
army cantonments throughout the country, most of them from the American South. Black
draftees would then join other recruits to form the sixteen regiments newly created during
this period. However, they realized that Southern congressmen like Mississippi's James
Vardaman and others opposed the training of armed blacks in the region.

After Southern congressional fears materialized into racial violence at Camp Logan
in Houston, Texas (see appendix), Secretary of War Newton Baker signaled his approval
of the War Department's plan to pare down the number of regiments in order to form a
combat division. The remaining portion of black draftees and enlistees would be assigned
to auxiliary units, such as service battalions, or placed in services of supply organizations.[5]
"The colored race, knowing that a combatant division is being formed, will realize that
in the non-combatant service, they are doing no more than their share along with similar
white troops, and there can be no reasonable cause for ill feeling," army staff members
contended.

General staff officers within the War Department quickly discovered that the creation of a black division gave rise to another staffing problem—namely, the employment

of officers to lead its regiments. The War Department announced plans to open an officer training camp at Fort Des Moines, Iowa, in late May of 1917. After it opened on June 18, more than 1,200 men passed through its gates. From June to October, college-educated men from universities like Howard, Cornell, Tuskegee, Cornell, and Wilberforce trained with business leaders, government employees, attorneys, letter carriers, and brick masons. Each was deeply determined to seize the mantle of leadership and advance the cause of the race. Recognizing the opportunity that the camp provided for a generation of young black men, one aspiring candidate from Lincoln University observed, "It is the height of my ambition to do credit to my country and my race."[6]

Meanwhile, the fate of Charles Young hung in the balance. As prospective black officers rushed to the colors at Fort Des Moines, Iowa, black leaders and organizations looked to the legendary Regular Army officer to lead troops into battle, as well as to serve as the exemplar for its expanding junior officer corps. Just two years earlier, Young had received the NAACP's Spingarn Medal, an honor accorded to the nation's Talented Tenth for distinguished achievement. The seasoned officer had become a rising star, receiving a promotion to lieutenant-colonel for his invaluable service in Mexico in 1916. As the highest-ranking senior black officer in the Regular Army, Young had received high praise from General Pershing and others, and was slated to be promoted to full colonel, making him eligible for advancement to brigadier general in the near future.

> "It is the height of my ambition to do credit to my country and my race."

However, the forty-nine-year-old career soldier soon found himself engulfed in military racism. Albert A. Dockery, a white first lieutenant with the 10th Cavalry, had complained to the War Department that he "found it not only distasteful but practically impossible to serve under a colored commander." Secretary of War Newton Baker initially suggested that the junior officer either "do his duty or resign." Baker also reassured Wilson that he would avoid what he perceived to be a potentially "embarrassing situation" for the president. Not long afterward, the situation was resolved through a medical technicality. After a physical examination revealed that Young had Bright's disease (a historical classification of kidney disease, often accompanied by high blood pressure), he was promoted to full colonel and ordered to report to a retiring board, where he was subsequently retired from the active list and reassigned to the Ohio National Guard as a military adviser.[7]

W. E. B. Du Bois wrote a letter to his distraught friend, telling him that *The Crisis* and the NAACP would "take all possible steps to bring [Young's] case to the attention of the authorities." Throughout the fall of 1917, NAACP officials tried unsuccessfully to persuade the Secretary of War to reverse the War Department's decision regarding Young's retirement. Not to be outdone, Young sought to demonstrate his fitness by riding five hundred miles on horseback from his home in Ohio to Washington, DC, where he hoped to personally present his case to the Secretary of War. His pleas fell on deaf ears.[8]

Young's removal shook the black public to its core. Not only did many view his forced retirement as a dastardly tactic employed by Wilson and the War Department, meant to cast aspersions on black leadership, but they also correctly perceived that the Young issue would cast a dark cloud over the actions taken by black enlisted men and officers once they reached Europe. Young's retirement also raised questions as to what would be considered honorable conduct in battle for black GIs who saw extensive action along the Western Front. The die was thus cast for all black servicemen who entered the armed forces during the European conflict.

"HE DIDN'T WAIT FOR NO DRAFT"

Training for World War I

A tumultuous story of foreign and domestic upheaval, born of war and race, structured the World War I experiences of African-American soldiers who saw action on the battlefields of Europe. In November of 1917, camps at Funston, Kansas; Grant, Illinois; Upton, New York; Dix, New Jersey; Meade, Maryland; Dodge, Iowa; and Sherman, Ohio, received thousands of black soldiers. Together, they formed the principal elements of the 92nd Infantry Division of the American Expeditionary Forces (AEF). Most of the black recruits with the 92nd Division were assigned to the 365th, 366th, 367th, and 368th Infantry Regiments, with a smattering of the inexperienced GIs reporting to indirect and service units. A month later, black National Guardsmen from the states of New York, Illinois, Connecticut, Maryland, Massachusetts, Ohio, Tennessee, and the District of Columbia assembled at Camp Stuart, Virginia, to form the 93rd Infantry Division (Provisional). The division's brigades were supplemented by conscripts from the state of South Carolina.

The assigned men were then organized into the 369th, 370th, 371st, and 372nd Infantry Regiments, along with an assortment of machine-gun, field artillery, medical, ordnance, and veterinary companies, battalions, and brigades. Altogether, each division had about 27,000 enlisted men and officers, with each regiment consisting of nearly 3,700 men, including several groups of train, engineering, sanitary, and field signal servicemen.[9]

Since the War Department announced that it had no desire to expand the number of black Regular Army units, most of the division's regiments were composed of National Guard units. Among the principal state-based units that were federalized during the war was the 15th New York Infantry Regiment. Organized in 1913 by Col. William Hayward, the son of a Republican senator, the 15th New York included men who largely came from Deep South states like Virginia, North Carolina, Georgia, and South Carolina. Quite a few had joined the regiment after moving from the rural South to the Empire State.[10]

This was the case with Henry Johnson, a poor black railroad porter from Winston-Salem, North Carolina, who joined the regiment in 1917 and would later distinguish himself in action during Allied fighting on the Western Front. Although little is known about Johnson's prewar life, he had already fought a war against a formidable foe—namely, white supremacy. As a young teenager, he, along with his parents, migrated north, eventually settling in Albany, New York. In 1915, Johnson landed work at the city's Union Station as a red cap and quickly plunged into local civic activities sponsored by his church and the Colored Benevolent Society. After marrying Edna Jackson, Johnson promptly registered for the Selective Service in 1917. He obviously found tradition and the call to duty virtually irresistible, as less than two months after congressional approval of war, he volunteered for the army. He reported to active duty with the 369th Infantry as the unit massed at Camp Whitman in New Jersey, just a few weeks before Congress federalized the unit. His wife observed at the time, "If you say anything about Henry, I want you to say Henry enlisted—he didn't wait for no draft. That ain't Henry's speed, no siree, not when Uncle Sam calls."[11]

Johnson's prewar activities and his sentiments regarding duty and honor were hardly atypical. Many of the men assigned to the regiments of the 92nd and 93rd (Provisional) Divisions came from polyglot backgrounds that included Northerners, Southerners, Easterners, and Westerners. Coming from all walks of life, they emerged from the levees of Mississippi, the coal mines of West Virginia, and the workshops and factories of the Midwest and the Northeast. Still others worked in kitchens as cooks and bakers, on docks as longshoremen and stevedores, on railways as Pullman porters and red caps. They came in every type of clothing imaginable—some in rags and tatters, others in overalls, still others in suits. Loaded down with diverse expressive folkways and cultures, recruits and draftees descended on the national army camp, some carrying their guitars and banjoes, while speaking dialects derived from every part of the country. Others came from beyond the borders of the United States, with nearly a thousand hailing from the British and Dutch West Indies, Cuba, Canada, Puerto Rico, and Panama.

While most of the soldiers had a vague understanding of the European conflict or its underlying cause, quite a few shared a broad interpretation of what was at stake: They felt that the war offered them a chance to strike a blow for a new world—one they hoped to see come into being. The war, in short, opened for them the possibility of a new world where they could live and breathe as *black men*. Like Chester Heywood, a captain with the 371st Infantry, most framed their experiences in the army encampments in the following manner: "Everybody talked overseas, A.E.F., France, the Boche, and swanked about the camp and town as if they had already seen months of service in the trenches." Others felt their families, relatives, and neighbors in their respective communities were depending on their honorable service during the fighting. They were staking their own abstract notions of freedom on their service in this war. W. Allison Sweeney, contributing editor to the *Chicago Defender*, observed that black intellectuals and the black press placed a great deal of importance on the loyalty and heroism of black troops who served during the period, writing, "How splendid was the spectacle of their response! Theirs not to ask the WHY; theirs but to do and die."[12]

But training black patriots for military service proved to be a battle in and of itself. Upon entering the camps in Whitman, New Jersey, and Newport News, Virginia, recruits marched to a processing area where they received brand-new uniforms and regular infantry equipment. Afterward, the men received instruction from watchful yet demanding officers on the intricacies of military training, including close-order drill, formal guard mounting, parade reviews, signaling, and marching. Then the men were put through the paces of small-arms practice and field exercises. Most of these soldiers had never shot a firearm before entering the camps. Not only that, but most of the companies and platoons of fledgling citizen-soldiers found themselves having to contend with the lice and cooties that accompanied trench-digging, the bane of all infantrymen fighting in World War I. Nonetheless, the new recruits and enlisted men embraced their training with grim determination. Arthur Little, a white officer with the 15th New York, observed at Camp Whitman, "Our men worked as few soldiers had ever before had to work in a mere camp of instruction. Every hour of daylight was devoted to drill and to rifle practice. We drilled and shot, rain or shine."[13]

> Every hour of daylight was devoted to drill and to rifle practice. We drilled and shot, rain or shine."

As their training progressed, thousands of black draftees and enlisted men with the 93rd Division (Provisional) quickly discovered that their introduction to military life included the familiar refrain of Southern racism that seemed to follow them at every turn. In October of 1917, most of the elements of the 93rd Division received orders to train at military facilities situated in the American South. The 8th Illinois reported to Camp Logan, the 15th New York was dispatched to Camp Wadsworth, and the District of Columbia's 1st Separate Battalion was dispatched to Camp Stuart—all located below the Mason–Dixon Line.

Black soldiers assigned to Spartanburg, South Carolina; Montgomery, Alabama; and Newport News, Virginia, heard speeches given by their commanders about the August insurrection staged by the 24th Infantry in Houston. But they also witnessed the "cake" and "custom" of Jim Crow discrimination firsthand. Almost immediately upon their arrival for training at Camp Wadsworth in early October 1917, men of the 15th New York reported to an assembly area. There, Col. William Hayward read a statement the mayor of Spartanburg had recently given to the *New York Times*, indicating the depth of fear and resentment that townspeople felt regarding the presence of armed black men near their city. Hayward implored the black soldiers to refrain from violence and conduct themselves as gentlemen and representatives of their race, but to no avail.

For most Northern black soldiers with the unit, such events proved to be rather unsettling. Although they had read or heard about Southern racism from the black press and family members and friends, when they encountered such affronts to their dignity firsthand, they found it hard to accept. After Spartanburg racists brutally accosted two of their most esteemed officers—Capt. Napoleon Bonaparte Marshall and regimental drum major Noble Sissle—some outraged members of the 15th decided to answer the insults and provocations with deadly force by gathering in small armed groups to storm the city. The potentially riotous encounter between black soldiers and the people of Spartanburg was dispelled only because Lt. James Reese Europe and the regiment received orders from Washington to be deployed overseas. On October 24, the regiment boarded troop transport trains bound for Hoboken, New Jersey.[14]

But not before another potential racial explosion rocked the unit. Once they had reported to Camp Mills, the men of the 15th almost came to blows with the all-white 167th Infantry, an Alabama National Guard regiment that was assisted to the famed 42nd "Rainbow" Division. The 167th had revealed their racist proclivities when some of the men reportedly placed "Whites Only" signs in the area. They had also severely beaten and blinded a black resident who sat in their railcar alongside the Long Island Rail Road. Racial tensions boiled to the point of becoming a full-scale confrontation between the two units as the 15th arrived in the Garden City area. Only after William Hayward managed to convince a troopship captain to set sail for Europe did the threat of violence lessen for all parties involved. Shortly thereafter, the men boarded the ship and headed for France, where fate and fortune awaited them.[15]

BLACK DEATH IN THE ARGONNE FOREST

The Heroism of Henry Johnson

New Year's Day of 1918 began with great anticipation for the men of the 93rd Division's 15th New York Infantry. As the "Fighting 15th's" band played "Auld Lang Syne," returning the salutes given to them by the ship's company, the enlisted men and officers debarked from the troopship *Pocahontas* in Brest before marching to a nearby station to board trains that would take them to Saint-Nazaire. As they trudged aboard the crowded freight cars, they understandably had much on their minds. Of course, they missed the comforts of home and hearth and good conversation with relatives and neighbors. They had just spent nearly three weeks on the Atlantic Ocean, avoiding near misses from friendly vessels and surviving rumored attacks from German submarines and raiders. But their spirits had never flagged. They were finally in France, about to confront the German enemy in a war to end all wars. The 15th's commander, Col. William Hayward, wrote in his diary, "December 27, landed at Brest. Right side up." Arthur Little, an officer with the unit, claimed, "We were ready to look up to John J. Pershing—almost as a god."[16]

Unbeknownst to Hayward, Little, and the rest of their comrades, the train ride into Saint-Nazaire would bring them face-to-face with disappointment and dismay. No sooner had they arrived at the depot area that they learned their unit had been assigned as Services of Supply troops with the American Expeditionary Forces (AEF), receiving assignments to build docks, lay railroad tracks, haul lumber, dig ditches, construct roads, and unload ships. Because virtually all of the newly arrived soldiers wished to get right into the action, those who received these noncombatant-duty orders were sorely disappointed. Emmett J. Scott, civilian aide to the Secretary of War, wrote at the time, "The fact of being in the country 'where the war is' helped the impatient soldiers to endure their lot for a while, but before long there was a general feeling that 'while stevedoring may be all right, it is not war,' and the officers were besieged with apologetic and respectful queries, 'When do we fight?'"[17] Their disillusionment was compounded when an element of the regiment was shuttled to the nearby town of Coëtquidan and given orders to guard a German prisoner-of-war camp—hardly an honorable assignment for soldiers who yearned to fight at the Front.

Although they didn't realize it, even before they had arrived in France the commander of the AEF had made other plans for them. In the days leading up to the 15th New York's arrival on European soil, Pershing and General Staff members had planned to disband the 93rd Division and reorganize its troops as pioneer infantry regiments. In his mind, they would work on lines of logistics and communication, as well as build roads, salvage battlefields, remove ammunition, rebury the dead, dig trenches, construct ammunition depots and bomb shelters, and perform other service and supply duties for frontline units. Pershing's

"We were ready to look up to John J. Pershing— almost as a god."

motivations for disbanding the unit and dispatching its components in such a manner remain unclear. While his prewar impressions of the conduct of black soldiers, stemming from his service with the celebrated 10th Cavalry, were highly complimentary, other forces may have contributed to his decisions as AEF supreme commander. While some scholars have pointed to the racial sensitivities of his senior commanders, others have indicated that diplomatic entreaties between Official Washington and European powers over manpower policies may have played a role.

Whatever lay behind Pershing's decision, it had a dampening effect on black troops stationed at port cities in France, including Brest, Saint-Nazaire, Bordeaux, Marseilles, and Le Havre. As 8th Illinois chaplain William Braddan recalled, "The most dejected-looking men I ever saw in uniform, and the most unsoldierly, are the stevedores. Truly, I would rather be a dog than such a soldier."[18]

Fate, and the dire military situation in Europe, soon forced a significant change in War Department policy. By early 1918, the French military had suffered a string of humiliating setbacks. During the previous spring, widespread mutinies had taken place within the French Army in the wake of its disastrous Nivelle Offensive. More than twenty thousand troops from over fifty divisions had deserted from the ranks. What's worse, German commanders had planned a major offensive along the Western Front that spring. Aimed at dividing the British and French forces, the Germans hoped to end the war in its favor before American troops could be assembled and used to reverse the Allied losses. Pressed to find fresh troops, Marshal Foch, recently named Allied commander in chief, pleaded with the War Department, met with Pershing, and requested that American soldiers be used as replacements. The French cared very little about race, having enlisted African troops from Morocco, Algeria, and West Africa from the beginning of the war.

Little did the French commander realize that machinations within AEF headquarters were at work in his favor. Around the same time, Pershing received a letter from Col. William Hayward from Saint-Nazaire, describing the demoralizing effect that labor duties were having on the 15th New York's morale and demanding a frontline assignment for the regiment. Although Pershing initially resisted the idea of integrating American troops into French formations, he reassigned the regiments of the 93rd (Provisional) Division to the French Army.

Describing the placement of the division's four regiments with the French at the time, Pershing later recalled, "I consented to send temporarily to the French four colored Infantry regiments of the 93rd Division. Some of the units had arrived, and others were expected soon to be en route, but they did not have in France even the beginning of a brigade or divisional organization. One regiment was to go to each of four divisions, with the provision that they were to be returned for the formation of the 93rd Division when called for."

While Pershing may have thought that the regiments would later be returned to the AEF and reconstituted as an American division, the French thought otherwise. The regiments of the 93rd would serve with French forces for the remainder of the war.[19]

On March 12, 1918, the first elements of the 15th New York moved from Connantre to Givry-en-Argonne, where they were assigned to the French 4th Army's 16th Division for field training. The men were upbeat. Upon their arrival at the sleepy town in central France, they received word that their unit had been renamed the 369th Infantry. For most of the soldiers, the reassignment to the French Army offered a real opportunity to fire guns, and, most importantly, to gain the notoriety of being the first American unit to strike a blow against the Germans as members of the French Army. But for many, the French Army experience soon proved to be as disconcerting as their arrival on the European continent. First, they lacked adequate interpreters in the ranks and had to adjust to the unfamiliar language spoken by their new French comrades. Then they were ordered to replace their American equipment with French uniforms, helmets, weaponry and ammunition, knapsacks, and gas masks. What's more, their units were reorganized in order to meet the requirements of the French Tables of Organization.

As if that wasn't enough, the feelings of bewilderment GIs experienced while receiving their new gear were no doubt accompanied by a profound sense of dislocation as French drill sergeants and corporals instructed them on the tactics inherent in the monotonous grind of trench warfare along the Western Front. For nearly a month, the men learned how to distinguish between different kinds of poison gas by smell, and the ways to approach the heavily armed enemy trenches that dotted the European battlefields. This instruction would prove to be essential, even as it conveyed the sobering possibility of death, since the training exercises often took place in close proximity to the sounds of enemy guns along the Front.

> The regiments of the 93rd would serve with French forces for the remainder of the war.

As the 369th Infantry received their introduction to trench warfare, disparate elements of the 93rd Division began to show up in France. During the month of April, Brest served as the landing point for the 370th and the 372nd Infantry Regiments. Upon their arrival, each regiment reported to different units within the French Army. While the 370th moved on to Grandvillars, where it was attached to the French 73rd Division, the 372nd debarked from the USS *Susquehanna* at Saint-Nazaire and headed for Condé-en-Barrois, where it trained with the French XIII Corps until late May.

Around the same time, Freddie Stowers and the 371st debarked and marched to the Pontanezen Barracks, an outpost that rested on the heights just beyond the port city. By the end of June, all of the units with the division were in central France and would report to active sectors in or around the Argonne Forest, where German shelling occurred on a daily basis. For the newly arrived soldiers, the Front marked a clear departure from anything they had ever experienced. Endless stories about impending German raids and artillery concentration filled the air as the soldiers moved into regimental sectors along the Front. Most of the division members were very inexperienced; as one newspaper correspondent who covered the unit's activities put it, "They did not know the use of rockets, and thought a gas alarm and the tooting of sirens meant that the Germans were coming in automobiles."

The men and junior officers in the 371st Infantry saw things differently. Trenton, New Jersey, native Needham Roberts, a soldier with the 369th, stated, "Green troops, though we were, who had never heard a shell burst, had never smelled gas, everyone was eager to write the first letter home and say, 'I am in the frontline trenches.'" Chester Heywood, a captain with the 371st, recalled, "Orders were received to prepare to march, surplus equipment was to be evacuated, and we were one step nearer an active participation in the war."[20]

To a man, soldiers in the newly designated 369th Infantry translated Heywood's sentiment into action. As the unit concluded a three-week stint of training along the Front, the regiment was dispatched to Mains de Massages, an area west of the Aisne River and northwest of the Champagne region. There, they participated in the occupation of the *Afrique* Sector, a zone that lay just west of the Argonne Forest. Under the command of

Colonel Hayward, they remained in the active sector until they received orders to take part in the Champagne-Marne Defensive in July. The purpose of the Allied action was to stave off the massive German offensive that was aimed at destroying the French 16th Division. The 369th's mission was to operate in tandem with the French unit to probe and recapture the weakest German trenches west of the Argonne Forest.

Upon entering the zone, black soldiers in the unit quickly discovered the enemy was just as intractable as the barbed-wired entrenchments they faced along the Front. The commander of the 369th assigned individual GIs to be relay runners who risked life and limb to cover an area of approximately three kilometers along the well-fortified front line. They did this to maintain a close liaison with their French comrades. The horrors of war were heightened considerably with both sides carrying out daily and nightly raids against each other, as well as patrols into the wide swath of land between the Allied trenches and the German defensive redoubts, often resulting in numerous casualties.

Finally, the soldiers battled the treacherous weather and the climate just as much as the German enemy. Horace Pippen, a twenty-nine-year-old corporal with the unit, remembered, "The 'Oregon Forest' [*sic*] was dark and rainy almost all the time. We took to them lonely, cooty, muddy trenches, water seeping everywhere; you went to bed wet and woke up the same. At night you could not see your hands before you . . . In the Day time it were Dark, even, we could not see anyone coming, but you could hear them."[21]

On a dark and gloomy night in May, a German raid near the western edge of the Argonne Forest prompted the courageous actions taken by Henry Johnson and Needham Roberts, two privates with the 369th Infantry. The two soldiers were standing guard at a small outpost near the German lines when Johnson heard what he thought was the shearing of barbed wire in the vicinity. When asked about the source of the noise, Johnson calmly responded, "They are Germans getting ready—they are going to take this hill," before shouting to his fellow sentry, "Turn out the guard!"

Almost instantly, a raiding party of almost twenty Germans appeared in the area, firing on and wounding both soldiers. Undaunted, Johnson—known as "Black Death" by his fellow servicemen for his intense fighting in France—returned immediate fire. For his part, Roberts tossed hand grenades at the enemy while lying prone on the ground, but to no avail. The German party continued to push the surprise attack and captured the belea-guered soldier. The events that followed have become a matter of conjecture, but have also entered black collective memory. Seeing his comrade in danger, the five-foot-four Johnson emptied the magazine of his rifle before grabbing his bolo knife, "a short, heavy weapon with a razor-sharp edge, the weight of a cleaver, and the point of a butcher knife." Armed with just the bolo, Johnson fiercely engaged the Germans in deadly hand-to-hand combat. With that, the "Battle of Henry Johnson" ensued.

After splitting the head of one of the enemy combatants, Johnson disemboweled the German leader of the raid who was dragging Roberts away, thus freeing the severely wounded soldier in his grasp. The heroic actions taken by the former railway porter so stunned the German party that they promptly gathered up their dead and wounded and hastily fled the outpost altogether. Johnson pressed the attack a bit further, using his emp-tied rifle as a club and throwing hand grenades at the fleeing enemy before being forced to succumb to the severity of his own wounds.

Shortly afterward, the two soldiers were transferred to a French hospital where they convalesced. Word of their acts of bravery began to attract the attention of French and American commanders throughout Europe. On May 20, Johnson and Roberts received the highest French military medal—the Croix de Guerre with Palm and Star from Gen. Henri Gouraud, the French Army commander—thus earning the distinction of being the first Americans to receive such an honor in the war. At the same time, they received special commendation from AEF headquarters. In an account that publicized their act of valor and devotion to duty, Gen. John J. Pershing openly voiced his admiration for the two men, stating, "The two colored sentries should be given credit for preventing by their bravery the taking prisoner of any of our men." Little did the two men realize at the time, but their valor and sacrifice would become the stuff of legend among various sectors of the black community once they returned home.

But as we shall see, American recognition of Johnson's heroic deed would take place much later.

THE MEUSE-ARGONNE OFFENSIVE

The Indomitable Courage of Freddie Stowers

On April 7, 1918, a regiment of all-black troops stood on a pier in Newport News, Virginia. H hour quietly approached as the harmonic melody of "Over There" filled the air. Darkness descended on the sleepy Southern town while companies with the 371st Infantry Regiment trudged up the gangplanks toward the *President Grant*, bound for France. For the men who marched in the ranks that evening, the moment was filled with great excitement intermingled with feelings of relief. For most of the conscripts, just getting to the Hampton Roads port of embarkation had tested the patience of even the most seasoned soldier.

Organized as an element of the First Provisional Colored Regiment in August 1917, the men in the unit had been forced to wait for nearly seven months before receiving orders from the War Department to report to Camp Upton, New York, for training in the combat arms. Official Washington had delayed their initial orders due to a severe labor shortage in the American South, harvesting the year's cotton crop. Since most of the men hailed from South Carolina, such noncombatant duties smacked of considerable irony, and must have produced profound feelings of disillusionment, not to mention anger and frustration. "'This man's army certainly doesn't want us,' was heard on all sides," a chaplain assigned to one of the 93rd Division's all-black regiments recalled.[22]

Twenty-two-year-old Freddie Stowers from Sandy Springs, South Carolina, may have shared those sentiments. Stowers had witnessed firsthand the harsh realities of race and class in the Deep South. Born in January 1896 to Wiley and Annie Stowers, both ex-slaves, he was raised in Anderson County, where nearly two centuries of cotton picking and share-cropping had shaped the lives of most members of the black community. As the twentieth century moved toward the end of its second decade, Stowers married and took on various forms of backbreaking, unskilled farm labor to support his expanding family.

In October of 1917, however, Stowers decided to quit the farming life altogether and join the army. His reasons for enlisting are unclear; he had no prior knowledge of army discipline and culture, nor did anyone in his family or neighborhood have any military experience. It's quite possible that he was interested in the brewing worldwide conflict that became known as the Great War, and was sufficiently impressed by the "close ranks" rhetoric of racial leaders like W. E. B. Du Bois that he decided to enlist. If that was the case, receiving labor assignments outside of the infantry, such as picking cotton, must have left Stowers and other soldiers feeling understandably underwhelmed.[23] As Stowers and the men gathered along the decks of the troop transport steamer, expressions of exasperation and cynicism surely wafted through their conversations.

Around the time that Henry Johnson and Needham Roberts were about to enter the pantheon of immortality, the men of the 371st Infantry boarded railcars that summer, bound for Vaubecourt, just west of the Saint-Mihiel salient. Shortly after their arrival, they, like their sister regiments formerly with the 93rd (Provisional) Division, were attached to the French 154th Infantry Division of the French XIII Corps. They, too, exchanged their US government–issued rifles, packs, helmets, and uniforms for French equipment. French advisers put the infantrymen through the same intricacies of training, including hours of instruction in the trenches. More often than not, their training took place in areas where they could hear artillery fire at close range. Shortly afterward, the outfit marched north-west through Sivry-la-Perche, Bois Borrus, and Vigneville, to the Bois de Bethlainville, before being assigned to the newly created French 157th "Red Hand" Division under the command of Gen. Mariano Goybet.[24]

As they approached the Front, the newly arrived soldiers of the 371st Infantry could not help but notice the multinational composition of the French Army. As soon as they reached Bois de Bethlainville, they met soldiers from all over the world, including Italians, French, Chinese, and Arabs. The Argonne Forest involved troops not only from France and Britain, but also Dominion forces from Canada, Australia, and New Zealand. In addition, they were deeply impressed by the pan-African sensibilities expressed by groups of Africans who hailed from French colonies like Senegal and Morocco, attached to the French divisions.

'It is a regular Tower of Babel, isn't it?'

The strange mélange of languages, customs, practices, and traditions assaulted their senses like no other, and encouraged them to think about the world anew. A black officer writing home to his family during the period described the transnational character of their experiences in the following manner: "The Italians all speak French pretty well, and a few words of English. We all jabbered in French, Italian, and English, and as one of the Italian officers said, 'It is a regular Tower of Babel, isn't it?'"[25]

From the moment the soldiers of the 371st regiment moved to the area north of Somme-Bionne with the French 4th Army to the days leading up to the Meuse-Argonne Offensive that fall, the consciousness-raising moments the soldiers experienced while interacting with their international counterparts were put to the test during the month of September of 1918. Upon their arrival, the infantrymen were ordered to take part in one of the most critical stages of the final and greatest Allied offensive along the entire Western Front, from the Swiss border to the Belgian coastline. The mission was to lay siege to the vaunted Hindenburg Line and seize the Carignan-Sedan-Mézières Railroad—a critical point in the German line of supply—thereby forcing the surrender of the German Army. The Argonne Forest was pivotal in the initiative, as its dense woods, barbed wire, and damp and narrow dugouts precluded passage by vehicle.

On September 25, the men of the 371st received orders to move forward to the Front, where they had been assigned as reserve forces for the French 157th Red Hand Division as it advanced south of Ripont. As the men approached the area, they discovered that the horrors of war awaited them. Enemy artillery fire erupted as a previously dormant Argonne Forest was transformed into an active theater of operation. During a nine-day period, elements of the 371st Infantry, along with the 372nd, fought German forces, advancing nearly five miles against well-organized enemy defenses. They captured over six hundred prisoners of war, along with fifteen heavy guns, twenty Minenwerfers, and scores of machine guns, engineering supplies, and artillery ammunition. But they paid a dear price for their gallantry, with more than five hundred of their men wounded, gassed, or killed in the process.[26]

One of the most costly battles fought during the Meuse-Argonne Offensive took place on September 28 at Cote 188, a key strategic point in the Hindenburg Line that lay near Beausejour (Bussy) Farm, and involved C Company squad leader Freddie Stowers. After receiving orders to launch an all-out assault on the hill, Stowers and the men of his company managed to move through the area virtually unscathed before encountering the most unlikely sight. Upon their arrival, the South Carolina native and his comrades discovered that the enemy had ceased firing upon them. They had actually begun climbing out of their dugouts, proclaiming their surrender.

But to their consternation, Stowers and his men found that all was not what it seemed. As they moved to reciprocate the gesture, the enemy jumped back into their positions and proceeded to lay down indiscriminate fire on the unsuspecting company, practically annihilating most of the unit's officers. The dire situation also gave rise to a critical moment of heroism for one soldier. Undaunted, Stowers stepped forward and provided inspired leadership for fellow members of his company, spurring them forward in a desperate battle against enemy trenches and the elements of the hill. With total disregard for any danger to himself, the intrepid squad leader moved his fellow soldiers toward the enemy position, until the Germans dropped their weapons and staged a hasty retreat to the Sechault-Ardeuil Line.

Stowers and his men seized Hill 188, captured many German prisoners, and secured precious machine guns, railroad cars, and enormous quantities of lumber and supplies. In addition, they shot down three German airplanes during their attack. Stowers would not live long enough to see the fruits of his courageous act. When the assault ended, he, along with more than 40 percent of his two-hundred-man company, had been brought down during the battle, gravely wounded by machine-gun fire.

LOST IN TRANSLATION

The Plight of Black World War I Ex-Servicemen

The legacy of Stowers's courage that day would long outlive his physical presence. His actions earned him many French honors from the Red Hand Division commander, Gen. Mariano Goybet. For his distinguished service, Stowers received the Croix de Guerre, France's highest military decoration for fortitude on the field of battle. Stowers, the grandson of slaves, was laid to rest in the Meuse-Argonne American Cemetery in France. The French memorialized the heroic deeds performed by Stowers and his 371st comrades who fell at Bussy Farm, Ardeuil, Montauxelle, and Triers Ferme by erecting an obelisk statue in their memory. His regimental commander also recommended the young patriot, along with six members of the all-black regiment, for the Distinguished Service Cross, and pushed for Stowers to receive the Medal of Honor, the nation's highest citation for valor.

In most instances, Stowers's courageous exploits would have generated the same outpouring of praise from observers in the United States, but this was not the case. As Stowers's family members and the survivors of the Meuse-Argonne Offensive would soon discover, their acts of bravery produced only a sort of Pyrrhic victory. The legacy of his valiant actions, along with the heroism displayed by other black soldiers in World War I, would be virtually erased from our nation's memory until the waning years of the twentieth century.

But like Henry Johnson and other black heroes of the World War I era, Stowers's path to glory would take many twists and turns before attracting the attention of congressional members and prompting the actions of a sitting president.[27]

Unlike Freddie Stowers, Henry Johnson managed to make it back home in one piece. In February of 1919, the former railroad hand returned to the United States and received a hero's welcome. During a parade along New York's Fifth Avenue, throngs of people lined the streets to catch a glimpse of their Albany hero. One can only wonder what Johnson was thinking as he rode along in an open-top automobile to shouts of "Oh, you, Henry Johnson! Oh, you, "Black Death." He had come a long way from Winston-Salem, North Carolina, through the streets of New York, to battles in France, only to wind up back in New York, greeted with adoring applause and lasting fame.

He was the first US soldier to be accorded a major decoration for bravery in the war when he received the Croix de Guerre. Former president Theodore Roosevelt heaped praise on him, describing the World War I veteran as "one of the five bravest" lads to serve in the war. On March 26, Johnson spoke at the State Armory on Washington Avenue about his wartime experience. He sat for seemingly endless rounds of interviews with members of both the black and the white national press corps, all of whom were anxious to hear about the exploits of the 369th and their authentic hero. By the end of that month, Johnson's celebrity had reached even greater heights when he appeared before the Albany State Legislature to speak in support of a bill to provide veterans' preference for ex-GIs who sought civil service employment.[28]

Shortly afterward, Johnson was discharged from the army. He soon discovered that new challenges awaited him. His war wounds had left him permanently crippled, preventing him from being able to secure employment in his old position as a baggage handler. Penniless, and denied a veteran's pension, Johnson died a destitute alcoholic in July of 1929 at the age of thirty-two. He was buried with full military honors in Arlington National Cemetery. Although he received a posthumous Purple Heart, the Medal of Honor still eluded him. As his wartime deeds entered the realms of local mythology, the Albany Chapter of the 369th Regiment Veterans traveled to the state capitol, urging lawmakers to push for legislation to honor the New York native. Assemblyman Michael McNulty and Senator Alfonse D'Amato also introduced bills in their respective chambers of the house, calling for the Medal of Honor for Johnson, to no avail.

But in June of 2015, at the behest of New York senator Charles Schumer and a host of prominent scholars, President Barack Obama finally bestowed the nation's highest honor for valor on Henry Johnson. Staff members and honored guests attended the ceremony, pregnant with meaning, in the East Room of the White House.[29] Command Sgt. Maj. Louis Wilson of the New York National Guard accepted the medal on behalf of the long-since-fallen soldier. President Obama stated that the country needed to express its gratitude, even ninety-seven years after the soldier's act of courage. "It takes our nation too long sometimes to say so," he added. "We have work to do as a nation to make sure that all of our heroes' stories are told."[30]

"We have work to do as a nation to make sure that all of our heroes' stories are told."

Obama's words signify how the quality of valor requires a revaluation of American democratic principles, and how its meaning has been transformed over time to meet the challenges of each war. How the nation arrived at such a re-estimation of courage and what circumstances forced such reinterpretation is the subject for a later chapter.

Members of an artillery unit stand by and check their equipment
while the convoy takes a break.

CHAPTER 5

Seizing the Hero's Mantle

HEROES IN WORLD WAR II, 1941–1945

I was an angry young man. We were all angry, but we had a job to do and we did it. It was very frustrating to be a soldier. But when the fighting started, all of that was gone. The uppermost thought in my mind was getting the job done and keeping myself alive.

—Vernon Baker, former first lieutenant, 92nd Infantry Division, 1996

In March of 1947, the Argonne Chapel in Cheyenne, Wyoming, was the scene of great solemnity and reflection. Col. Andral Bratton and fellow members of the Transportation Training Sub-Center, along with nearly seventy townspeople, were attending a religious service where they heard the word of God and exhortations about the challenges of public service. They were particularly moved by Chaplain Louis Beasley, one of the foremost religious leaders in the nation's military at the time. "Loyalty, Duty, and Country," Beasley intoned, "has no price in the larger battle for our rights." As a black chaplain with the 92nd Infantry Division during World War II, Beasley had encountered the struggle for equality firsthand. While stationed at Fort Huachuca, Arizona, during the early 1940s, he and his wife were personally insulted when they entered a post restaurant and a white colonel said, "They don't serve your kind here." When the pair protested, the ranking officer ordered them to leave the premises.

"It's not enough to be the first officers in tomorrow's military," Beasley told those in attendance that day. "We have to be long-distance runners on the path of freedom." As the congregants nodded their heads in approval, Beasley beckoned offstage. Vernon J. Baker—considered one of the city's most revered citizens—strode toward the rostrum. Baker had just returned home from an extended tour of duty with the 3373rd Quartermaster Corps in Italy after enduring nearly two years of fighting against the German Army in northern

Italy as a member of the 370th Regimental Combat Team. Like the rest of his uniformed comrades in the chapel, he was a member of the segregated army of the era, having served with the all-black 92nd Infantry Division.[1]

Baker was a twenty-three-year-old railroad porter when he joined the army in 1941, among the thousands of other young black men that year destined to wear specially made dog tags labeling them government personnel of the US military. Shortly after enlisting, Baker went through basic training at Camp Wolters, Texas—but not before receiving a rude introduction to Jim Crow racism. While boarding a bus heading to the southwestern Texas facility, he dropped his duffel bag on a front seat, only to be sternly admonished by the driver: "Hey, nigger! Get up and go to the back of the bus where you belong!"

At every turn, race and rank discrimination dogged the steps of the soldiers in the 92nd Infantry Division. As they trained in Indiana, Alabama, and Arizona, Baker and other black infantrymen lived their "fight for the right to fight" mantra. As Baker later recalled, "Instead of imbuing our men with a sense of accomplishment—gaining the right to fight—it brought unrest. We considered our homeland imperfect, but still considered it the best country in the world."

Once Baker and his comrades arrived in Italy in 1944, they quickly discovered that the fight for first-class citizenship had taken on new meaning. Those who stood in the ranks of the segregated army at the time were being labeled by Official Washington and senior army commanders as "unreliable [. . .] soldiers who run away in the heat of battle," even before they had begun to engage the enemy and confront the horrors of modern war.

As with previous medal recipients, the war in Europe and Asia offered black servicemen like Vernon Baker the rare opportunity to carry guns and ammunition, and the chance to strike back at their oppressors. Like those who had experienced racism and class oppression while fighting against the Confederate Army, the American Indian nations, the Spanish empire, and the armies of previous wars, World War II GIs came to regard Hitler, Mussolini, and Hirohito as representatives of their oppressors at home. They also realized they were being asked to pay a price for all who lived under the threat of racism and class antagonism at home.

"FIGHT FOR THE RIGHT TO FIGHT"

Joining World War II

The World War II experiences of Baker and his fellow Medal of Honor recipients were forged in the crucible of the Great Depression and the New Deal years of the late 1930s and early 1940s. Between 1925 and 1930, the labor-participation rate for black working-class males (between the ages of sixteen and twenty-four) dipped from 85 percent to 82 percent. By 1940, the proportion had dropped even lower, reflecting the loss of thousands of jobs in the agricultural, service, and industrial sectors due to massive layoffs and firings. Meanwhile, young black men contemplated serving in a racially segregated military, whose ongoing discriminatory practices since World War I had given them little reason for hope.

Prior to November of 1940, army planners had conducted studies that supported World War I commanders' disparaging perceptions of black troops. War Department officials had stubbornly upheld the military's long-standing practice of segregating black soldiers, relying on racial prejudice and vicious stereotypes and innuendo to denigrate the combat capabilities of African-American enlisted men and officers. African Americans were also barred from enlisting in the navy, marines, or the air corps. As branch officials stipulated in 1940, "The policy of the War Department is not to intermingle colored and white enlisted personnel in the same regimental organizations."

Black Americans were confined to separate training facilities and combat and service and supply units, with limited opportunities for promotion to field-grade officer positions. In addition, the United States had greatly reduced the strength of its army after World War I. The War Department typically adopted this practice after every war, but the aftermath of World War I brought a new set of harsh realities for black recruits. Throughout the 1920s and 1930s, the four black regiments established after the Civil War–the 9th and 10th Cavalry and the 24th and 25th Infantry–were chronically understaffed, and they faced the constant threat of being converted to service and support units, or being demobilized altogether.[2] By 1940, there were only 4,700 African-American enlisted men and five African-American officers serving in the Regular Army.[3]

By the late 1930s, African Americans across the country reacted in various ways to the outbreak of war in Europe. During the first few weeks, their initial responses ranged from cynical isolationism to outright patriotism. George Schuyler, syndicated columnist for Pittsburgh's *Courier*, pointed to the similarities between the German invasion of Austria and British colonialism in Asia, stating, "War is a toss-up." Publications such as the *Annals of the American Academy of Political and Social Science*, *Scribner's Commentator*, *PM*, *Common Sense*, *People's Voice*, *Opportunity*, and black newspapers carried stories with headlines like "Should the Negro Care Who Wins the War?" and "A White Folks' War?" In a pamphlet titled "Why Negroes Should Oppose the War," noted Afro-Caribbean scholar and human rights activist C. L. R. James proclaimed that no matter who won the war, blacks would continue to face discrimination, police brutality, and poverty worldwide.

In the months leading up to and through the Japanese bombing of Pearl Harbor, most African-American views hinged on the black struggle for equality and the military's discriminatory policies. Few NAACP and other civil rights leaders were willing to follow W. E. B. Du Bois's 1918 advice—to embrace "First Your Country, then Your Rights." Instead, they stressed that blacks should embrace a "fight for the right to fight" strategy to gain racial equality. From the 1940 presidential election through Asa Philip Randolph's 1941 March on Washington Movement, black leadership advanced the central idea that total African-American support for the war campaign required federal guarantees calling for the inclusion of blacks in the defense industries and the end of segregation in the armed forces.

INTO THE CRUCIBLE

Training and Deploying of Soldiers of Valor

On the heels of the Selective Service Act of 1940, African Americans came out in droves to register for the armed forces. As the war intensified in Europe and Asia, the number of black servicemen in the army increased from 3,640 in 1939 to nearly 500,000 by December of 1942. On the eve of the 1940 presidential election, Franklin D. Roosevelt promoted

Col. Benjamin O. Davis Sr. to the rank of brigadier general, making him the country's first African-American general officer in the Regular Army. The War Department also announced the appointment of Judge William Hastie as civilian aide to the Secretary of War, and named Maj. Campbell C. Johnson as the special assistant to the director of the Selective Service. Shortly after Pearl Harbor, the War Department created an air corps, two infantry divisions, a cavalry division, several tank battalions, and a women's army corps unit, all of which accepted black soldiers. By 1944, an increasing number of black soldiers attended officer candidate schools and special training programs on a limited-integrated basis.[4]

Despite the rapid expansion of the army, black soldiers found that true equality still escaped their grasp. More often than not, African Americans held positions in the military that were similar to those they occupied in civilian society. Black GIs were largely segregated along racial lines, confined to non-combat units and training schools, and placed in separate camp facilities located far from large cities and towns. Numerous racial clashes took place between black GIs and white military and civilian law enforcement officials in military hospitals, post exchanges, theaters, and camp buses located on army and navy bases throughout the country. And in many cases, African-American enlistees and inductees received substandard instruction and faced bouts of discrimination meted out by the white Southern officers, who perceived their assignment to black units as a form of punishment. When asked years later how he and others felt about it at the time, a black soldier stated, "Right away, we said, what are we doing this for?"[5]

> "Right away, we said, what are we doing this for?"

These day-to-day confrontations with army discrimination may have reinforced the determination of black men who served in the ranks of World War II military. Streaming into training sites in the Deep South, the Midwest, and the Southwest, young African Americans were stationed largely at facilities like Camp Croft, Camp Wolters, Fort Huachuca, Fort Breckinridge, Fort McClellan, Fort Lee, and Fort Swift. There, they were trained under the watchful eye of talented veteran noncommissioned officers.

The seven soldiers who eventually earned the nation's highest award for valor in World War II came from all over the country: George Watson and Charles Thomas grew up in Alabama; Ruben Rivers, in Oklahoma; John Fox hailed from Ohio; Vernon Baker, from Wyoming; Willy James, Missouri; and Los Angeles–born Edward Carter spent time in China before returning to California.

As the young soldiers progressed toward the advanced stages of their combat training, a combination of forces calling for overseas deployment of black troops pushed them forward. Throughout the spring and summer months of 1943, numerous military installations like Camp Dorn, Mississippi; Lake Charles, Louisiana; Camp Stewart, Georgia; Fort Huachuca, Arizona; Fort Bliss, Texas; and Camp Shenango, Pennsylvania, became the sites of racial violence involving black soldiers and white troops and military and civilian townspeople. At the same time, members of the black press corps and War Department civilian aides William Hastie and Truman K. Gibson Jr., along with several members of the Advisory Committee on Negro Troops, clamored for the employment of black troops in active theaters of operation.

By early 1944, the 24th Infantry Regiment had been deployed into action in the Pacific, and infantry teams from the 92nd and 93rd Infantry Divisions were designated for combat assignments overseas. As their deployment attracted the attention of punditry and public alike, War Department officials and army commanders offered their racially biased perceptions of how black soldiers would perform on the field of battle. Indeed, as noted historian Ulysses G. Lee pointed out, "The careers of Negro combat units were, there, as atypical as were the circumstances of their commitment to overseas duty."[6]

SAVING LIVES IN THE PACIFIC RIM

The Heroism of George Watson

Not long afterward, everyone had their answer. In the months following the Japanese attack on Pearl Harbor, Washington strategists hastily dispatched nearly 80,000 troops aimed at protecting the supply and communication routes between Hawaii, Australia, and vast areas of the Southwest Pacific. By the end of 1942, nearly 300,000 soldiers would be mobilized and deployed to the Pacific. Aboard the converted transports were hundreds of black GIs assigned to engineering and quartermaster units. Once they arrived in the Pacific, most of these soldiers performed backbreaking labor, including stevedoring, guarding air bases, loading and unloading ships, and roadbuilding at various island ports stretching from Samoa and Fiji to New Caledonia and New Guinea.[7]

For black troops arriving on converted landing crafts, just being able to reach the Pacific Rim safely was clouded with uncertainty. Hazardous weather at sea and bombing attacks by Japanese aircraft and submarines proved to be just as much of a test as the jungle warfare that awaited them. Japanese nighttime attacks also spelled endless round-the-clock evacuation drills and heightened feelings of anxiety among the men.

In the words of one black soldier who journeyed aboard a transport ship at the time:

This was a long and anxious trip for those of us who were poor sailors or who were not able to pass the time in poker. I was often seasick but had to struggle out at odd times during some of the days for "abandon ship" practice. If a suspicious submarine or airplane was sighted or heard, everyone went on the alert. At night the ship was in complete "black out"; to get from one area to another after dark one had to go through a series of dark room curtains or staggered door. If the night watch on deck saw one flicker of light from a cigarette, flashlight, or electric, the offender was apprehended and questioned. Every military man knows how important this precaution is, since submarines along the marine route can see a light in the dark for miles and miles.[8]

On the night of March 8, 1943, precaution gave way to a moment of heroism for George Watson, a private assigned to the 29th Quartermaster Regiment. Born in Laurel, Mississippi, and raised by his grandmother in Birmingham, Alabama, Watson moved to Colorado in the late 1930s. He attended Colorado Agricultural and Mechanical College before entering the army in 1942, at the tender age of twenty-four.

Watson and his fellow GIs in the quartermaster unit had been aboard a Dutch converted luxury liner named *Jacob* for nearly a month after leaving San Francisco. As they coasted near Porlock Harbour, New Guinea, on March 8, they suddenly found themselves under all-out attack by Japanese bombers. After sustaining serious damage to its hull, the transport ship listed back and forth before capsizing, forcing all occupants to abandon ship. A fair number who had never learned to swim drowned in the process.

Watson decided to take matters into his own hands. Instead of moving directly to safety, he swam from ship to shore several times, saving soldiers struggling to get free of the ocean current. His courageous efforts came at a tremendous cost. Weakened by exertion and overcome with muscle fatigue, Watson drowned as the undertow from the sinking ship dragged him below the surface. While his body was never recovered, his valorous actions, exemplary leadership, and selfless devotion earned him the army's second-highest decoration, the Distinguished Service Cross. Watson was the first African American to be recognized for such an honor, and later, he became the only black soldier who served in the Pacific War to receive the Medal of Honor.[9]

Ruben Rivers

Charles Thomas

BLACK PANTHERS AT THE SIEGFRIED LINE

The Heroism of Ruben Rivers and Charles Thomas

After crossing the English Channel and landing at Omaha Beach in the fall of 1944, black soldiers with the 761st Tank Battalion were transformed into the shock troops for freedom on the battlefields of Europe. They bivouacked at Les Pieux, France, where they were assigned to Lt. Gen. George Patton's 3rd Army and attached as a supportive unit to the US 26th Infantry Division, commanded by Maj. Gen. Willard S. Paul. With their morale running at an all-time high and buoyed by the chance to finally strike a blow against the enemy, most of the well-trained soldiers quickly realized their stake in the war's outcome.

Advancing at a breakneck pace, the flamboyant Patton had reached a critical stage in the execution of the war. His tanks were running short on gasoline and supplies that were necessary for making an assault during the Lorraine Campaign of northeastern France, and the three-star general desperately needed fresh manpower, guns, and equipment to complete the Allied race across Europe.

Specifically calling for the 761st Tank Battalion, Patton visited the soldiers on November 3 and addressed them while standing on a half-track:

> Men, you're the first Negro tankers to ever fight in the American Army. I would never have asked for you if you weren't good. I have nothing but the best in my Army. I don't care what color you are, so long as you go up there and kill those Kraut sonsabitches. Everyone has their eyes on you and is expecting great things from you. Most of all, your race is looking forward to you. Don't let them down, don't let me down.[10]

But Patton's words of encouragement belied his true feelings about the capabilities of black soldiers in battle. When he returned to his headquarters, he noted, "They gave a good first impression, but I have no faith in the inherent fighting ability of the race."[11]

Patton's disparaging attitude toward black soldiers was soon put to the test. The 761st entered combat on November 7 and would see continuous action on the front lines for the next 183 days. During this period, the unit largely fought through the Lorraine region as forward elements. The men battled German tanks, losing fourteen of their own in the process, and sustaining the loss of 113 men either killed or wounded during its first month of combat.

It was during the unit's all-out assault on enemy forces at Vic-sur-Seille that Staff Sgt. Ruben Rivers first came to the attention of his superior officers.

Born in Tecumseh, Oklahoma, Rivers was the son of Willie, an African American, and Lillian, a Cherokee. Growing up in nearby Hotulka with eleven brothers and sisters, the twenty-three-year-old had worked on the family farm and as a railroad porter, and had enrolled with the Civilian Conservation Corps before joining the army in 1942. After undergoing basic training, he reported to Fort Hood, Texas, where he was assigned to the 761st Tank Battalion.[12]

On November 8, 1944, Rivers and fellow A Tank Company members of the 761st, along with the 104th Infantry Regiment, moved into armed positions against the German position near Vic-sur-Seille. As they reached a railroad crossing adjacent to the town, they confronted a roadblock of felled trees in which enemy forces had placed mortars, rifles, and land mines to obstruct the movement of tank columns and infantrymen. As the troopers advanced, several soldiers accidentally tripped the mines, drawing enemy fire, disabling several of their tanks, and pinning the infantrymen down during the fighting.

Despite being struck in the leg during the action, Rivers, a tank platoon sergeant, declined medical treatment and refused to be evacuated to safety. Instead, he took command of another column, attaching a cable to one of the felled trees and removed it from the road. He continued to use his tank to deliver direct fire on enemy tanks, allowing A Company to move forward and successfully assault and capture the town without sustaining further loss of life and limb. His courage and devotion to duty brought great distinction to the talented noncommissioned officer and his unit.

Less than a week later, his military career came to an abrupt end. While advancing toward the town of Guebling, France, his lead tank was hit by several deadly rounds from German guns, killing the sergeant instantly. The staff sergeant stayed at his post until his death. Capt. David Williams, his company commander, remembered Rivers telling him over the radio just minutes before he was mortally wounded that he had spotted enemy antitank positions in the area, exclaiming, "I see 'em! We'll fight 'em!"

"I see 'em! We'll fight 'em!"

On November 20, Captain Williams recommended Rivers for the military's highest award, the Medal of Honor, but it would take nearly sixty years for a grateful nation to finally recognize the leadership qualities and selfless actions taken by this intrepid young soldier.[13]

Meanwhile, the performance of another soldier with the 761st in the European Theater of Operations would bring additional luster to the African-American experience in the war. On a cold, foggy morning in early December 1944, a task force of tankers with the 614th's C Company, along with a reinforced rifle company from the 411th Infantry Regiment, advanced through northeastern France. Their assignment: to storm and seize the German-occupied village of Climbach, an area centrally located in an open valley approximately five miles from the Siegfried Line. Capturing the heavily wooded stronghold would cut off the enemy line of communications, thus bolstering Allied chances of knocking Germany out of the war altogether. Their mission was hampered by limited visibility in the valley and lack of reconnaissance regarding the enemy's whereabouts.

This select platoon was commanded by Lt. Charles Thomas. Born in Birmingham, Alabama, Thomas was a former molder for the Ford Motor Company, and had been attending Detroit's Wayne State University when he decided to join the army in January of 1942. While undergoing basic training with the 614th Tank Destroyer Battalion, his leadership qualities and assertive personality caught the attention of his senior officers, and they encouraged the intense twenty-two-year-old soldier to attend Officer Candidate School at Fort Benning, Georgia. Thomas successfully negotiated the twelve-week program and earned his commission the following spring.

Thomas and his men left Preuschdorf, France, in the early-morning hours that day and climbed the rugged hills. They had no sooner achieved the high ground southeast of the village than they drew fierce enemy fire from German artillery in the area. The initial hail of bullets disabled Thomas's lead jeep and severely wounded him in the chest, legs, and left arm. Undaunted, the determined commanding officer rallied his troops, signaling them to halt in the face of enemy fire. Despite his severe wounds, Thomas refused medical attention and directed the dispersal and emplacement of two of his antitank guns before ordering his platoon leader to train his guns on the enemy gun positions. Only after stabilizing his unit's situation, permitting the men to outflank the enemy, did Thomas allow himself to be treated for his wounds.

Thomas's courageous action enabled the unit to capture the town and forced German troops to withdraw below the Siegfried Line. For his extraordinary heroism in France that day, twenty-four-year-old Thomas was awarded the Distinguished Service Cross by the War Department, becoming the second African American to be so honored during actual fighting. Not long afterward, the humble GI returned home to wide acclaim, downplaying his newfound celebrity status. "I know I was sent out to locate and draw the enemy fire, but I didn't mean to draw that much," he said.[14]

John R. Fox

Vernon Baker

FIGHTING ON TWO FRONTS

John R. Fox, Vernon Baker, and the 92nd Infantry Division in Northern Italy

Meanwhile, black troops with the 92nd Infantry Division received their first taste of war in northern Italy in the fall and winter months of 1945. Arriving in Naples at the end of July, 1944, the newly constituted 370th Regimental Combat Team reported to the 1st Armored Division. There, the men prepared to cross the Arno River in order to breach the southern slope of the Gothic Line that stretched along the northern Apennines. Their mission was to maintain contact with enemy forces, thus allowing Gen. Mark Clark's 5th Army to launch a coordinated effort in the Bologna area to outflank the German Army, puncture the Gothic Line, and reach the Po Valley.

Before leaving the bivouacked area, the 370th Regimental Combat Team quickly discovered that their operation was part of a multinational effort involving soldiers from all over the world, including South Africans, Italian partisans, and Brazilians, Indians, Canadians, and British forces, all of whom had made their way to the northern Apennines to fight Hitler and Mussolini.[15]

They soon discovered that the weather and the jagged rock of the northern Apennines would prove to be just as daunting as the enemy they faced. Running from south of La Spezia to the Foglia Valley in the west, the Gothic Line consisted of crests and peaks reaching as high as seventy feet. They stretched to the Adriatic Sea and then dropped sharply into the Arno River valley and the narrow coastal plain south of Massa. The deep valleys and irregular terrain provided ample cover for more than two thousand machine-gun nests, casemates, bunkers, observation posts, and artillery-fighting positions. Developed by German field marshal Albert Kesselring, these fortified enemy redoubts were designed to withstand any assault mounted by Allied forces. Finally, weather considerations dictated that the 5th Army must launch a successful attack on this heavily fortified position before the onset of winter.[16]

On September 1, the men of the 370th Infantry, commanded by Capt. Charles Gandy, crossed the Arno River near Pisa and secured Mount Pisano, before moving on to capture the towns of Lucca, Bagni di Lucca, La Lima, and San Marcello. They destroyed enemy resistance and successfully breached the Gothic Line south of Abetone, a small ski resort. By the end of October, the men in the unit had participated in several offensive operations that bordered the Ligurian Sea, most notably at Mount Cauala, where some of the most staunchly defended positions of the Gothic Line were located. All told, by the end of autumn, the regiment had advanced more than thirty miles into enemy territory. Seven men distinguished themselves on the field of battle and were awarded the Silver Star for gallantry in action.

But the combat team suffered dearly. While advancing the front line, black soldiers with the 370th suffered nearly 300 casualties, including 225 wounded and nearly 70 killed in action. As the men quickly realized, army commanders were reluctant to provide adequate replacements for their diminished numbers. Jehu Hunter, a former 92nd Infantry Division GI, reflected years later: "The human cost of this effort pointed out the need for trained black infantry replacements, and they were nowhere to be found. It is my opinion that the failure of Army Ground Forces to provide for suitable replacements was an extension of the Army's plan to limit the utilization of blacks in combat roles."[17]

During the Serchio River Valley Campaign that winter, manpower issues and the army's lack of confidence in black soldiers' fighting abilities were exposed. On the night of December 26, a company of the 366th Infantry Regiment arrived in Sommocolonia. As an element of the 92nd Infantry Division, the unit was part of the division's all-out attack on the enemy to support the 5th Army's drive toward Bologna. The 366th attack was to take place along the Serchio River in conjunction with its sister outfit, the 370th Infantry, in order to secure the water crossing for supporting troop movements through the area. But no sooner had the company arrived in Sommocolonia and attempted to move into position than they were forced to abandon their plans for the Christmas Day attack. Almost instantly, the men were greeted by enemy antitank and machine-gun fire from the village. The GIs' field of fire was greatly hampered by enemy soldiers who fired on them while dressed as civilians.[18]

As the fog of war thickened and the situation at Sommocolonia worsened, one courageous soldier stepped forward. Lt. John R. Fox was a soldier with the 92nd Infantry Division. Originally assigned to the 366th's Cannon Company, he had been transferred to the 598th Field Artillery Battalion as a forward observer. In late December, the Wilberforce University graduate, along with several other forward observers, volunteered to be a part of the company to indirectly support the mission. As enemy mortar and artillery fire steadily increased that morning, Fox called for artillery fire perilously close to his own position. After discovering that large numbers of the enemy had encircled the dwelling, he issued a last radio request directing an artillery strike on his own position, and for a smoke screen to provide adequate cover for his withdrawing troops. When asked whether his call for fire was accurate, Fox answered, "Fire it! There are more of them than there are of us. Put fire on my Observation Post."

With that, Fox's radio went silent, and the rest of his observer party was never heard from again. Days later, soldiers with the 366th discovered his body, along with one hundred dead Germans, near the demolished building. The 366th Infantry regimental commander recommended Fox for the Distinguished Service Cross, but the 92nd Division Headquarters never forwarded it to the 5th Army Corps. It would take nearly forty years and an intense investigation by a former 92nd Division GI before the racial injustice and pain of nonrecognition would be fully resolved.[19]

Wyoming native Vernon Baker was born in 1919. He hardly knew his parents, having lost both of them when he was just four years old. Years later he would learn that he was the child of an interracial couple; his father Manuel Caldera came from New Mexico and worked as a carpenter, and his mother Beulah's family had labored as black farmers in the cornfields of Clarinda, Iowa, prior to his birth. After his parents died in a tragic car accident, Baker and his two older sisters moved to Cheyenne, where they were raised by their grandparents in a blacks-only boardinghouse.

Although Fort D. A. Russell in Cheyenne served as a principal training site for African-American GIs, members of the black community greeted them with ambivalence. Baker never heard anyone mention the Buffalo Soldiers of the Indian Fighting Army, and when he saw soldiers from the base "walking down the streets of Cheyenne as a child," he received a stern warning from his grandfather, Joseph Samuel Baker: "Those are ruffians . . . stay away from them." According to Baker, "Nobody talked of their heroics."

But in June of 1941, past, present, and destiny intervened in Baker's life in the form of love, and Uncle Sam. Eager to wed his hometown sweetheart, Leola Sassler, and start a family of his own, he joined the army. After basic training in Camp Wolters, Texas, he reported to the 92nd Infantry Division at Fort Huachuca, Arizona. His stellar performance as a service and supply sergeant earned him a recommendation from his company commander to attend Officer Candidate School at Fort Benning, Georgia. After completing the training program, he earned his lieutenant's bars on January 11, 1943.[20]

A small man at five-foot-five, Baker responded to the call of honor during the Spring Offensive of 1945. The Allies had decided to use the 92nd Infantry Division to launch a diversionary attack aimed at containing the German forces along the Ligurian Coast, clearing the 5th Army to stage an offensive toward Bologna and force the German Army to relinquish its stranglehold on the areas south of the Po River. If accomplished, the event might trigger the end of Germany's control of northern Italy, an area that Hitler hoped to retain at all costs. Code-named "Second Wind," the division's components no longer fought as a single all-black unit. After reorganization, it now included the white 473rd Infantry and the Japanese-American 442nd Infantry Regiments. Only the 370th, along with its complementary assortment of artillery, combat engineering, medical, cannon, and air observation units, remained with the all-black division. By the time the division launched its initial attack on April 5, most of the black soldiers were led by white commanders, whose ambivalent views regarding black soldiers' fighting abilities led to numerous moments of uneasiness, distrust, and uncertainty.[21]

Such was the case with Company C of the 370th on Hill X in the spring of 1945. Before dawn on April 5, Capt. John F. Runyon led his infantrymen west of the hill in hopes of surprising enemy forces in the area. But as the GIs launched their attack, they found themselves facing a severe bombardment of mortar and machine-gun fire from an enemy that had been alerted to their presence. Pinned down by intense shooting, Runyon ordered the unit forward, but not before calling for indirect fire to aid their advancement.

What ensued next was not for the fainthearted. The company moved swiftly toward Castle Aghinolfi, proceeding nearly one hundred yards beyond friendly lines, stopping only to cut enemy wire communications. It was only then that the men learned from central headquarters that they had overrun their artillery support. They were also told not to expect ample reinforcements, even though they had fallen headlong into a well-fortified enemy outpost. Facing increased enemy fire and mounting casualties among his men, the company commander decided to personally withdraw five hundred yards to the battalion lines, leaving behind a group of enlisted men and one sole officer to press the attack.

It was at this point that the hazards of war gave birth to a moment of heroism. Lt. Vernon Baker instantly gathered his wits and commanded his men to form a defensive perimeter, volunteering to cover the withdrawal of a group of wounded soldiers as they made their way to the rearguard area. Covered by one of his subordinates who was armed with a Browning Automatic, Baker crawled toward the enemy, lobbing hand grenades into their machine-gun emplacements, destroying the entrenchments and killing several Germans in the process. The diminutive soldier continued on, single-handedly knocking out an enemy observation post and mortally wounding its occupants.

By the end of the ordeal, Baker had destroyed four enemy machine-gun nests, secured the battalion's objective, and managed a successful evacuation of the surviving members of his company. For his inspiring action during the assault on Castle Aghinolfi that day, and for providing valuable leadership in the capture of a key position coveted by Allied forces,

Baker was promoted to the rank of first lieutenant, and 5th Army commander Lt. Gen. Lucian Truscott Jr. presented him with the Distinguished Service Cross. Nonetheless, years later Baker said, "I am haunted by the memory of nineteen men—men I left on a ridge in northern Italy five decades ago."[22]

Edward Carter Jr.

Willy James Jr.

HEROISM FOR A NEW ARMY

Edward Carter Jr., Willy James Jr., and the Allied Race across the Rhine

Around the same time, black GIs serving in the European Theater of Operations were given a glimpse of equality and liberation. By December of 1944, events at the Front had reached a critical stage. Army Ground Forces Headquarters began to experience severe shortages of infantry rifle replacements. That month, the German Army launched its last offensive in the Ardennes, and the Battle of the Bulge caught Allied forces completely off guard. While the offensive ended in a stalemate, American forces suffered tremendous casualties. During the first week of fighting alone, nearly 50,000 soldiers were killed or wounded. All told, between 60,000 and 125,000 soldiers would end up injured from enemy fire, missing in action, or victimized by the harsh winter conditions they had experienced after a month of the fighting.

By late winter, army commanders' search for trained infantrymen became so acute that men who were serving in service and support units, such as truck drivers, stevedores, and engineers, were now being placed into rifle companies and battalions slated for duty at the Western Front. Even that was not enough. Pressed by the extreme situation, Supreme Allied Commander Dwight D. Eisenhower issued a call for a limited number of volunteers to serve as infantrymen regardless of race or color. Thousands of black troops responded enthusiastically. By February of 1945, nearly 5,000 black troops volunteered, and 2,500 soldiers were reorganized into rifle companies commanded by white officers. These units were led by veteran black noncoms who accepted a reduction in rank to private, relinquishing their sergeant's stripes in order to provide valuable leadership for those who stood in the ranks.[23]

Edward A. Carter Jr. was among those who answered the call to duty. Born in Los Angeles, California, in 1916, he was the son of itinerant Holiness Church missionaries. At the age of five, he traveled to China with his parents, attending schools with the offspring of diplomats. His wanderlust led him to run away at sixteen and join the Chinese Army, where he served until they discovered he was underage. He and his parents returned to LA during the mid-1930s, where Carter became interested in left-wing causes. Convinced that Generalissimo Francisco Franco posed a fascist threat, Carter went to Spain and enlisted in the Loyalist Army as a volunteer with the Abraham Lincoln Brigade. He was captured by Germans and held in a prison camp for several months before returning to serve with the Loyalists for two and a half years. Carter returned to LA in 1940, where he married a young violinist. In the midst of raising a family, he felt the irresistible call to duty. Alarmed by the war in Europe and Asia and the real possibility of US intervention, Carter joined the army, reporting to Camp Wolters, Texas, for basic training in 1941, several months before Pearl Harbor.

After initial training, he was sent to Fort Benning, Georgia, and assigned to the 35th Quartermaster Truck Company, rising to the rank of staff sergeant. While willing to fight against Nazism and fascism abroad, like so many other young black recruits, Carter realized that their "war within the war" was just beginning. After encountering Jim Crow discrimination in the army and among the civilian white population in places like Texas and Georgia, Carter observed, "They don't treat us at all like soldiers. It's more like slaves. When this war is over, you'll see plenty of tough and bitter boys coming home."[24]

> "The harder I work and fight to draw this war to a speedy close, the sooner my return home."

In November of 1944, Carter and his company shipped out to southern France, assigned to transport supplies to Allied fighting forces. They soon heard about Eisenhower's appeal for volunteers among black troops. When the 7th Army requested an all-black platoon to serve with larger white units, army recruiters quickly realized Carter's leadership abilities and recommended he be placed among the first soldiers to be offered the assignment. Finally able to realize his deepest ambition, he wrote home to his wife Mildred: "The harder I work and fight to draw this war to a speedy close, the sooner my return home."[25]

That spring, Carter's unit, now the 1st Provisional Company, was assigned to the 12th Armored Division before being merged into the 56th Armored Infantry Battalion. The company was attached to General Patton's 3rd Army, which stood poised to cross the Rhine River and advance into Germany. In late March, Carter, along with fellow members of the 12th Armored Division, received an order to move from Saint-Avold to an area near Sierck-les-Bains, where they were attached to the 3rd Army's XX Corps. There, they were ordered to attack German forces at the city of Speyer and to secure the bridge over the Rhine River.[26]

On March 23, reaching the heavily wooded area that surrounded the city, Carter and other black volunteers were pinned down by German antitank rockets and fierce machine-gun fire. Taking refuge behind a road embankment to decide upon a course of action, they realized that a warehouse was the source of most of the enemy rocket fire, and that seizing the stronghold meant negotiating an open field. The veteran noncommissioned officer volunteered to lead a three-man patrol for the mission.

He and his men faced an increasingly dire situation, with steady enemy fire. After witnessing the deaths of two of his men and the severe wounding of the third, Carter continued on alone, despite being wounded himself. Forced to take cover, he waited several hours before fate intervened. When an eight-man patrol of German riflemen emerged from the warehouse to reconnoiter the area, Carter emptied his .45 caliber Thompson submachine gun on them, killing six of the soldiers. Capturing the remaining two, and using them as human shields, Carter marched them back across the open field to his company, where they were detained as prisoners of war.

But Carter's exploits did not stop there. Upon returning to the command outpost, he refused medical attention until he was able to obtain valuable information from the captured soldiers as to the location and strength of enemy troops in the area. Based on Carter's interrogation, the 12th Armored Division was able to clear an essential pathway into Speyer, thus facilitating the Allied drive into the heart of Germany. After recovering from his wounds, Carter returned to his unit and continued fighting until the end of the war.

Carter's bravery and undying devotion to his comrades attracted attention. For his extraordinary heroism and inspired leadership in the 7th Army, the staff sergeant was awarded the Distinguished Service Cross.[27]

★ ★ ★

The clarion call of freedom and a deep devotion to country also beckoned Pvt. Willy F. James Jr. Born in Kansas City, Missouri, in 1920, James worked as a deliveryman before entering the army in late 1942. He trained to be a scout, and was assigned to a unit with the 104th "Timberwolf" Infantry Division. After arriving in Germany in early 1945, James and his comrades in Company C were given orders on April 7 to cross the Weser River and secure a group of houses near Lippoldsberg, Germany. Possessing the enemy stronghold would allow American forces to establish and secure a bridgehead for launching an all-out attack on the rest of the town.

Private James was walking apart from his squad when he stumbled upon a well-fortified machine-gun nest manned by enemy snipers. Despite drawing furious crossfire, James unhesitatingly volunteered to reconnoiter the area to get a better sense of the enemy position. After maneuvering approximately two hundred yards across open, contested terrain,

James managed to pinpoint the enemy's whereabouts before returning to cover, where he gave a full and detailed report to his platoon leader. His heroics were short-lived, however. After his platoon leader was struck down, the intrepid soldier took charge of the mission. He was moving across an open field to come to the aid of his fallen commander when he himself was struck and killed by enemy fire.

> James's extraordinary act of valor proved to be instrumental in his unit's ability to achieve its mission.

James's extraordinary act of valor proved to be instrumental in his unit's ability to achieve its mission, greatly aiding the 413th's efforts to establish a bridgehead over the Weser River. His fellow servicemen recovered his body, and his remains were interred in the Netherlands. His selfless spirit continued to inspire those who served in the theater of operations long after his demise. On May 26, his platoon leader recommended the infantry scout for the Distinguished Service Cross, and James received the honor posthumously less than four months later.[28]

HONOR DEFERRED

The Legacies of Edward Carter and Vernon Baker

As James's body was being lowered into the ground, fierce discussion ensued within the military over the very meaning of his military service and sacrifice. Although it is beyond doubt that his selfless actions should have earned him greater attention beyond the battlefields of Europe, few Americans had heard of Willy James Jr., or anything about African-American combat experience in Europe. Deeply immersed in Jim Crow practices, European and Pacific theater commanders either neglected or completely dismissed the battlefield performances of black GIs.

This was even more evident in the postwar period. In 1948, Maj. Gen. Edward Almond prepared a preliminary report on the performance of black troops in the European Theater of Operations. According to a top-secret wartime study conducted by a board of senior white officers, the former commander of the 92nd Infantry Division downplayed the army's experiment with desegregated units at the end of the war. Almond stated that black soldiers in the unit repeatedly demonstrated their inability to be trained "in modern combat methods," and that "no amount of training of the Negro infantry rifleman will insure his application of sound principles under fire, or even in the forward combat area." Almond wrote to his superiors: "My experience of three and a half years in an attempt to create a combat infantry division comprising of negro units convinces me that it is a failure."[29] Almond's staunch adherence to the military's segregationist policies may have foreshadowed the immediate postwar experiences of black GIs like Edward Carter and Vernon Baker, who returned home to discover that their "war within the war" was just beginning.

Arriving in Los Angeles in late 1945, although Edward Carter felt his wartime experience had produced fundamental changes in him, he found the social and political climate in America basically unchanged. After struggling to find work and trying his hand at private business, Carter reenlisted in the army and reported to Camp Lee, Virginia, where he was assigned as a staff sergeant for a special service unit. But the army's system of segregation seemed to follow the talented soldier. Based on his previous tour of duty, Carter was assigned to an all-black engineering combat battalion in the California National Guard. As his biographer later wrote, "Eddie's assignment was ironic and exciting. The irony was that during the war Eddie had fought side by side with white soldiers and only a year earlier he was working on plans for black and white veterans to work together, but he now found himself assigned by the Army to a segregated National Guard Unit. He could not have thought of this as progress. Nevertheless, it was exciting to be training young men (and other men of color) in an environment where the best he had to offer would shine."[30]

After receiving his Distinguished Service Cross—the only black soldier in his division to receive such a recommendation—Vernon Baker was reassigned to a unit in the quartermaster corps before being rotated back to the United States in 1947. Back home in Cheyenne, Wyoming, he too rejected civilian life. He reenlisted in the army and reported to Fayetteville, North Carolina, where he was assigned to a company in the 82nd Airborne Division. But Jim Crow also dogged the steps of this former platoon leader. When he volunteered to go to Korea, the army refused his request, telling him they were not sending any Distinguished Service Cross recipients to the armed conflict. "I didn't know what to believe," Baker said. "I knew there were few black Distinguished Service recipients. But white Distinguished Service Cross recipients had gone to Korea. Was this about color, in the sense that the Army wanted a few decorated black soldiers around to prove it had a broad, inclusive outlook?"[31]

> People have considerable expectations of heroes.

Although Baker was one of the most highly decorated black soldiers of World War II—years later, he would accept the long-delayed Medal of Honor from President William Jefferson Clinton—he wore his status with great humility. "After years of trying to forget, or regretting many deaths, I have been handed the hero's mantle," Baker said. "I wear it uneasily. People have considerable expectations of heroes. We are not to falter in the spotlight; we are not to have made many mistakes in the past. Being a black American raises the ante."[32]

Baker's musings about the army's changing perceptions provide an apt metaphor for how black honor was being reshaped to meet the demands of a new period—namely, the

Cold War. No longer would black GIs be expected to "fight for the right to fight" in segregated units; rather, the merits of their performance under fire would be judged in the context of a new environment, and in the face of a new enemy. This perplexing set of circumstances and the changes they wrought for a different generation of heroes also, in turn, greatly

Black honor was being reshaped to meet the demands of a new period.

altered black perceptions of military service in America. As a result, new definitions of honor would be created.

The war in Korea serves as an important example of how these notions of bravery were translated into action.

Korean War, African-American Marines

CHAPTER 6

Cold War Civil Rights Warriors

THE KOREAN WAR AND BLACK PORTRAITS OF BRAVERY, 1950–1953

Thousands of Negro boys would have done the same thing as Connie did if they had been put in the same spot as he was. My son did not give his life in vain. His bravery has been recognized by the President of the United States and the whole country. And even those persons in America who have felt that the Negroes are second-class citizens must in their hearts now know that this isn't so. My son has proved that the Negro is worthy of the country's highest honor.

—*Van Charlton, 1952*

On a warm, sunny day in July 1952, a Gold Star mother shed tears of pride during a ceremony honoring her recently fallen son. In the midst of whistle blasts and geysers of water emanating from fireboats in New York harbor, Clara and her husband Van were on hand to witness the launching of the Merchant Marine's latest sea vessel, a handsome ferryboat called the *Sergeant Cornelius H. Charlton*. The army vessel had previously plied the waters of New York Harbor between 1st Army Headquarters on Governors Island and the Battery under a different nameplate, but it was now being rechristened after the Bronx, New York, infantryman who had recently been posthumously awarded the Medal of Honor for his outstanding act of valor near Chipo-ri during the Korean War. Charlton joined fellow New York State native William Henry Thompson as one of only two African-American soldiers to be so honored.

The whole Charlton family was there, along with members of the Bronx American Legion and the Unknown Soldiers Post, and a whole host of Defense Department officials. Perhaps Lt. Gen. Willis D. Crittenberger, 1st Army commander, provided the ideal eulogy for the occasion when he said, "In giving Sergeant Charlton's name to this craft, we of the Army are dedicating a memorial to symbolize our highest respect for his deed."[1]

Unfortunately, the gratitude that Crittenberger and those in attendance expressed that day did not extend to Charlton's unit. At the time, the 24th Infantry Regiment was fighting a multiple-front war—first, as ideological shock troops in an emerging civil rights insurgency; then, as black patriots fighting against the Communist enemy, along with racism within their own ranks, during the actual shooting; and later, as pivotal figures in the nation's historical memory of the Cold War era. As Charlton and his comrades no doubt realized, Southeast Asia served as the battleground upon which these struggles would be bitterly contested.

While the public dedication of the *Sergeant Cornelius H. Charlton* was a wonderful tribute to the man, recognition of his unit's monumental role in America's first shooting war after 1945 has been largely erased from the nation's collective memory. Until recently, historians have tended to accept Roy Appleman's negative depiction of black soldiers' performance as presented in the army's 1961 official history of the Korean War. Largely based on judgments rendered by army officers and mass media outlets, the battlefield actions of the 24th have been described as "frightened and demoralized," exhibiting a "tendency to panic," "and straggling in retreat." History textbooks and social science literature have used these negative depictions to highlight Executive Order 9981, which marked the desegregation of the military and the end of Jim Crow racism in the US Army.[2] In some ways, the legacy of Cornelius Charlton's valor and the misrepresentation of the 24th Infantry have moved in tandem with each other. It would take nearly forty years and a long quest for equality, both within and without the American military, to revise that interpretation.[3]

As the presence of American troops expanded in Europe and Asia at the end of World War II, African Americans contemplated their place in the postwar military establishment.

In the months immediately following the end of World War II, African-American men and women found themselves confronting a sharp downturn of personal fortune, as military demobilization spelled massive unemployment and the reinstitution of discriminatory hiring practices in the workplace. As a result, large numbers of African Americans were barred from the nation's auto, steel, and electronics industries, leaving them impoverished and embittered.

Black GIs who had fought Fascist and Nazi enemies abroad now faced a more-familiar adversary. Immediately upon their return home, many former servicemen were harassed, beaten, and murdered by white civilians and law enforcement, with vicious impunity. Episodes of racial violence erupted up and down the Eastern Seaboard: Isaac Woodard was blinded in South Carolina; a police officer killed two former black servicemen in Nassau County, New York; and James Stephenson was violently beaten upon his arrest in Columbia, Tennessee.

The plight of African Americans worsened as relations chilled between the United States and the Soviet Union. Mounting anti-Communist hysteria at the end of 1946 resulted in months of government harassment for many black progressive organizations and leaders. As the country began to pivot from wartime to peacetime status, the tentacles of segregation and discrimination reasserted themselves, reaching nearly every facet of American society, and leading black men to openly debate their status in postwar America.[4] World War II and its bitter aftermath influenced many young black veterans to remain in the military. They had come to believe it offered greater economic and social opportunity than what they could find in civilian life. In many ways, the army still offered what it had provided black men since the Civil War: steady employment and a viable pathway toward achieving respectable black manhood.

At the end of World War II, black reenlistment in the army had outpaced the wartime percentage projected by War Department planners, rising from 9.7 percent of its enlisted strength to well over 14 percent in 1946. As the military strength declined sharply from 1,891,000 men in 1946 to 550,000 in 1948, black enlistment climbed steadily during the same period. The Secretary of War and army staff officials began to contemplate the issue of black employment in the peacetime army. Launched by the adjutant general in late 1945, army ground and service forces, along with the air force, began to evaluate the performance of black troops in the previous war. The War Department issued questionnaires to senior commanders to gauge the performance of black troops and to solicit recommendations for their use in the postwar period.

Unsurprisingly, their responses were negative. While acknowledging the valorous acts performed by the small black outfits that served alongside larger all-white units during the latter stages of the war, most officers ignored the heroism of soldiers like Vernon Baker, John Fox, and countless others. They largely derided the performance of black officers and enlisted men and questioned their conduct under fire, couching their arguments in claims of military cohesion and efficiency.

> Noel Parrish, senior officer of the Tuskegee Army Airfield in Alabama, stated that by developing racial guidelines that focused entirely on black GIs, the army may have erred.

Not all commanders subscribed to these views, however. Some, like Noel Parrish, senior officer of the Tuskegee Army Airfield in Alabama, stated that by developing racial guidelines that focused entirely on black GIs, the army may have erred. Policies that called for the end of segregation but acknowledged the individual capabilities of black soldiers might be more feasible, Parrish noted.[5]

In October of 1945, Secretary of War Robert P. Patterson asked Chief of Staff George Marshall to appoint a group of senior officers to develop a policy for the future employment of black manpower in the postwar period. Headed by Lt. Gen. Alvan Gillem Jr., the board, mostly composed of Southern-born officers, convened for nearly six weeks before rendering its report to the chief of staff. After interviewing more than sixty witnesses and collecting a wealth of evidence, the board concluded that black soldiers had a constitutional right to fight, and that the US Army must live up to its obligation to develop more-effective employment policies for African-American service personnel. But while they advised the

War Department to abandon its practice of developing division-size all-black units, they emphasized the continued employment of smaller black outfits to serve alongside white combat elements.[6]

When released in the spring of 1946, the Gillem Board's findings drew scorn from nearly every quarter of the black community. NAACP officials and other civil rights organizations excoriated the report, correctly claiming that it merely continued the military's practice of segregation. Roy Wilkins, the NAACP's assistant executive secretary, called the board's recommendations an absolute "failure" in *The Crisis*. Under the headline "Still a Jim Crow Army," Wilkins concluded, "The basic policy is still Jim Crow. Instead of having big Jim Crow units like the 92nd and the 93rd Infantry Divisions (15,000 to 18,000 men), we are to have nothing larger than Jim Crow regiments (3,000 men)."

By the end of 1948, international events would combine with presidential politics to galvanize public debate over military service. A Communist coup in Czechoslovakia had increased tensions between the United States and the Soviet Union, raising the possibility of a shooting war between the two adversaries. American military officials became even more concerned about US troop strength when the Soviet Union imposed a full-scale blockade on West Berlin. Military leaders and the Senate Armed Services Committee held hearings about instituting universal military training, and worried about how African Americans would react to serving yet again in a segregated army.

On July 26, 1948, President Harry Truman, facing the prospect of massive black resistance to a segregated draft and military while anticipating the ominous threat of renewed war, signed Executive Order 9981, calling for "the equality of treatment and opportunity for all persons in the Armed Services without regard to race, color, religion, or national origin." When asked whether his order spelled the eventual demise of segregation in the armed forces, Truman emphatically responded "Yes."[7] When the President's Committee on Equality of Treatment and Opportunity in the Armed Services suggested that the army break up its all-black units in late 1948, the service branch demurred. As a result, large segregated units were deactivated and black infantry and artillery battalions were simply merged into white regiments and divisions. Staffed by white senior commanders, racial prejudice manifested within these units.

By the time the Korean War erupted in 1950, black men who had enlisted in the army stood in the ranks of segregated platoons, companies, and battalions. As one veteran soldier noticed when he was reassigned to active duty to American occupational forces in Japan during the period, "It was still a Jim Crow Army. Segregation was practiced routinely and administered religiously. Training was slipshod and routine—not a serious or focused professional activity. The senior officers were there essentially to get their tickets punched for promotion to higher rank or pass the time until retirement."[8]

The subterfuge inherent in the US military's delayed response to Truman's executive order was soon unveiled for all to see in the post–World War II experiences of the 24th Infantry Regiment. At the end of the war, the regiment moved across the Pacific Ocean to Okinawa, joining American occupational forces there. They had just completed a series of mopping-up operations on Saipan and on the Kerama Islands, where they had accepted the first formal surrender of Japanese troops in the area. The regiment had remained in Okinawa until January 1947, when they were ordered to the island of Honshu, attached to the 8th Army's 25th Infantry Division. Their stint of duty proved uneventful. As the army began its postwar conversion to peacetime status, the men engaged in seemingly end-

> The constant rotation of enlisted men and officers in the unit created feelings of instability and a lack of discipline for men who had become accustomed to the stresses of war.

less retraining exercises, including dismounted drill, military courtesy and discipline, physical training, and interior guard duty. The constant rotation of enlisted men and officers in the unit created feelings of instability and a lack of discipline for men who had become accustomed to the stresses of war.

Jim Crow segregation also impacted the men in Okinawa and Japan, as they encountered separate post exchanges and officers' clubs on the military posts. They were discouraged from patronizing Japanese businesses whenever they left the base, and military commanders forbade them from bringing Japanese women to their quarters. Fistfights broke out frequently between the men of the 24th Infantry and other regiments, as black GIs reacted to racial slurs like "blackbirds," "niggers," and "boys."

When the 24th Infantry left the southern part of Japan for the shores of Korea, they essentially had two separate identities: While they were seen as bulwarks in the fight against international communism and symbols of equality and first-class citizenship in American life, they still faced racial segregation at the hands of skeptical white commanders and staunch segregationists.

The heroic acts performed by William Henry Thompson, Cornelius Charlton, and others during the Korean War would support blacks' persistent claims of equality during war and directly refute long-standing white beliefs of African-American dysfunction and cowardice in the face of battle and overall unfitness for citizenship. To best understand these heroes, we must look into their past and the events that inspired them.

"IF I CAN'T GET OUT, I'LL TAKE A LOT OF THE ENEMY WITH ME!"

William Henry Thompson and the Battle of Masan, August 1950

Born in 1927, William Henry Thompson experienced hard times throughout his early years. His mother, Mary Henderson, raised him in an impoverished tenement neighborhood in Brooklyn, New York. Thompson dropped out of high school and worked as a menial laborer in a textile factory. The low wages he earned were not enough to sustain an adequate living, and when a minister saw him wandering aimlessly in the street, he placed him in a homeless shelter where he stayed until the age of eighteen.

In October of 1945, Thompson struck out on his own. He decided to join the army, apparently in an attempt to escape abject poverty. After undergoing basic training, he was attached to units stationed in Adak, Alaska, and Honshu, Japan, where he served for a year and a half before receiving an honorable discharge from military service in late 1947. But after discovering that civilian life afforded little comfort, Thompson reenlisted in January of 1948, reporting to South Korea where he was assigned to the US 6th Infantry

Division. He remained there until he was reassigned to Company M of the 24th Infantry Regiment.

On June 25, 1950, the 24th Infantry had just completed heavy weapons exercises at Mount Fuji and were returning to their barracks at Gifu, Japan, when the guns of war erupted on the Korean peninsula. Elements of the North Korean People's Army (NKP) had crossed the 38th parallel, initiating an all-out attack on South Korea. Approximately ninety thousand men, supported by a full complement of infantry divisions, an armored brigade, tanks, and artillery, deployed along the south side of the defensive perimeter in an overt attempt to capture South Korea's capital city of Seoul. Encouraged by the Soviet Union, the invasion by the NKP was such that it caught the Republic of Korea Armed Forces (ROK) and the United States totally by surprise. Hasty efforts were made to rush ground and air forces and equipment from Japan to the Korean peninsula. By the end of the month, the men of the 24th Infantry had received orders to move across the Korean Strait and proceed to Pusan, on the southeastern tip of the Korean peninsula. Once they arrived at the port, they boarded railcars, heading 110 miles north to P'ohang-dong. From there, they received orders to move into the Kumchon area before eventually taking up a position in the vicinity of Yechon.[9]

At Pusan harbor, the 24th Infantry realized they had hurdles to overcome. First, there were not enough railcars to take them to the forwarding areas. Second, there were not enough trucks to transport them to the front. Third, they were underequipped; their field packs contained only a change of socks and underwear, a few personal items, and a meager supply of combat rations. Fourth, confusion and uncertainty reigned. The combat readiness of the 8th Army proved to be woefully abysmal during the opening of hostilities.

The 25th Infantry Division's initial mission was to set up its headquarters at Yongchon, halfway between Taegu and Pohang. From there, two of the division's infantry regiments, the 27th and the 25th, respectively, were to block enemy movement south from Taejon and Chonju sectors. But as the regiments moved into position, deteriorating circumstances at Kumchon dictated that the 1st and 2nd Battalions of the 24th Infantry be moved to retake the higher ground north of Yechon. The small town was of primary importance to American and South Korean forces, for it possessed strategic roads that would allow the enemy to move east or west.[10]

In the summer of 1950, William Thompson experienced a baptism by fire near the Pusan Perimeter. In late July, Thompson's unit, the 25th Infantry Division, received orders to move south to Masan, a port city located thirty miles west of Pusan, where enemy forces were massing for a possible attack. The assignment proved to be easier said than done. On August 2, the unit attempted to leave Sangju, but discovered that their southward movement was partially blocked by the continuous flow of refugees into the area. The regiment's convoy of trucks stood in the pathway of one of the supporting cavalry divisions, and this caused episodes of confusion and delays. These setbacks failed to deter the flow of division forces to Masan, however. After arriving at the port city, battalions of the regiment took up positions west and northwest of the city and began to carry out patrols ostensibly aimed at offsetting guerrilla activities and enemy infiltration into the area.[11]

After nearly a month of waging countermeasures against the enemy, the 2nd and 3rd Battalions staged countless patrols in areas south of Haman. These missions came at a tremendous cost, as they encountered enemy parties and sustained numerous casualties. During a patrol, a platoon from the 3rd Battalion's Company L engaged a group of approximately thirty North Korean soldiers, and both sides were practically annihilated. The company commander, recently arrived to assume leadership in the unit, and two enlisted men were killed while leading the mission. Eleven men with the outfit were wounded, and two others were listed as missing in action.[12]

Pvt. 1st Class William Thompson's valiant actions while engaging the enemy would become firmly enshrined in the collective memory of his fellow servicemen. On August 6, Thompson's heavy-weapons platoon, along with Company M, was providing support for the 25th Infantry Division's night advance near Haman when it was ambushed by an overwhelming number of NKP troops. Pinned down by a steady stream of automatic-weapons fire, the platoon leader ordered the men to withdraw to higher ground and regroup under the cover of darkness. Despite being severely wounded, Thompson ignored the order, setting up his machine gun in the path of the approaching enemy and laying down withering suppressive fire until his unit was able to secure a more-tenable position.

Thompson sacrificed himself while defending his comrades on the rough ground of Sobuk-San. Although gravely injured, he resisted his fellow GIs' efforts to get him to withdraw to safety. Thompson's war came to an abrupt end when he was struck by an enemy grenade, killing him instantly. While making his final stand, the twenty-two-year-old New York native had taken the lives of numerous North Koreans before succumbing to his own wounds.

Thompson's role in the fighting impressed enlisted men and officers alike. His platoon leader, Lt. Herbert Wilson, later recalled: "When the order was given to withdraw, I ordered Thompson to withdraw with the rest. At the time, I saw he had been wounded in several places and was bleeding profusely. Thompson told me that he had been hit and was not going to move back, but would cover the movement of the rest of the men; then if he couldn't get out, he would take a lot of the enemy with him."[13] Thompson's achievement was honored by senior officers throughout the Far East Command. Recognizing the Korean War veteran posthumously, Gen. Matthew Ridgeway cited the black machine gunner as "a splendid soldier who fought with distinct gallantry and fortitude for the ideals of freedom and the protection of his fellow soldiers."[14]

Thompson's heroic actions that day were overshadowed by white officers' reservations about the 24th Infantry Regiment's conduct on the field of battle. Battalion commander Lt. Melvin Blair withheld his recommendation for the Medal of Honor because he and other senior commanders looked rather unfavorably upon the overall performance of the men in the 24th Infantry. Thompson's action simply confirmed their shared belief that black junior officers took questionable risks and often disobeyed orders on the battlefield. Only after interviewing many eyewitnesses who corroborated Thompson's act of valor did Blair relent and recommend him for the Silver Star citation and the Medal of Honor.

On June 21, 1951, Chairman of the Joint Chiefs of Staff, Gen. Omar Bradley, awarded the Medal of Honor to Thompson's mother, Mary Henderson, at the Pentagon. Thompson was recognized by black scholars as the first African American to be honored with the medal for bravery in the Korean War, and the first black soldier to be accorded the nation's highest military honor since the Spanish-American War.[15] (African-American heroes who fought during World War I and World War II would not be accorded the Medal of Honor until the 1990s and 2000s.)

"LET'S GO!"

The 24th Infantry and Sgt. Cornelius Charlton during Operation Piledriver, June 1951

Cornelius Charlton was born in 1929 to a large family in East Gulf, West Virginia. His father Van struggled to provide for his family for nearly thirty years as a coal miner for the Gulf Smokeless Coal Company. Charlton and his family lived in West Virginia until 1940, when they moved to the Bronx, New York, after his father landed a job as an apartment building superintendent. After graduating from high school, Charlton enlisted in the army in November of 1946. He completed his basic training and was assigned to occupied Germany for a few years before reporting for stateside duty with a military engineering outfit at Aberdeen Proving Ground in Maryland. There he remained until he was deployed to Okinawa in 1950,[16] eventually heading to Korea to serve in the war.

As the weeks turned into months, the men of the 24th Infantry participated in some of the most hotly contested battles in the latter stages of the Korean War. From Battle Mountain to the breakout from the Masan Perimeter to Chongchon, to the Han River Crossing, the unit fought valiantly against tremendous odds. From their arrival in Korea through the winter months of 1951, the men had withstood numerous casualties. Nearly 1,200 of the 3,200 men who composed the unit were wounded on the battlefield, reflecting a nearly 40 percent casualty rate. As a result, the unit suffered severe shortages of enlisted men and officers, as the availability of replacement soldiers was extremely limited. Manpower shortages became even more acute over time, for unlike their white counterparts, the men of the 24th did not rotate from combat to rearguard areas; rather, they stayed at the front for more than 120 days, from July until the dead of winter, without any relief.

The shortage of battle-hardened troops made it even more urgent for the army to find seasoned noncommissioned sergeants and corporals who could provide leadership at the front. By the spring of 1951, the situation was so dire that a black correspondent who covered the unit's activities reported that the outfit "was hit hard by the staggering casualties, and this crack regiment is continually being sent into the line without the vital resources necessary for combat."

One of these moments happened during the 8th Army's Operation Piledriver in May of 1951. Earlier that spring, Chinese Communist troops had forced the 25th Infantry Division to withdraw from the Hant'an to Line Kansas, just north of the Yongp'yong River. Hoping to slow the enemy from launching a major attack, the 25th Infantry Division, in concert with other elements of I Corps, launched an attack north of the towns of Chorwon and Kumhwa. The purpose was to block the enemy's main avenues of approach to the eastern front, as well as to mitigate pressure that the Chinese and the North Koreans had been applying to Allied troops in the area. Based on this reasoning, the limited action would force the enemy to the peace table.

As part of the assault, troops in the 24th Infantry were assigned to provide support to the eastern flank of the 25th Infantry Division and to move incrementally toward Kumhwa. That spring, however, the climate was a pressing concern for military commanders, with the rainy, warm days leading up to the advance punctuated by temperatures that dipped sharply at night.

By the time the regiment's battalions had moved into position, they were encountering fierce enemy machine-gun and mortar fire and were forced to withdraw. As a company of its 3rd Battalion attempted to capture a hill north of the area, near the village of Chipo-ri, they fell headlong into a well-fortified Chinese entrenchment manned by enemy soldiers who were armed with numerous heavy automatic weapons. They took tremendous casualties, losing their platoon leader in the process.

It was under these taxing circumstances that Sgt. Cornelius Charlton stepped forward. The talented noncommissioned officer had reported to the platoon just weeks before, following an assignment with an engineering service unit in Korea. His considerable leadership skills had been recognized by his superiors, and his second lieutenant had recommended him for a battlefield commission. After learning that the platoon leader lay mortally wounded, Charlton took command of the beleaguered men and led them up the hill. Attempting to advance three times and suffering heavy casualties in the face of crushing mortar and rifle fire, the West Virginia native single-handedly destroyed two Chinese positions and killed six enemy soldiers. All the while, Charlton exposed himself to heavy fire, sustaining wounds to his chest while advancing the attack.

> Charlton took command of the beleaguered men and led them up the hill.

The war hero's actions inspired eyewitnesses who were present during the fighting that day. As one enlisted man in the company recalled, "Charlton was wounded in the chest, but he refused to be evacuated. He got the rest of the men together, and we started for the top. The enemy had good emplacements. . . . We couldn't get to him. Grenades kept coming at us and we were chased back down again. Again we tried but no luck. Sergeant Charlton said he was going to make it this time and he yelled, 'Let's go.' I saw the sergeant go over the top and charge a bunker on the other side. He got the gun but was killed by a grenade." Charlton's selfless act saved most of the men in his platoon.

As Charlton's comrades recovered his remains for the final trip home, word of his brave deed reached the ears of public leaders and pundits. Each eulogized the fallen soldier's act of valor, ascribing different meanings to its significance. To black weeklies like the *Los Angeles Sentinel*, Charlton's actions demonstrated the 24th's ability to perform admirably under fire against tremendous odds. In fact, before Charlton was killed on June 2, 1951, he and his fellow soldiers with the regiment had been largely responsible for the United States' first important victory at Yechon. For other mainstream periodicals, like *Redbook* magazine, the sergeant's daring exploits served as an enduring testament to the US military and the youth of America. Still others believed that Charlton's intrepid action gave new meaning to black claims of equality in American society.

On March 12, 1952, Cornelius Charlton was posthumously awarded the Congressional Medal of Honor.[17] Republican senator Irving M. Ives of New York used the medal presentation to call attention to the seventh anniversary of the New York State law against discrimination. "This simple but moving ceremony emphasized deeply the fact that when loyalty and heroism and sheer patriotism are demanded of Americans, there is no distinction among us," Ives told his Senate colleagues.

This perspective was also expressed by Charlton's father. After he and his family journeyed to the District of Columbia to accept the nation's highest military honor from Secretary of the Army Frank C. Pace, on behalf of their son, Van Charlton stated, "My boy's action in combat and his death make a liar out of Paul Robeson and others who have claimed the Negro will not fight for this country."[18]

THE RETURN OF THE COLORS

The Ordeal of Cornelius Charlton

After his heroic death, Charlton was laid to rest in an American Legion cemetery located in his boyhood town of Beckley, West Virginia. During his funeral, townspeople gathered to pay tribute to the fallen soldier, honoring him with a parade, a twenty-one-gun salute, and the playing of "Taps." The decorated soldier was buried at the top of a hill, alongside some 250 white soldiers.

Secretary of the Army Frank Pace with the
family of Sergeant Cornelius H. Charlton,
March 12, 1952.

Shortly after his funeral, however, a battle over his legacy began. Charlton had only
been buried for a few months when his parents demanded that he be reinterred with full
military honors in Arlington National Cemetery. The response they received from Official
Washington left a lot to be desired. Army officials stated that they had not offered to rebury
the fallen GI at Arlington or at another location because of an administrative oversight.
His family members tell a different story. "They say it was an administrative error," his
brother Arthur Charlton recalled years later, "but I say it was discrimination."

The fight between Charlton's family members and the army over his burial continued
for nearly forty years. In 2008, a group of white veterans from Beckley's American Legion
post petitioned members of Congress, urging them to address the apparent oversight. And
in May of that year, Korean War veterans and Charlton's surviving family members assembled for the reburial of Charlton's remains at the national cemetery. Among those in attendance were an assistant secretary of state, a local congressman, two army generals, and a
full honor guard from Fort Knox, Kentucky. While some in the audience had gathered to
honor a soldier who fought and died in a war that took place more than forty years earlier,
for others, Charlton's life—and death—held more significance. Sgt. Maj. Lindsey Bowers,
president of the 24th Infantry Regiment Association, commented, "This guy should have

had some kind of hero's ceremony. If it had been a white soldier who won the Medal of Honor, somebody would have come forward immediately."[19]

The forty-year-old fight over the reburial of Charlton's remains reflected the larger battle being waged over the historical legacy of the 24th Infantry Regiment in Korea. The regiment was disbanded on October 1, 1951, marking the end of the last segregated combat regiment in the Regular Army. But as the unit faded into history, its conduct in the shooting war remained a matter of public discussion, as military commanders and army historians debated the service record of the celebrated unit. Almost to a person, they downplayed the army's long-standing system of racial discrimination, focusing instead on senior officers' disparaging reports of black soldiers' conduct and the many court-martial proceedings meted out to African-American servicemen in Korea. All the while, black press correspondents who had covered the fighting in Korea, and black Korean War veterans themselves, refused to be silent on the matter. To a person, they cast doubt on the negative assessments of the regiment's performance. Instead, they pointed to poor decisions made by white commanders on the field of battle, inadequate equipment, insufficient rest and relaxation periods for black soldiers at the front, and biased coverage by mass media as the root of the unit's negative image.[20]

Ironically, both sides based their judgments of the 24th Infantry on the number of medals won by black GIs on the battlefield during the war, noting that their perceptions of bravery played a major role in their assessments. As the military began to slowly change the composition of their ranks, each side reassessed the meaning of valor to fit the exigencies of the post–Korean War period.

To fully understand this phenomenon, we must now explore the integration of the armed forces, and society's efforts to understand bravery, in the context of American military involvement in Southeast Asia.

Vietnam: US Army soldiers in action during the 1968 Tet Offensive at Hue, central Vietnam.

CHAPTER 7

Soldiers in the Second Indochina War

THE VIETNAM WAR AND BLACK HEROISM
UNDER FIRE, 1965–1973

> I really think about the ones that gave their life and going back to my
> team sergeant, he gave his life. And he gave the ultimate sacrifice. That's
> my real hero. And all the ones that gave their lives, they are not here to
> accept the decoration and honor. They gave it their all, and I often dwell
> on that. And I'm glad I'm receiving this honor in honor of them.
>
> —*Melvin Morris, 2014*

"His whole life was centered on being a minister and working for the Lord. That was his purpose," said Mary Anderson, reflecting on her brother, James, in 1984. In 1966, James Anderson Jr. had been attending Los Angeles Harbor College and was on his way toward receiving an associate's degree in theology when he made a momentous life decision: to enlist in the US Marine Corps. For James's family, his choice was unsettling. Just a year earlier, the introspective nineteen-year-old had adamantly stated that he would never be able to take a life, under any circumstances.[1]

While it's unclear exactly what prompted the Compton resident to make such an abrupt career change, Anderson worked diligently to make the best of it. After venturing to nearby San Diego for basic training at the Marine Corps Recruit Depot, he reported to the 2nd Infantry Training Regiment for advanced instruction. In late 1966, he reported to the I Corps Tactical Zone in South Vietnam and was assigned as a rifleman to a company in the 3rd Marine Division's 3rd Battalion.

Anderson had no sooner arrived in the area than he learned that he and his unit had a two-pronged mission: to carry out combat operations against Vietcong and North Vietnamese along the demilitarized zone, and to conduct a counterinsurgency effort against enemy forces in the Quang Tri and Thua Thien provinces. This was easier said than done against the intractable enemy forces. North Vietnamese mortar and rocket attacks pounded American positions throughout the region, inflicting heavy enemy casualty rates among United States forces. The situation was so complex that an officer with the 3rd Battalion noted, "We were ordered to proceed . . . knowing full well we were walking into a hornet's nest. Based on the number of enemy forces we had already encountered and the vast amounts of equipment, new weapons, and ammunition, we knew we were outmanned and outgunned. One could almost smell the enemy forces."[2]

On February 28, 1967, Anderson, who had recently turned twenty, and his platoon were negotiating a densely covered jungle northwest of Cam Lo. Their mission was simple: Extract a beleaguered reconnaissance patrol that had come under heavy enemy attack. As the private and his fellow corps members quickly discovered, the heavy brush made them susceptible to small-arms and automatic weapons fire. After advancing approximately two hundred meters, they stumbled into an ambush. A fierce firefight ensued, and several of the men were wounded. Anderson and his comrades were bunched together some twenty meters from the enemy position when a grenade suddenly landed near their defensive redoubt. With total disregard for his own physical safety, Anderson jumped forward, pulling the explosive into his chest and curling his body around it as it detonated. He died instantly. But by absorbing the full destructive force of the blast, he managed to shield several marines from the majority of its shrapnel.[3]

Anderson was awarded the Medal of Honor several months later for his personal heroism, extraordinary valor, and inspirational leadership. While his selfless act placed him head and shoulders above his fellow corpsmen, he also gained the distinction of becoming the first African-American US Marine in United States history to receive the nation's highest award for valor. His loved ones were well aware of the significance of this honor, along with James's altruistic nature. Decades after receiving the medal from Secretary of the Navy Paul R. Ignatius on a hot, humid, day in 1967, his father James Sr. made the following observation of his long-departed progeny: "My son was a sensitive person with an unusual concern for the welfare of others. He never cared for himself."[4]

Young black men serving in Southeast Asia during the 1960s encountered a new military environment. Sociologist Charles C. Moskos is one of many scholars who believe that

Vietnam was the first war since the American Revolution where the armed forces were integrated from the beginning. There was a promise of equal opportunity for black service personnel that paralleled what was ostensibly enjoyed by their white counterparts. No longer constricted by Jim Crow racism and discrimination, African Americans were now free to pursue duty assignments and promotion, and to gain recognition as first-rate fighting soldiers.

During the Civil War, "black valor" meant preserving a unit's flag; in the Indian-fighting army, it referred to fulfilling notions of frontier honor; in World Wars I and II and the Korean War, it meant upholding a unit's reputation. In the Vietnam War era, black valor meant trying to save one's comrades from serious injury or death. In the eyes of James Anderson and a generation of African-American Medal of Honor recipients, it didn't matter whether your blood was black or white—it all flowed from the same river of freedom. All lives mattered in an increasingly racially diversified military.

> In the Vietnam War era, black valor meant trying to save one's comrades from serious injury or death.

Yet, as James Westheider reminds us, the racial component that had historically shaped military traditions and practices still encroached on the Vietnam War experiences of black GIs like Anderson and other MOH recipients. They still had to "fight for the right to fight."

We must begin with what led these black men to the "killing fields" of Laos and South Vietnam in the first place.[5]

OPENING THE RANKS

The Drive for Black Civil Rights

The bravery of black soldiers during the Vietnam War era was forged during student-led acts of civil disobedience in the early 1960s, an era impacted by the Kennedy administration's policies regarding racial integration. While Freedom Riders staged nonviolent direct action in an attempt to integrate buses, many African Americans pointed to the plight of blacks in the armed forces as a symbol of the federal government's acceptance of segregation on and near military bases at home as well as abroad. Black military personnel complained bitterly to civil rights spokesmen such as Michigan congressman Charles Diggs about the inequalities of promotion, duty assignments, and housing. They found it especially galling when they rode public buses near the military installations where they were stationed.

When John Kennedy took office, a group of nearly fifty black leaders petitioned the young president, demanding that the federal government withdraw its support of communities and organizations near military posts that supported segregation. The Congress of Racial Equality (CORE) wrote to the Department of the Army in 1962, demanding that military personnel avoid segregated restaurants in Aberdeen, Maryland.[6] There were mixed results. While somewhat sympathetic to the injustices that blacks faced in society, the Kennedy administration was unable to prevent commanders from endorsing segregation in communities near military bases.

On the other hand, the Department of Defense waged a two-pronged campaign: First, they published a list of the number of high-ranking black officers in order to mute public criticism; second, Kennedy appointed Gerhard Gesell, a young lawyer from Washington, DC, to head the President's Committee on Equal Opportunity in the Armed Forces. Its members included John Sengstacke, noted publisher of the *Chicago Defender*; Whitney Young Jr. of the Urban League; Benjamin Muse, a staunch civil rights activist; and Abe Fortas, a Washington attorney and future Supreme Court nominee, to name a few. The group was tasked with gathering vital information regarding issues of racial discrimination, to be used by Defense Secretary Robert S. McNamara to draft a specifically defined equality-of-opportunity directive for all branches of the military.

On July 26, 1963, fifteen years after Truman's Executive Order 9981, McNamara issued the directive, which stated that the department would openly promote equal opportunity for military personnel. In addition, the secretary of defense would use the vast powers of his office to compel military commanders to enforce anti-discriminatory policies. McNamara's racial policies failed to produce the results he desired, however. With

President Kennedy's death in November 1963, the directive lay moribund, greeted with congressional opposition and mild disinterest from the Washington press corps.[7]

Not all of the committee's findings were ignored. One area that benefited from the investigative energies of the Gesell Committee was the enlistment and assignment practices of different branches of the military. The racial policies of the navy, air force, and Marine Corps came under intense scrutiny. The committee found that between 1949 and 1962, the percentages of black military personnel in these branches were markedly lower than in other service organizations. By the mid-1960s, the discrepancy had become even more acute for black enlistments. While the army slowly increased its numbers through the draft, the percentage of African Americans in the navy and air force continued to lag behind. Between 1962 and 1968, the promotion of black enlisted men in the Marine Corps did rise sharply, from 7.6 percent to nearly 12 percent. The number of black officers in each branch of the military was equally abysmal. As of 1966, there were no black admirals in the navy, and only one black general in the air force, Lt. Gen. Benjamin O. Davis Jr.[8]

> The racial policies of the navy, air force, and Marine Corps came under intense scrutiny.

In the months that followed, the armed forces worked feverishly to devise new strategies to attract large numbers of young blacks into the military. They also strove to improve the image of those already in the ranks. In August of 1964, the army launched a special training and enlistment program aimed at enhancing "the military training, education, and physical rehabilitation of men who cannot meet current mental or medical standards for regular enlistment in the Army." Providing for the enlistment of nearly 10,000 men, the program faced fierce resistance from Congress, and was tabled before it could be effectively launched.[9]

Two years later, the Department of Defense created its own initiative to increase the number of soldiers in the armed forces. Labeled Project 100,000, it was designed to accept men who had failed to qualify for military duty under the previous standards. According to Defense Secretary McNamara, the program's purpose was "to broaden opportunities for enlistment, to equalize military service obligations, to assure foresighted mortuary planning, and through Project Transition, help 'new standards' men become productive citizens when they return to civilian life." For McNamara and other White House officials, the goals were quite simple. Young men could be "salvaged" so that once they received the benefits of Defense Department on-the-job training, they would be transformed into efficient military personnel. Young blacks would also acquire new skills and attitudes that would enable them to break out of the grinding cycle of poverty once they had completed their service.[10]

Among the program's advocates was thirty-nine-year-old policy expert and future senator, Daniel Patrick Moynihan. He had just written a major policy report for President Lyndon Johnson that outlined what he believed to be the ills that blacks faced while living in America's major urban areas. Titled "The Negro Family: The Case for National Action," the report contended that the real problem blacks faced was not segregation or lack of voting power; rather, Moynihan placed the blame on the matriarchal structure of black families. He cited statistics that revealed black men were largely absent from nearly two million of the nation's five million black families, in which some 25 percent of all births were illegitimate. He also claimed that young boys who grew up in fatherless households could not adjust to the patriarchal nature of American society. He argued that military service was one way blacks could be inculcated with the social mores of middle-class American society. "The draft is one of the greatest institutions ever invented by the United States. [. . .] For the young Negro boy from the slums, military service is an escape hatch out of the ghetto into the main current of American life."[11]

But many young black men were witnessing a different reality. Because of the growing economic disparity between blacks and whites and the discriminatory implementation of the draft laws, undereducated and working-poor blacks were more likely to make an appearance before their draft boards, ultimately shouldering much of the burden of military service throughout the 1960s. While young African Americans made up approximately 11 percent of the general population, they were drafted at rates that increased incrementally throughout the Vietnam War. In 1963, the percentage of black men who were drafted reached 18.5 percent. By 1967, the President's National Advisory Commission on Selective Service found that black draftees comprised nearly 30.2 percent of the whole, as compared with only 18.8 percent of their white counterparts. "The position of the Negro in the nation's military manpower picture is in several ways inequitable," advisory members told Johnson.

As the draft escalated in black communities and neighborhoods across the country, the high rates had a dampening impact on the lives of young African Americans. As one white priest whose ministry reached into Chicago's South Side noted, "Knock on any door and you will probably find a family that has a son, nephew, or cousin in Vietnam. Add them all up and you have a community that is fighting more than its share of the war in Vietnam. It's a brutal fact." The growing number of blacks inducted into the military service was reflected in the increasing percentages of African-American combat personnel in Southeast Asia. While black troops accounted for only 11 percent of the total enlisted personnel in Vietnam, 40 to 50 percent of black enlisted men served in frontline combat units, a proportion considerably higher than white GIs in the war.[12] And for young black men who served in such a capacity, their presence in forward areas did not always translate into opportunities for promotion.

> "Knock on any door and you will probably find a family that has a son, nephew, or cousin in Vietnam."

As America's involvement in Southeast Asia deepened, many black leaders expressed ambivalence about the disproportionate numbers of black servicemen in the ranks. In May of 1966, New York congressman Adam Clayton Powell held a press conference where he roundly criticized the existing draft-deferment program implemented by the Selective Service System. Calling it a "foundation for racial aristocracy," Powell argued that "implicit in the draft deferments is the theory of a race of Aryan supermen and the belief that rare great minds alone are fit to direct the destinies of a nation and to dispose of the lives of its untutored masses."

While speaking at a news conference at the University of Pittsburgh that fall, Reverend Dr. Martin Luther King Jr., the head of the Southern Christian Leadership Conference, called for a complete overhaul of Selective Service exemptions. Pointing to the socioeconomic components that contributed to the overwhelming number of blacks in infantry battalions, companies, and platoons in Vietnam, King stated, "It may not be a conscious thing, but it goes back to the economic programs in the country. [. . .] Negroes were drafted because they didn't have sufficient education to gain an exemption or could not afford to attend college. It seems to me this is totally unfair."

Other black political figures also voiced their opposition to the inequities that existed in the draft. In April of 1967, Whitney Young Jr. announced that the advisory commission on the Selective Service had recommended broad changes to the draft system. "As anyone who watches televised newscasts or sees photos in the newspapers knows, Negroes are doing much of the fighting in Vietnam," Young observed. "Although only 11 percent of the population is Negro, 14.5 percent of the US Army in Vietnam are Negro. In some of the line companies, the proportion is far higher, as reflected in the fact that Negroes comprise 22.4 percent of combat deaths."

After citing the extraordinary act of heroism performed by a young black medic named Lawrence Joel, Young observed, "Can we ask so much from these men without doing something about the discrimination which limits their opportunities in civilian life?"[13]

"A SPECIAL KINSHIP"

Lawrence Joel and Operation Hump

Army specialist Lawrence Joel was a paratrooper originally from Winston-Salem, North Carolina. Like so many of his MOH compatriots, he was no stranger to grinding poverty. Born in 1928, Joel was one of ten children in an ever-expanding working-class family that lived in a series of shanties near the Norfolk and Western Railway line. Working an assortment of jobs, his father struggled to provide a living for Joel and his siblings, to no avail. Some of Joel's most vivid childhood memories include having to miss days of elementary school because he lacked appropriate clothing. At the age of eight, a caseworker placed him in a foster home.

Joel made average grades and graduated from high school. At the age of seventeen, he was anxious to get away from the poverty-stricken areas of east Winston-Salem, so in 1946, he joined the Merchant Marine. After a year in New York City, he joined the US Army and served with occupational forces in France, Germany, and Italy. After three years of active duty, he was discharged in 1949. He soon discovered there was little opportunity for young blacks like himself in civilian society, so Joel reenlisted in 1953, returning to military life just as the Korean War was ending.

The military was in the midst of desegregating its ranks. By the time the army had begun to expand its role in Vietnam, Joel had become a seasoned soldier. He attended airborne school at Fort Bragg, North Carolina, and advanced rapidly up the chain of command, achieving the rank of specialist in a headquarters company of the 503rd Airborne Infantry Regiment.[14]

Soon after Joel and his comrades reported to Bien Hoa, South Vietnam, in July 1965, they received orders to conduct search-and-destroy operations with several elements of the Army of the Republic of Vietnam (ARVN) against Vietcong-controlled areas in the Central Highlands. As part of the 173rd Airborne Brigade, their regiment was participating in Operation Hump, a full-blown offensive designed to protect designated bases and to conduct a series of deep patrolling, offensive, and reserve operations aimed at disrupting enemy advances in the region.

Joel's company was part of a wider mission to carry out interdicting operations against Vietcong units and strongholds in the countryside. On a hot day in early November, the stocky medical aide, along with three squads of the 1st Battalion's Company C, had journeyed out from their staging area. They planned to spend the early hours of the day in search of Vietcong forces in the jungles within Zone "D" of the Third Corps area.[15] For the unassuming thirty-nine-year-old airborne medic, it was the last day of real combat after enduring four months of training in a corps area west of Saigon. Up to that point, his company had seen little action.

All of that would change in a flash. No sooner had they advanced two hundred yards into the jungle than they found themselves in an ambush staged by a Vietcong regiment of nearly seven hundred soldiers. Despite being vastly outnumbered and losing nearly every man in its lead squad, Joel's company fought desperately to maintain their position in the midst of a deadly stream of gunfire. The intrepid sixteen-year veteran provided treatment and blood plasma to many wounded soldiers, even though he was wounded twice during the deadly exchange, one round striking him in the calf, another hitting him in the thigh. "I found a stick on the ground with a little crook in it," he recalled. "I broke it about waist-high and sort of cradled my arm in it so I could hobble around. That way I could make it from one man to the next—sort of fall down beside him, then pull myself up on a tree or something when I finished."

As the bullets continued to rain down, Joel successfully treated thirteen additional men while shouting words of encouragement. When the firing ceased nearly twenty-four hours later, Company C had turned back the Vietcong attack, and 410 enemy soldiers lay dead. Shortly afterward, Joel and numerous other wounded GIs were airlifted to a Saigon hospital.[16]

On November 8, 1965, Lawrence Joel received the Silver Star, and less than five months later, the unassuming war hero and his family stood on the White House lawn as President Lyndon Johnson presented him with the Congressional Medal of Honor. Joel was the first medic in the country's history to earn such distinction, and the first living African American to be so honored since the Spanish-American War of 1898. As President Johnson draped the nation's highest award for bravery around the neck of the paratrooper medic, he remarked that the "soldier's heroism in Vietnam indicates as nothing else could the willingness of his country to sacrifice, to stand and to persist in freedom's cause."

In 1967, Winston-Salem held a parade to pay tribute to their native son. After Robert Scott, North Carolina's lieutenant governor, introduced Joel to the crowd, the humble, bespectacled paratrooper stepped forward and made the following statement: "I don't consider myself a hero. I just consider myself a soldier doing my job . . . saving lives."[17]

> "I don't consider myself a hero. I just consider myself a soldier doing my job . . . saving lives."

THE WOLFHOUNDS

Capt. Riley Pitts in Ap Dong, South Vietnam

In the fall of 1967, another black GI defined honor by saving lives. In October, a company of the 27th Infantry Regiment had been assigned to take part in a counteroffensive aimed at clearing enemy forces that were concentrated in Ap Dong, just north of Saigon. Working in conjunction with the US 1st Infantry Division, the 27th Infantry Regiment was supplemented by the 11th Armored Cavalry Regiment and South Vietnamese troops. They hoped to maintain contact with the enemy in order to minimize its presence in areas that lay in close proximity to Laos and Cambodia. This was an arduous task. Throughout the month, the Vietcong had struck a Special Forces camp at Loc Ninh with devastating force. By October 31, companies with the 27th Infantry Regiment received orders to launch an airmobile assault to divert enemy forces from the area.[18]

Among the men who received this assignment was Capt. Riley Pitts, a native of Fallis, Oklahoma. Born in 1937, Pitts had grown up in Lincoln County, graduating from Wichita State University with a bachelor's degree in journalism. He had married and moved to

Oklahoma City, where he worked with the Boeing Corporation, but military service called to the twenty-four-year-old father-to-be. Years earlier, he had attended an officers' basic course, so he was commissioned as a second lieutenant. By December of 1966, he had risen to the rank of captain in the US Army Reserves when he received orders to report to Vietnam. The young information officer relished the assignment, as it afforded him the opportunity to lead a company into combat while on active duty. Five months later, Pitts was transferred to C Company, a combat unit aptly nicknamed "the Wolfhounds." On October 31, his dreams of leading a unit into battle were realized when his outfit received orders to reinforce another company that was already carrying out operations in the Ap Dong area.[19]

As he and his men soon discovered, the situation carried dire consequences. They had just arrived in the forwarding area when they were attacked by well-placed Vietcong automatic and artillery fire. The talented company commander led an assault, overrunning the enemy positions before directing his men to move north toward another company that had come into contact with Vietcong forces. As Pitts's company moved forward, they ran headlong into fierce enemy fire from three directions, preventing them from maneuvering. Pitts picked up a grenade launcher and began firing on an enemy bunker. When one of the explosives landed near his men, the young captain immediately pounced on the grenade to shield his men from possible injury, only to discover that it had failed to discharge. Shortly afterward, however, Pitts's luck came to an end. He died while laying down suppressive fire and urging his men forward against the fiercely determined enemy forces.

For his conspicuous gallantry and bravery under fire, the Oklahoma City native gained immortality when he was posthumously awarded the Medal of Honor on December 10, 1968. Pitts's widow, along with his son and daughter, journeyed to Washington, DC, accepting the medal on behalf of their fallen loved one, along with heartfelt condolences from President Lyndon B. Johnson. By giving his life to safeguard the lives of other servicemen, the martyred company commander followed in the footsteps of his fellow MOH recipients from nearly a century before, becoming the first black commissioned officer to receive the nation's highest award for valor.[20]

"IF THEY CALLED, I WENT AFTER THEM"

Clarence Sasser and the Rice Paddies of the Mekong Delta

For companies and battalions of the 9th Infantry Division's 3rd Battalion, valor assumed an all-too-familiar character. As part of a series of operations, the division had been assigned to the III Corps' Tactical Zone of Vietnam, where it carried out operations against Vietcong-controlled rivers and canals of the Mekong Delta in the Dinh Tuong and Long An provinces. The overall purpose was to provide countervailing forces against Communist insurgents and to lend support for the rural pacification campaigns developed by South Vietnamese regular and territorial forces against Vietcong guerrillas. The Military Assistance Command and American troops were dismayed to learn that these operations proved difficult to execute in the delta, due to the presence of a very intransigent and formidable enemy. North Vietnamese troops brought forces to bear against American and South Vietnamese forces in the tactical zone, inflicting numerous casualties in the process.[21]

Such was the case for a company with the 9th Division's 60th Infantry in the Dinh Tuong Province in the winter of 1968. While serving with the Brown Water Navy's Riverine Force at Dinh Tuong, members of A Company had just ventured out as part of a search-and-destroy mission, providing support for patrolling units. The soldiers thought it would be another typical day in Vietnam. As medic Clarence Sasser recalled, "For once, in our opinion, [we were] lucky. We were the backup company. If any other company had a problem, or became engaged with the enemy, we [. . .] would be helicoptered in to help these people out, to try to get them out of the situation they were in."[22]

Specialist Clarence Sasser was particularly well-trained for such an assignment. Born in 1947, the Chenango, Texas, resident had been drafted into the army despite receiving a college deferment while attending the University of Houston. He had hoped to become a physician, but fate intervened. After discovering that he lacked funding to continue his education, and facing the prospect of irregular work, he dropped his student status to part-time, anticipating his impending induction into the military. "I like to think I was drafted into the service, but if truth be told, I volunteered to be drafted. I wanted to discharge that obligation."

After entering the army in 1967, he went on to receive advanced training as a medic at Fort Houston. By the end of 1967, Sasser was in Vietnam and well into a six-month assignment with an infantry unit in Company A when the unit received orders to report to the Mekong Delta. "My job specifically was to accompany my platoon when they went outside of the perimeter area, the base camp grounds. I of course went on every mission [. . .] And of course, I went on some of the search-and-destroy and reconnaissance missions they had, the nightly ambush[es] that were done."[23]

Sasser and his comrades would discover that the reconnaissance mission of January 10, 1968, would be unlike any other they had ever encountered. No sooner had the unit arrived in the delta area than it suddenly came under heavy small-arms fire. One of the helicopters carrying servicemen directly in front of them had been brought

> Sasser was struck through his right leg as he departed his helicopter.

down by enemy antiaircraft fire. To make matters worse, Sasser was struck through his right leg as he departed his helicopter. As billows of flame and smoke filled the air around them, the capable medic quickly ran across an open rice paddy through a hail of bullets to assist the wounded, despite being wounded himself.

The situation took a turn for the worse when Sasser, helping a man to safety, was struck yet again in the left shoulder by shrapnel from an exploding rocket. Undaunted, the determined soldier refused medical attention for himself, continuing to aid others while braving constant rocket and automatic-weapons fire. Even after suffering additional wounds to his legs, Sasser continued to assist his fallen comrades, dragging himself over considerable distances—between one hundred and two hundred feet, in some instances—to give them much-needed medical treatment. One of Sasser's most powerful memories provides a vivid depiction of that harrowing day: "One of the worst things I remember about that day was spending [the] night there, and listening to the guys call for their mothers, their daddies: 'Somebody help me; I'm dying. Please help me.' That's probably the worst thing that I remember about the whole day."[24]

After five hours, the deadly exchange with the enemy had produced numerous casualties on both sides. All told, the majority of Sasser's company was killed during the fighting, and many more wounded were evacuated to nearby hospitals where they received extensive treatment for their wounds.

For his part, the Texas youth experienced agonizing pain and a tremendous loss of blood. After being transported to a Saigon hospital, Sasser was medevacked to Camp Zama, Japan, in March of 1968, where he received treatment for his wounds before being airlifted back to the United States. His tour of duty in Vietnam lasted fifty-one days, but his acts of bravery resonated well beyond the war in Southeast Asia. On March 7, 1969, he appeared in the East Room of the White House for a special ceremony, during which he and two other soldiers who fought in Vietnam received the Medal of Honor for gallantry from President Richard M.

"I am proud that my medal was for saving lives as a medic."

Nixon. "These three young men have demonstrated to us that we can be very proud of our younger generation," Nixon proclaimed.

For the slender combat medic, his service meant something else. Years later, Sasser would state, "I am proud that my medal was for saving lives as a medic, rather than destroying lives. . . . It's a source of pleasure with me to have received it for that."[25]

BRAVE FAR BEYOND THE CALL OF DUTY

Charles C. Rogers and Firebase "Rita"

Located near the Cambodian border, Firebase "Rita" drew some of the fiercest fighting of the war. Despite the fact that fighting in South Vietnam had steadily declined by this point in the war, American and South Vietnamese forces continued to engage the enemy by conducting search-and-destroy missions along the border. In early 1968, components of the 1st Infantry Division directed extensive operations in support of forward support bases in the area. North Vietnamese forces subjected these bases to continuous bombardment from heavy mortar, rocket, and rocket-propelled-grenade fire. These barrages were often followed by human wave attacks.[26] In the fall of 1968, Lt. Col. Charles C. Rogers and soldiers assigned to Firebase "Rita" would witness such an assault.

Born in 1929, Charles Rogers attended West Virginia State College while undergoing military training as an army ROTC cadet. After graduating in 1952, he served briefly in Korea, followed by duty at a number of military outposts. He developed quite a reputation among enlisted men and senior officers as a very determined and capable officer, willing to do whatever it took to accomplish the mission at hand. By 1968, he had advanced rapidly. He was promoted to lieutenant colonel and given command of the 1st Battalion, 5th Field Artillery Regiment almost upon his arrival in Vietnam.[27]

Late on the night of October 31, 1968, Lieutenant Colonel Rogers and his men were struck by a human wave ground assault launched by seasoned North Vietnamese and Vietcong soldiers. During the initial attack, enemy forces used Bangalore torpedoes to penetrate the firebase perimeter, which caused a great deal of concern among the base defenders. As fragments of enemy shells exploded on his position, Rogers, with complete disregard for his own well-being, aggressively rallied his beleaguered men to their howitzers and directed their fire toward the assaulting enemy. Although knocked down and painfully wounded by an exploding round, Rogers sprang to his feet and led a counterattack against the North Vietnamese soldiers who had infiltrated the base position. Pressing the attack, Rogers managed to reestablish and reinforce the defensive perimeter while killing several enemy troops and driving the remainder from their positions.

This proved to be temporary. Almost instantaneously, a second human wave attack was launched against another sector of the perimeter. Undeterred, Rogers provided the type of leadership his superiors had long expected of him, leading the charge and inspiring his men. Rogers directed artillery fire on the assaulting troops and led a second counterattack. During the fighting, he moved from position to position, encouraging his men to return enemy fire.

As dawn broke on November 1, the enemy launched yet another assault to overrun the position, but to no avail. Rogers continued to rally his troops, providing timely direction as they withstood the desperate attack. Although he was too severely wounded to physically lead the defenders, he continued to encourage his soldiers in the heat of battle until the enemy retreated from the forward position.[28]

As a result of his unselfish efforts during the fighting, Lt. Col. Charles C. Rogers was nominated by his commanding officer for the Medal of Honor. Upon approval of his nomination, the West Virginia native became the highest-ranking black officer to be accorded the nation's most esteemed award for bravery. Shortly afterward, Rogers, along with eleven other servicemen, received the Medal of Honor from President Richard Nixon on May 14, 1970. As he bestowed the nation's most prestigious honor upon the venerable officer, Nixon commented, "Today we honor the brave men, the men who, far beyond the call of duty, served their country magnificently in a war very far away, in a war which is [often] not understood and not supported by some in this country."[29]

How would the nation respond to them now?

We can only wonder what was going on in the minds of Rogers and other black Medal of Honor recipients who had survived the battlefields of Vietnam. Of course, they had sacrificed a great deal in defense of their country; they must have yearned for home cooking, familiar settings, and their loved ones while they were serving. But as President Nixon referenced, they were also returning to a country that was deeply divided over the war, along with other pressing social and political issues. How would the nation respond to them now? How would the country respond to them as recipients of a medal given for honor, which they had earned for fighting a war that was not well-received at home? To what extent would Rogers and his contemporaries be perceived as killing machines and exemplars of American colonialism abroad, as opposed to thinking and feeling human beings—or in their case, citizen-soldiers?

These soldiers had reported to Vietnam from diverse life streams and duty stations. And as we shall see, they also returned to different situations at home.

Webster Anderson

Dwight Johnson

THE ROAD HOME

Webster Anderson and Dwight Johnson Navigate Life after Vietnam

With artillery shells still exploding in Indochina at the end of the Vietnam War, fifteen of the twenty black Medal of Honor recipients paid the ultimate price for their bravery on the battlefield. The ages of the fallen heroes ranged from eighteen (the youngest) to thirty-seven (the oldest); most were in their early to late twenties. The fifteen soldiers killed in action represented a diverse group that included Northerners and Southerners, semi-illiterate and college-educated, unemployed workers and semiskilled laborers. While they took different paths into military service, all had participated in missions that ended with selfless acts performed out of concern for their comrades in the heat of battle.

Between 1966 and 1969, the provinces of Quang Nam, Quang Tri, Tan Ninh, and Pleiku would be the final destinations for Rodney Davis, Robert H. Jenkins, Ralph H. Johnson, Garfield M. Langhorn, and John Warren Jr. These men hurled themselves onto hand grenades to protect the lives of their fellow soldiers. Among this group were marines

John Warren Jr.

James Anderson Jr.

that included James Anderson Jr. and Oscar P. Austin, who unselfishly and without hesitation threw themselves between their fellow corpsmen and the enemy in order to absorb the full impact of explosion. By the fall of 1969, the remains of most of these martyred heroes had made the long trek back to the United States, arriving at different stateside locations for public ceremonies before they were interred in their final resting places.

For those who survived the war in Vietnam and managed to make their way home, the fighting simply continued on in different ways. Many of the returning MOH recipients probably had the same immediate experience as Webster Anderson—a hero's welcome, followed by an overriding desire to give new meaning to their wartime experiences. A native of Winnsboro, South Carolina, Anderson distinguished himself in Vietnam while serving as a staff sergeant with the 101st Airborne Infantry Division's 320th Artillery Regiment. On October 15, 1967, Anderson's unit had been under attack from a North Vietnamese Army Infantry unit near Tam Ky. Undaunted, the section chief and veteran soldier immediately took charge of the situation by mounting the parapet of his howitzer position and leveling deadly fire toward the enemy position. While putting down suppressive fire,

Anderson sustained serious injury to both of his legs when two enemy grenades exploded near him, knocking him to the ground. Despite his wounds, he refused medical evacuation and encouraged his men to press the attack, even though he was wounded again in another explosion. For his conspicuous gallantry and intrepid action on the battlefield, Staff Sergeant Anderson received the Medal of Honor on November 24, 1969. Shortly afterward, he was discharged from the army.[30]

Anderson paid dearly for his selfless act. His wounds on the battlefield caused him to lose both of his legs and part of an arm. Despite his personal hardships, however, the venerable soldier stubbornly took up the "good fight." Within a year, he was fitted with prosthetic limbs, returned to school, and moved to Philadelphia, where he worked with city youth and for veterans' causes as a member of the Vietnam Veterans Against Drugs organization, until his death in 2003. Of his postwar life, he later reflected, "I lost my legs thirty years ago—understand what I'm fixing to say—I have been totally independent. Drive my own car, fix cars . . . cut my own grass . . . run my own electronics business . . . totally independent."[31]

The antiwar movement produced many hand-wringing moments for some returning black MOH recipients. Between 1965 and 1967, soldiers serving in Vietnam were buffeted by the explosion of riots in Selma, Alabama; Milwaukee, Wisconsin; Watts, California; and Newark, New Jersey. These events were especially powerful for black enlisted men and junior officers. While stationed at Long Binh, Vietnam, in 1968, Specialist 4 Charles Parks voiced what may have been the opinion of many young black soldiers: "What some of our fellow soul brothers are doing in an effort to bring about equality for the black men of America, the land of the free. . . . Though I'm in Vietnam, I'm with the patriots of Milwaukee, 100 percent, in their efforts to obtain a fair housing law."

Some soldiers expressed a great deal of ambivalence or were at complete odds with the antiwar rhetoric voiced by some civil rights and black power activists. While serving a tour of duty in Vietnam, Pvt. David Parks observed, "Frankly, I'm mixed up. The stateside news bugs me. On the one hand, you have Stokely Carmichael saying Negroes shouldn't be fighting for this country. On the other hand, some Negro leaders think just the opposite. I doubt that most of them have ever been to war. One thing's for sure: I have been, [and] I'm fed up with it."

Still others took a more-direct approach. When MOH recipient Lawrence Joel returned stateside in 1967, he went to Philadelphia and addressed a rally supporting American involvement in the Vietnam War.[32]

After his Medal of Honor ceremony, Dwight Johnson was greeted by an antiwar protester who pointed at him before making the following statement: "The army used this guy because of the color of his skin to recruit more black young men for cannon fodder."[33] For Johnson, the Vietnam War and its aftermath carried deadly consequences. In 1968, the Detroit, Michigan, native had returned home only to struggle with his inner demons. Drafted into the army in 1967, he was assigned as a tank driver in the infantry company in Vietnam.

"Though I'm in Vietnam, I'm with the patriots of Milwaukee, 100 percent, in their efforts to obtain a fair housing law."

On the eve of the Tet Offensive in 1968, Private Johnson's performance during a battle in the Kontum Province became the stuff of legend. On January 15, he and his platoon members were headed toward Dak To in the Central Highlands, near the Cambodian border and the Ho Chi Minh Trail, when they were ambushed by a battalion-size North Vietnamese force. As the minutes stretched into hours, the situation became increasingly tenuous for the defenders. During its initial contact, the enemy was intent on destroying several tanks. Johnson promptly climbed out of his half-track and, armed with a .45 caliber pistol, proceeded to kill several North Vietnamese soldiers, expending all of his ammunition. The twenty-one-year-old GI then ran through heavy crossfire to one of the burning tanks, pulling men out from the wreckage along the way. After returning to his half-track, he located a submachine gun and proceeded to hunt down the enemy on foot. At one point, he stood face-to-face with a Communist soldier, shooting and killing him at close range. Johnson returned to his half-track and continued firing on the enemy until the rest of his platoon arrived on the scene. By acting so decisively in the face of the enemy, showing concern for his fellow soldiers and complete disregard for his own safety, he was awarded the nation's highest award for valor on November 19, 1968.[34]

Dwight Johnson's ordeal was just beginning. His actions during the Dak To Campaign had taken a toll on the celebrated soldier, both physically and mentally. After the fighting, Johnson was given morphine, and when he showed signs of psychiatric distress, he was sent in a straitjacket to a hospital in Pleiku for observation.

After returning home and receiving the Medal of Honor, Johnson was widely sought after, with many clamoring for his attention, including Gen. William C. Westmoreland, army chief of staff and commander of US Forces in Vietnam; entertainer Bob Hope; and Detroit's chapter of the American Legion. It didn't take long for Johnson's battlefield struggles to resurface in his postwar life. He suffered from a variety of health issues, and after undergoing a battery of medical evaluations, military physicians at Valley Forge Army Hospital in Pennsylvania determined that Johnson still suffered from the psychiatric distress he had first experienced in Vietnam. To make matters worse, he had gone into debt after writing bad checks and missing several public appearances.

On a cool night in late April of 1971, his wartime struggles came to an ignominious end. During an attempt to rob a grocery store less than a mile from his Detroit home, the store manager shot and killed the war hero. On May 6, the Vietnam veteran was buried with honors at Arlington National Cemetery. As his body was being interred, one of his childhood friends remarked, "They [the Vietnam veterans] get quiet. It's like they don't have too much to say about what it was like over there. Maybe it's because they've killed people and they don't really know why they killed them."[35]

On the surface, it might appear that the postwar struggles of MOH recipients like Dwight Johnson led to a somewhat mixed legacy for black heroes who served during the Vietnam War era. But, similar to their predecessors, black MOH recipients during the Vietnam War turned out to be significant trailblazers in the American struggle to better comprehend valor in an ever-changing world. For them, the military was the one place where they could pick up guns and prove their manhood, as well as openly challenge the forces of racism and injustice that threatened their daily existence.

More important, even before arriving in Southeast Asia, many of them clearly understood that their neighborhoods and communities expected them to become shock troops in a larger war—one that might possibly determine the fate for people of color both near and far in the years to come. Out of the crucible of war, they fashioned a new sense of American promise and what their conduct in the heat of battle might mean for successive generations.

What are the larger lessons that late twentieth- and early twenty-first-century Americans gleaned from black heroism? It is to this final pivot in the story of African-American valor that we now turn.

Melvin Morris

Keeping the Faith

LESSONS OF BLACK HEROISM FOR TWENTY-FIRST-CENTURY AMERICA

I came along at a time when most of the barriers were down in the Army. While I was privileged, I will never forget those who went before me and those who were willing to serve their country, which was not willing to serve them.

—Gen. Colin L. Powell, US Army (Ret.), 1997

It was an auspicious moment that would live long in human history and collective memory. On a bright, sunny day in April of 1991, White House Cabinet members, distinguished dignitaries, congressional leaders, and former Medal of Honor recipients assembled in the East Room to pay homage to a fallen hero: Cpl. Freddie Stowers. Although the World War I veteran had died some seventy years earlier, his memory was clearly present in the room. Among those present was a veritable who's who of Official Washington, including Vice President Dan Quayle, Secretary of Defense Dick Cheney, Army Chief of Staff Carl E. Vuono, South Carolina senator Strom Thurmond, former representative Joseph J. DioGuardi, Secretary of the Army Michael Stone, and Chairman of the Joint Chiefs of Staff, Gen. Colin L. Powell. President George H. W. Bush summoned their attention by recounting the deeds performed by Corporal Stowers in France on September 28, 1918.

On that day, President Bush recalled, the young South Carolina native had rushed forward to meet his destiny. During an attack on Hill 188, Stowers's company received heavy machine-gun and mortar fire from enemy forces. In the midst of the chaotic battle, Stowers took charge of the situation and bravely led his men forward on a bayonet charge, destroying the German forces even as he was mortally wounded in the process. On that September day, Bush stated, the young enlisted soldier was alone, far from family members and home. "He had to be scared; his friends died at his side. But he vanquished his fear and fought not for glory, but for a cause larger than himself: the cause of liberty. [. . .] Today Corporal Freddie Stowers becomes the first black soldier honored with the Medal of Honor from World War I. He sought and helped achieve the triumph of right over wrong."

As the president paid tribute to the heroic performance of their loved one, nearly twenty members of Stowers's family—including his two surviving sisters, eighty-eight-year-old Georgiana Palmer and seventy-seven-year-old Mary Bowens—looked on with a great sense of pride and personal fulfillment. As Bush presented them with the long-overdue posthumous award, more than a few family members wiped away tears of relief and satisfaction. Their relative was being recognized as a citizen-soldier who gave his life in defense of family and country. Although his physical being had long since left the earth, they must have felt his spiritual presence that day. Stowers's role in the War to End All Wars had inspired several successive generations of his family, including two present in the East Room that day. Two great-grandnephews stood there in uniform: Tech Sgt. Odis Stowers, who had made the trip from Langley Air Force Base in Virginia, and Staff Sgt. Douglas Warren of the 101st Airborne, who had trekked thousands of miles from his duty station in the Persian Gulf.

There are several elements that we must consider about Freddie Stowers's Medal of Honor ceremony. First, his path to the Medal of Honor ceremony was similar to the one experienced by his distant relatives, and just as arduous. For Stowers's selfless act in 1918, his commanding officer recommended the South Carolina native for the Medal of Honor, but the paperwork was never processed. His story was relegated to the scrap heap of history and remained shrouded from view. Second, public recognition emerged from below. In the late 1980s, after receiving complaints from Texas congressman Mickey Leland and others in early 1990 that pointed toward the racist impetus behind the lack of awards, Defense Secretary Frank Carlucci ordered the Department of the Army to launch an investigation, acknowledging that the oversight may have been racially motivated. After going to France to investigate the events surrounding Stowers's distinguished act of bravery, the Army Decorations Board approved the Medal of Honor for the long-deceased army veteran.[1]

Such was also the case for black soldiers who served with distinction during World War II. In 1992, Acting Secretary of the Army John Shannon commissioned an independent study to investigate the circumstances surrounding the lack of Medal of Honor recipients from World War II. Led by Elliott V. Converse III, Daniel K. Gibran, John A. Cash, Robert K. Griffith Jr., and Richard H. Kohn, the panelists uncovered the fact that senior army commanders like Douglas MacArthur and Edward Almond developed and implemented separate policies to recognize the performances of black soldiers as opposed to white. Theater commanders also imposed a general policy of excluding black GIs from combat that prevented them from qualifying for awards of combat distinction. Despite their disproportionate numbers on the battlefield, promotions and awards were not as forthcoming.

The panelists recommended that the army review all cases where black soldiers were accorded the Distinguished Service Cross for their action under fire. They also urged the Department of the Army to nominate GIs for the Medal of Honor if they had lost their lives while performing an act of gallantry in service to their country. After meeting in October of 1993, the Army Decorations Board met to consider further action in this regard. From their deliberations, the names of Vernon Baker, Edward A. Carter Jr., John R. Fox, Willy F. James Jr., Ruben Rivers, Charles Thomas, and George Watson attracted their immediate attention.

> "[These] Medal of Honor recipients were denied the nation's highest honor, but their deeds could not be denied."

After Congress waived the 1952 statute that barred the heroic deeds of future World War II veterans, President William J. Clinton held a special ceremony at the White House on January 13, 1997, to present the Medal of Honor to the seven soldiers whose deeds had earned the admiration of an adoring country. In the presence of members of the Joint Chiefs of Staff, various Cabinet members, veterans, and relatives of the deceased soldiers, President Clinton stated, "[These] Medal of Honor recipients were denied the nation's highest honor, but their deeds could not be denied." Veterans Affairs Department Secretary and Vietnam War veteran Jesse Brown may have expressed the thoughts of most attendees when he stated, "In no small way, this is an act of healing at a time when it may very well mean more than it might have fifty years ago. We will all be better for it."

Vernon Baker, the only surviving World War II veteran in attendance, had more immediate impressions. A lot of time had passed, but vivid memories of his fallen comrades were forever seared in his memory. Tears streamed down his face as President Clinton draped the nation's highest award for valor around his neck. The humbled hero later reflected on the ceremony with a sense of irony. The octogenarian used the expression of "loss" to connect the physical absence of those long since departed to family members who could not attend the momentous gathering. "I felt the loss of those men, and I felt the loss of my children," Baker stated. "Like Private Watson, I had no blood relatives to stand with me. My only living sister was incapacitated by a stroke. And four of the most important people in my life, my daughters, were absent from this moment, this pinnacle of my life."[2]

Perhaps Baker's definitions of dignity and honor were being paid forward in certain respects. In May of 2014, President Barack Obama placed a call to a former GI for an oversight committed by the US government decades earlier. On the other end of the line was Melvin Morris, a Vietnam War veteran who hailed from Cocoa, Florida. Born in 1942, Morris was originally from Okmulgee, Oklahoma, and had been a member of the state National Guard before joining the army in 1959. A former Green Beret, Morris had served several tours in South Vietnam before he was wounded three times while recovering the body of a fallen comrade in the face of withering machine-gun fire during a firefight near Chi Lang in 1969. For his gallantry in action, Morris was awarded the Distinguished Service Cross in 1970. Receiving this honor hardly fazed the battle-hardened soldier. As he later reflected, "I never really did worry about decorations."[3]

Morris would become one of the beneficiaries of the government's new policies for assessing courage under fire. In 2002, the Defense Department, at the behest of members of Congress, launched an investigation into the historical prejudice against Hispanics and Jews who had served in the nation's military. They particularly focused on those who had received the Distinguished Service Cross for acts of valor during World War II, but later broadened their scope to include black GIs who had fought in the Korean and Vietnam Wars. Among those on their list was former staff sergeant Morris, who lived in Florida. Remembering Obama's call, Morris said, "I fell to my knees, I was so shocked. President Obama said he was sorry this didn't happen before. He said this should have been done forty-four years ago."[4]

Not long afterward, Morris appeared at the White House where a mass ceremony was held to honor twenty-four veterans, mostly of Hispanic or Jewish heritage. They had previously received the nation's second-highest award for valor, but had not been recognized with the Medal of Honor until that moment.

As the nation's first African-American president placed the prestigious medal around Morris's neck, those present were bearing witness to a new standard of honor,[5] enveloped in freedom and equality. With that, the brotherhood of valor initially founded by stalwarts like Christian Fleetwood, William McBryar, George Wanton, Cornelius Charlton, and Milton Olive welcomed a new member into their ranks.

How bravery will be translated into action by successive generations of African Americans has yet to be revealed.

> "I fell to my knees, I was so shocked. President Obama said he was sorry this didn't happen before. He said this should have been done forty-four years ago."

Pantheon of Heroes

A List of African-American Recipients of the Medal of Honor from the Civil War to Vietnam

THE CIVIL WAR

William H. Carney: DOB–February 29, 1840, Norfolk, Virginia; Hometown: New Bedford, Massachusetts; Unit: 54th Massachusetts Volunteer Infantry, 1863-1864; Rank: Sergeant; Place and Date of Distinguished Action: Second Battle of Fort Wagner, South Carolina, July 18, 1863.

Robert Blake: DOB–Unknown, Virginia; Hometown: Unknown; Unit: US Navy, USS *Marblehead*; Rank: Contraband Seaman; Place and Date of Distinguished Action: Legareville, Stono River, South Carolina, December 25, 1863.

Joachim Pease: DOB–1842, Fogo Island, Newfoundland, Canada; Hometown: Long Island, New York; Unit: US Navy, USS *Kearsarge*; Rank: Seaman; Place and Date of Distinguished Action: Cherbourg, France, June 19, 1864.

Decatur Dorsey: DOB–1836, Howard County, Maryland; Hometown: Hoboken, New Jersey; Unit: B Company, 39th US Colored Infantry; Rank: Corporal; Place and Date of Distinguished Action: Battle of the Crater, Petersburg, Virginia, July 30, 1864.

William H. Brown: DOB–1836, Baltimore, Maryland; Hometown: Unknown; Unit: US Navy, USS *Brooklyn*; Rank: Landsman; Place and Date of Distinguished Action: Fort Morgan, Battle of Mobile Bay, Alabama, August 5, 1864.

Wilson Brown: DOB–1841, Natchez, Mississippi; Hometown: Natchez, Mississippi; Unit: US Navy, USS *Hartford*; Rank: Landsman; Place and Date of Distinguished Action: Fort Morgan, Battle of Mobile Bay, Alabama, August 5, 1864.

John Lawson: DOB–June 16, 1837, Philadelphia, Pennsylvania; Hometown: Philadelphia, Pennsylvania; Unit: US Navy, USS *Hartford*; Rank: Landsman; Place and Date of Distinguished Action: Fort Morgan, Battle of Mobile Bay, Alabama, August 5, 1864.

James Mifflin: DOB–1839, Richmond, Virginia; Hometown: Unknown; Unit: US Navy, USS *Brooklyn*; Rank: Engineer's Cook; Place and Date of Distinguished Action: Fort Morgan, Battle of Mobile Bay, Alabama, August 5, 1864.

Thomas R. Hawkins: DOB–1840, Cincinnati, Ohio; Hometown: Washington, DC; Unit: 6th US Colored Infantry Regiment; Rank: Sergeant Major; Place and Date of Distinguished Action: Battle of Chaffin's Farm, New Market Heights, Virginia, September 29, 1864.

Milton M. Holland: DOB–August 1, 1844, Austin, Travis County, Texas; Hometown: Washington, DC; Unit: Company C, 5th US Colored Infantry Regiment; Rank: Sergeant; Place and Date of Distinguished Action: Battle of Chaffin's Farm, New Market Heights, Virginia, September 29, 1864.

Robert A. Pinn: DOB–March 1, 1843, Stark County, Ohio; Hometown: Massillon, Ohio; Unit: Company I, 5th US Colored Infantry Regiment; Rank: First Sergeant; Place and Date of Distinguished Action: Battle of Chaffin's Farm, New Market Heights, Virginia, September 29, 1864.

Alfred B. Hilton: DOB–1842, Harford County, Maryland; Hometown: Harford County, Maryland; Unit: Company H, 4th US Colored Infantry Regiment; Rank: Sergeant; Place and Date of Distinguished Action: Battle of Chaffin's Farm, New Market Heights, Virginia, September 29, 1864.

Christian A. Fleetwood: DOB–July 21, 1840, Baltimore, Maryland; Hometown: Washington, DC; Unit: Company G, 4th US Colored Infantry Regiment; Rank: Sergeant Major; Place and Date of Distinguished Action: Battle of Chaffin's Farm, New Market Heights, Virginia, September 29, 1864.

Charles Veale: DOB–1838, Portsmouth, Virginia; Hometown: Hampton, Virginia; Unit: Company D, US Colored Infantry Regiment; Rank: Private; Place and Date of Distinguished Action: Battle of Chaffin's Farm, New Market Heights, Virginia, September 29, 1864.

Powhatan Beaty: DOB–October 8, 1837, Richmond, Virginia; Hometown: Cincinnati, Ohio; Unit: Company G, 5th US Colored Infantry Regiment; Place and Date of Distinguished Action: Battle of Chaffin's Farm, New Market Heights, Virginia, September 29, 1864.

William H. Barnes: DOB–1840, Saint Mary's County, Maryland; Hometown: Indianola, Texas; Unit: Company C, 38th US Colored Infantry Regiment; Rank: Sergeant; Place and Date of Distinguished Action: Battle of Chaffin's Farm, New Market Heights, Virginia, September 29, 1864.

Edward Ratcliff: DOB–February 8, 1835, James City County, Virginia; Hometown: York County, Virginia; Unit: Company C, 38th US Colored Infantry Regiment; Rank: First Sergeant; Place and Date of Distinguished Action: Battle of Chaffin's Farm, New Market Heights, Virginia, September 29, 1864.

Alexander Kelly: DOB–April 7, 1840, Saltsburg, Pennsylvania; Hometown: Pittsburgh, Pennsylvania; Unit: Company F, 6th US Colored Infantry Regiment; Rank: First Sergeant; Place and Date of Distinguished Action: Battle of Chaffin's Farm, New Market Heights, Virginia, September 29, 1864.

James H. Bronson: DOB–1838, Indiana County, Pennsylvania; Hometown: Carnegie, Pennsylvania; Unit: Company D, 5th US Colored Infantry Regiment; Rank: First Sergeant; Place and Date of Distinguished Action: Battle of Chaffin's Farm, New Market Heights, Virginia, September 29, 1864.

James D. Gardiner: DOB–September 16, 1839, Gloucester, Virginia; Hometown: Clarks Summit, Pennsylvania; Unit: Company I, 36th Regiment, US Colored Troops; Rank: Private; Place and Date of Distinguished Action: Battle of Chaffin's Farm, New Market Heights, Virginia, September 29, 1864.

James H. Harris: DOB–1828, Saint Mary's County, Maryland; Hometown: Arlington, Virginia; Unit: Company B, 38th US Colored Troops; Rank: Sergeant; Place and Date of Distinguished Action: Battle of Chaffin's Farm, New Market Heights, Virginia, September 29, 1864.

Miles James: DOB–1829, Princess Anne County, Virginia; Hometown: Norfolk, Virginia; Unit: Company B, 36th Regiment, US Colored Troops; Rank: Corporal; Place and Date of Distinguished Action: Battle of Chaffin's Farm, New Market Heights, Virginia, September 30, 1864.

Andrew Jackson Smith: DOB–September 3, 1843, Livingston County, Kentucky; Hometown: Grand Rivers, Kentucky; Unit: 55th Massachusetts Voluntary Infantry; Rank: Corporal; Place and Date of Distinguished Action: Battle of Honey Hill, South Carolina, November 30, 1864.

Bruce Anderson: DOB–June 19, 1845, Mexico City, Mexico; Hometown: Albany, New York; Unit: Company K, 142nd New York Volunteer Infantry; Rank: Private; Place and Date of Distinguished Action: Second Battle of Fort Fisher, North Carolina, January 15, 1865.

Aaron Anderson: DOB–1811, Plymouth, North Carolina; Hometown: Philadelphia, Pennsylvania; Unit: US Navy, USS *Wyandank*; Rank: Landsman; Place and Date of Distinguished Action: The Clearing of Mattox Creek, Virginia, March 17, 1865.

INDIAN WAR CAMPAIGNS

Emanuel Stance: DOB–1843, Carroll Parish, Louisiana; Hometown: Nebraska; Unit: Company F, 9th Cavalry Regiment; Rank: Sergeant; Place and Date of Distinguished Action: Kickapoo Springs, Texas, May 20, 1870.

John Ward: DOB–1847, Arkansas; Hometown: Brackettville, Texas; Unit: 24th Infantry Regiment, Black Seminole Indian Scouts; Rank: Sergeant; Place and Date of Distinguished Action: Pecos River, Texas, April 25, 1875.

Adam Paine: DOB–1843, Florida; Hometown: Brackettville, Texas; Unit: 24th Infantry Regiment, Black Seminole Indian Scouts; Rank: Private; Place and Date of Distinguished Action: Canyon Blanco Tributary of the Red River, Texas, September 26-27, 1874.

Isaac Payne: DOB–1854, Mexico; Hometown: Brackettville, Texas; Unit: 24th Infantry Regiment, Black Seminole Indian Scouts; Rank: Trumpeter; Place and Date of Distinguished Action: Pecos River, Texas, April 25, 1875.

Pompey Factor: DOB–1849, Arkansas; Hometown: Brackettville, Texas; Unit: 24th Infantry Regiment, Black Seminole Indian Scouts; Rank: Private; Place and Date of Distinguished Action: Pecos River, Texas, April 25, 1875.

Clinton Greaves: DOB–August 12, 1855, Madison County, Virginia; Hometown: Columbus, Ohio; Unit: Company C, 9th Cavalry Regiment; Rank: Corporal; Place and Date of Distinguished Action: Florida Mountains, New Mexico, January 24, 1877.

Benjamin Brown: DOB–1859, Spotsylvania County, Virginia; Hometown: Washington, DC; Unit: Company C, 24th Infantry Regiment; Rank: Sergeant; Place and Date of Distinguished Action: Arizona, May 11, 1889.

John Denny: DOB–1846, Big Flats, Chemung County, New York; Hometown: Washington, DC; Unit: Company C, 9th Cavalry Regiment; Rank: Sergeant; Place and Date of Distinguished Action: Las Animas Canyon, New Mexico, September 18, 1879.

Henry Johnson: DOB–June 11, 1850, Boydton, Mecklenburg County, Virginia; Hometown: Washington, DC; Unit: Company D, 9th Cavalry Regiment; Rank: Sergeant; Place and Date of Distinguished Action: Milk River, Colorado, October 2-5, 1879.

Thomas Boyne: DOB–1849, Prince Georges County, Maryland; Hometown: Washington, DC; Unit: Company C, 9th Cavalry Regiment; Rank: Sergeant; Place and Date of Distinguished Action: Mimbres Mountains and Cuchillo Negro River, New Mexico, May 29, September 27, 1879.

George Jordan: DOB–1847, Williamson County, Tennessee; Hometown: Maxwell, Nebraska; Unit: Company K, 9th Cavalry Regiment; Rank: Sergeant; Place and Date of Distinguished Action: Fort Tularosa and Carrizo Canyon, New Mexico, May 14, 1880, August 12, 1881.

Thomas Shaw: DOB–1846, Covington, Kenton County, Kentucky; Hometown: Arlington, Virginia; Unit: Company K, 9th Cavalry Regiment; Rank: Sergeant; Place and Date of Distinguished Action: Carrizo Canyon, New Mexico, August 12, 1881.

Augustus Walley: DOB–March 10, 1856, Reistertown, Baltimore County, Maryland; Hometown: Reistertown, Maryland; Unit: Company I, 9th Cavalry Regiment; Rank: Private; Place and Date of Distinguished Action: Cuchillo Negro Mountains, New Mexico, August 16, 1881.

Moses Williams: DOB–October 10, 1845, Carrollton, Orleans Parish, Louisiana; Hometown: Vancouver, Washington; Unit: Company I, 9th Cavalry Regiment; Rank: First Sergeant; Place and Date of Distinguished Action: Cuchillo Negro Mountains, New Mexico, August 16, 1881.

Brent Woods: DOB–1855, Pulaski County, Kentucky; Hometown: Somerset, Kentucky; Unit: Company B, 9th Cavalry Regiment; Rank: Sergeant; Place and Date of Distinguished Action: New Mexico, August 19, 1881.

Isaiah Mays: DOB–February 16, 1858, Carters Bridge, Virginia; Hometown: Phoenix, Arizona; Unit: Company B, 24th Infantry Regiment; Rank: Corporal; Place and Date of Distinguished Action: Cedar Springs, Arizona Territory, May 11, 1889.

William McBryar: DOB–February 14, 1861, Elizabethtown, Bladen County, North Carolina; Hometown: Philadelphia, Pennsylvania; Unit: 10th Cavalry Regiment; Rank: Sergeant; Place and Date of Distinguished Action: Arizona Territory, March 7, 1890.

William O. Wilson: DOB–September 16, 1869, Hagerstown, Washington County, Maryland; Hometown: Washington County, Maryland; Unit: Company I, 9th Cavalry Regiment; Rank: Corporal; Place and Date of Distinguished Action: near Pine Ridge Agency, South Dakota, December 30, 1890.

SPANISH-AMERICAN WAR

Dennis Bell: DOB–December 28, 1866, Washington, DC; Hometown: Washington, DC; Unit: Troop H, 10th US Cavalry; Rank: Private; Place and Date of Distinguished Action: Battle of Tayabacao, Cuba, June 30, 1898.

Fitz Lee: DOB–June, 1866, Dinwiddie County, Virginia; Hometown: Leavenworth County, Kansas; Unit: Troop M, 10th Cavalry; Rank: Private; Place and Date of Distinguished Action: Battle of Tayabacao, Cuba, June 30, 1898.

William H. Thompkins: DOB–October 3, 1872, Paterson, New Jersey; Hometown: San Francisco, California; Unit: Troop G, 10th Cavalry; Rank: Private; Place and Date of Distinguished Action: Battle of Tayabacao, Cuba, June 30, 1898.

George H. Wanton: DOB–May 15, 1868, Paterson, New Jersey; Hometown: Paterson, New Jersey; Unit: Troop M, 10th Cavalry; Rank: Private; Place and Date of Distinguished Action: Battle of Tayabacao, Cuba, June 30, 1898.

Edward L. Baker, Jr.: DOB–December 28, 1865, Laramie County, Wyoming; Hometown: Los Angeles, California; Unit: 10th Cavalry; Rank: Sergeant Major; Place and Date of Distinguished Action: Battle of San Juan Hill, Santiago, Cuba, July 1, 1898.

Robert Penn: DOB–October 10, 1872, City Point, Prince George's County, Virginia; Hometown: Las Animas, Bent County, Colorado; Unit: US Navy, USS *Iowa*; Rank: Fireman First Class; Place and Date of Distinguished Action: Santiago de Cuba, July 20, 1898.

WORLD WAR I

William Henry Johnson: DOB–July 15, 1892, Winston-Salem, North Carolina; Hometown: Albany, New York; Unit: 369th Infantry Regiment; Rank: Sergeant; Place and Date of Distinguished Action: Combat operations during the Meuse-Argonne Offensive, Champagne, France, May 15, 1918.

Freddie Stowers: DOB–January 12, 1894, Sandy Springs, South Carolina; Hometown: Sandy Springs, South Carolina; Unit: Company C, 371st Infantry Regiment, 93d Infantry Division; Rank: Corporal; Place and Date of Distinguished Action: The attack on Hill 188, Champagne Marne Sector, France, September 28, 1918.

WORLD WAR II

George Watson: DOB–1915, Birmingham, Alabama; Hometown: Birmingham, Alabama; Unit: 2nd Battalion, 29th Quartermaster Regiment; Rank: Private; Place and Date of Distinguished Action: Near Porlock Harbour, New Guinea, March 8, 1944.

Ruben Rivers: DOB–1921, Tecumseh, Oklahoma; Hometown: Tecumseh, Oklahoma; Unit: 761st Tank Battalion; Rank: Staff Sergeant; Place and Date of Distinguished Action: During the Allied Advance toward Guebling, France, November 16–19, 1944.

John R. Fox: DOB–May 18, 1915, Cincinnati, Ohio; Hometown: Whitman, Massachusetts; Unit: 366th Infantry Regiment, 92nd Infantry Division; Rank: First Lieutenant; Place and Date of Distinguished Action: Sommocolonia, Italy, December 26, 1944.

Charles L. Thomas: DOB–April 17, 1920, Alabama; Hometown: Detroit, Michigan; Unit: 761st Tank Battalion; Rank: Second Lieutenant; Place and Date of Distinguished Action: Near Climbach, France, December 14, 1944.

Edward A. Carter, Jr.: DOB–May 26, 1916, Los Angeles, California; Hometown: Los Angeles, California; Unit: 56th Armored Infantry Battalion, 12th Armored Division; Rank: Sergeant First Class; Place and Date of Distinguished Action: Near Speyer, Germany, March 23, 1945.

Vernon Baker: DOB–December 17, 1919, Cheyenne, Wyoming; Hometown: Saint Maries, Idaho; Unit: 370th Infantry Regiment, 92nd Infantry Division; Rank: Second Lieutenant; Place and Date of Distinguished Action: Near Viareggio, Italy, April 5 and 6, 1945.

Willy F. James, Jr.: DOB–March 18, 1920, Kansas City, Missouri; Hometown: Kansas City, Missouri; Unit: Company G, 413th Infantry Regiment, 104th Infantry Division; Rank: Private First Class; Place and Date of Distinguished Action: Near Lippoldsberg, Germany, April 7, 1945.

KOREAN WAR

William H. Thompson: DOB–August 16, 1927, New York City, New York; Hometown: New York City, New York; Unit: Company M, 24th Infantry Regiment, 25th Infantry Division; Rank: Private First Class; Place and Date of Distinguished Action: Pusan Perimeter Operations, Haman, Korea, August 6, 1950.

Cornelius H. Charlton: DOB–July 24, 1929, East Gulf, West Virginia; Hometown: East Gulf, West Virginia; Unit: Company C, 24th Infantry Regiment, 25th Infantry Division; Rank: Sergeant; Place and Date of Distinguished Action: Operation Piledriver, Chipo-ri, Korea, June 2, 1951.

VIETNAM WAR

Milton L. Olive III: DOB–November 7, 1946, Chicago, Illinois; Hometown: Chicago, Illinois; Unit: 3rd Platoon, Company B, 2nd Battalion (Airborne), 503rd Infantry, 173rd Airborne Brigade; Rank: Private First Class; Place and Date of Distinguished Action: Pu Cuong, Republic of Vietnam, October 22, 1965.

Lawrence Joel: DOB–February 22, 1928, Winston-Salem, North Carolina; Hometown: Winston-Salem, North Carolina; Unit: Headquarters and Headquarters Company, 1st Battalion (Airborne), 503rd Infantry, 173rd Airborne Brigade; Rank: Specialist Fifth Class; Place and Date of Distinguished Action: Republic of Vietnam, November 8, 1965.

Donald R. Long: DOB–August 27, 1939, Blackfork, Ohio; Hometown: Blackfork, Ohio; Unit: Troop C, 1st Squadron, 4th Cavalry, 1st Infantry Division; Rank: Sergeant; Place and Date of Distinguished Action: Republic of Vietnam, June 30, 1966.

James Anderson Jr.: DOB–January 22, 1947, Los Angeles, California; Hometown: Los Angeles, California; Unit: US Marine Corps, 2nd Platoon, Company F, 2nd Battalion, 3rd Marines, 3rd Marine Division; Rank: Private First Class; Place and Date of Distinguished Action: Cam Lo, Republic of Vietnam, February 28, 1967.

Matthew Leonard: DOB–November 26, 1929, Eutaw, Alabama; Hometown: Birmingham, Alabama; Unit: Company B, 1st Battalion, 16th Infantry, 1st Infantry Division; Rank: Sergeant First Class; Place and Date of Distinguished Action: near Suoi Da, Republic of Vietnam, February 28, 1967.

Ruppert L. Sargent: DOB–January 6, 1938, Hampton, Virginia; Hometown: Hampton, Virginia; Unit: Company B, 4th Battalion, 9th Infantry, 25th Infantry Division; Rank: First Lieutenant; Place and Date of Distinguished Action: Hau Nghia Province, Republic of Vietnam, March 15, 1967.

Rodney M. Davis: DOB–April 7, 1942, Macon, Georgia; Hometown: Macon, Georgia; Unit: US Marine Corps, Battery C, 2nd Battalion, 4th Artillery, 9th Infantry Division; Rank: Sergeant; Place and Date of Distinguished Action: Quang Nam Province, Republic of Vietnam, September 6, 1967.

Webster Anderson: DOB–July 15, 1933, Winnsboro, South Carolina; Hometown: Winnsboro, South Carolina; Unit: Battery A, 2nd Battalion, 320th Field Artillery, 101st Airborne Infantry Division (Airmobile); Rank: Staff Sergeant; Place and Date of Distinguished Action: Tam Ky, Republic of Vietnam, October 15, 1967.

Riley Pitts: DOB–October 15, 1937, Fallis, Oklahoma; Hometown: Fallis, Oklahoma; Unit: Company C, 2nd Battalion, 27th Infantry, 25th Infantry Division; Rank: Captain; Place and Date of Distinguished Action: Ap Dong, Republic of Vietnam, October 31, 1967.

Dwight H. Johnson: DOB–May 7, 1947, Detroit, Michigan; Hometown: Detroit, Michigan; Unit: Company B, 1st Battalion, 69th Armor, 4th Infantry Division; Rank: Specialist Fifth Class; Place and Date of Distinguished Action: near Dak To, Kontum Province, Republic of Vietnam, January 15, 1968.

Clarence Sasser: DOB–September 12, 1947, Chenango, Texas; Hometown: Chenango, Texas; Unit: Headquarters Company, 3rd Battalion, 60th Infantry, 9th Infantry Division; Rank: Private First Class; Place and Date of Distinguished Action: Ding Tuong Province, Republic of Vietnam, January 10, 1968.

Eugene Ashley Jr.: DOB–October 12, 1931, Wilmington, North Carolina; Hometown: Fayetteville, North Carolina; Unit: Company C, 5th Special Forces Group (Airborne), 1st Special Forces; Rank: Sergeant First Class; Place and Date of Distinguished Action: near Lang Vei, Republic of Vietnam, February 6-7, 1968.

Clifford C. Sims: DOB–June 18, 1942, Port St. Joe, Florida; Hometown: Port St. Joe, Florida; Unit: Company D, 2nd Battalion (Airborne), 501st Parachute Infantry Regiment, 101st Airborne Division; Rank: Staff Sergeant; Place and Date of Distinguished Action: near Hue, Republic of Vietnam, February 21, 1968.

Ralph H. Johnson: DOB–January 11, 1949, Charleston, South Carolina; Hometown: Charleston, South Carolina; Unit: Company A, 1st Reconnaissance Battalion, 1st Marine Division; Rank: Private First Class; Place and Date of Distinguished Action: Hill-146, near Quan Duc Valley, Republic of Vietnam, March 5, 1968.

Charles C. Rogers: DOB–September 6, 1929, Claremont, West Virginia; Hometown: Munich, Germany; Unit: 1st Battalion, 5th Artillery Regiment, 1st Infantry Division; Rank: Lieutenant Colonel; Place and Date of Distinguished Action: Fishhook near Cambodian Border, Republic of Vietnam, November 1, 1968.

John E. Warren Jr.: DOB–November 16, 1946, Brooklyn, New York; Hometown: Farmingdale, New York; Unit: Company C, 2nd Battalion (Mechanized), 22d Infantry, 25th Infantry Division; Rank: First Lieutenant; Place and Date of Distinguished Action: Tay Ninh Province, Republic of Vietnam, January 14, 1969.

Garfield M. Langhorn: DOB–September 10, 1948, Cumberland, Virginia; Hometown: Riverhead, New York; Unit: Troop C, 7th Squadron, 17th Cavalry, 1st Aviation Brigade; Rank: Private First Class; Place and Date of Distinguished Action: near Plei Djereng, Pleiku Province, Republic of Vietnam, January 15, 1969.

Oscar P. Austin: DOB–January 15, 1948, Nacogdoches, Texas; Hometown: Nacogdoches, Texas; Unit: US Marine Corps, Company E, 2nd Battalion, 7th Marines, 1st Marine Division; Rank: Private First Class; Place and Date of Distinguished Action: West of Da Nang, Republic of Vietnam, February 23, 1969.

Robert H. Jenkins Jr.: DOB–June 1, 1948, Interlachen, Florida; Hometown: Interlachen, Florida; Unit: US Marine Corps, 3rd Reconnaissance Battalion, 3rd Marine Division; Rank: Private First Class; Place and Date of Distinguished Action: Fire Support Base Argonne, DMZ, March 5, 1969.

William M. Bryant: DOB–February 16, 1933, Cochran, Georgia; Hometown: Cochran, Georgia; Unit: Company A, 5th Special Forces Group, 1st Special Forces; Rank: Sergeant First Class; Place and Date of Distinguished Action: Long Khanh Province, Republic of Vietnam, March 24, 1969.

Melvin Morris: DOB–January 7, 1942, Okmulgee, Oklahoma; Hometown: Cocoa, Florida; Unit: Company D, 5th Special Forces Group, 1st Special Forces; Rank: Sergeant First Class; Place and Date of Distinguished Action: near Chi Lang, Republic of Vietnam, September 17, 1969.

PEACETIME PANTHEON OF HEROES:

John Johnson: DOB–1839, Philadelphia, Pennsylvania; Hometown: Philadelphia, Pennsylvania; Unit: U.S. Navy, USS *Kansas*; Rank: Seaman; Place and Date of Distinguished Action: near Greytown, Nicaragua, April 12, 1872.

Joseph B. Noil: DOB–1841, Nova Scotia, Canada; Hometown: Washington, DC; Unit: US Navy, USS *Powhatan*; Rank: Seaman; Place and Date of Distinguished Action: Norfolk, Virginia, December 26, 1872.

William Johnson: DOB–1855, Saint Vincent, West Indies; Hometown: Arlington, Virginia; Unit: US Navy, USS *Adams*; Rank: Cooper; Place and Date of Distinguished Action: Navy Yard, Mare Island, California, November 14, 1879.

John Smith: DOB–1854, Bermuda; Hometown: Bermuda; Unit: US Navy, USS *Shenandoah*; Rank: Seaman; Place and Date of Distinguished Action: Rio de Janeiro, Brazil, September 19, 1880.

John Davis: DOB–1854, Kingston, Jamaica; Hometown: Hampton, Virginia; Unit: US Navy, USS *Trenton*; Rank: Ordinary Seaman; Place and Date of Distinguished Action: Toulon, France, February 1881.

Robert Augustus Sweeney*: DOB–February 20, 1853, Montserrat, West Indies; Hometown: Queens, New York; Unit: US Navy, USS *Kearsarge*, USS *Yantic*; Rank: Ordinary Seaman; Places and Dates of Distinguished Action: Hampton Roads, Virginia, and Navy Yard, New York, October 26, 1881, December 20, 1883.

---

* Robert Augustus Sweeney is the only African American to be awarded the Medal of Honor for two separate acts of valor during peacetime service.

Daniel Atkins: DOB–November 18, 1866, Brunswick, Virginia; Hometown: Portsmouth, Virginia; Unit: US Navy, USS *Cushing*; Rank: Ship's Cook First Class; Place and Date of Distinguished Action: aboard U.S.S. *Cushing*, February 11, 1898.

Alphonse Girandy: DOB–January 21, 1868, Guadaloupe, West Indies; Hometown: Philadelphia, Pennsylvania; Unit: US Navy, USS *Petrel*; Rank: Seaman; Place and Date of Distinguished Action: aboard the USS *Petrel*, March 31, 1901.

Appendix

CHAPTER 1

The National Convention of Colored Men

Around the same time, the National Convention of Colored Men assembled in Syracuse, New York. Nearly a hundred delegates packed the Wesleyan Methodist Church during a four-day period. There they heard speeches given by a wide array of noted social, political, civic, religious, and fraternal organization leaders, including John M. Langston, Henry Highland Garnet, Frederick Douglass, and Peter Clark. During the meeting, Garnet, a longtime advocate for black emigration prior to the war, reversed his stance and clamored for greater public recognition of African Americans in American society, based on "the brave deeds of the colored soldiers and the effect their brave conduct had produced upon the public mind." Echoing Garnet's remarks, John Rock of Boston pointed out to rousing applause that "all we ask is equal opportunities and equal rights. This is what our brave men are fighting for. They have not gone to the battlefield for the sake of killing and being killed, but they are fighting for liberty and equality. We ask the same for the black man that is asked for the white man; nothing more, and nothing less."

Before the Syracuse meeting came to a close, delegates resolved to petition Congress, demanding black suffrage. They asked that the Congress "use every honorable endeavor to have the rights of the country's colored patriots respected, without regard to their complexion. [. . .] We believe that the generosity and sense of honor inherent in the great heart of this nation will ultimately concede us our just claims, accord us our rights, and grant us full measure of citizenship, under the broad shield of the Constitution," they concluded.[1]

Delegates of the National Convention of Colored Men felt obliged to treat the exploits of MOH aspirants on the battlefield as markers in progress.

Christian Fleetwood and the Plight of Black Civil War Soldiers

Disillusioned with the army, Christian Fleetwood harshly criticized its treatment of black troops, and wrote an angry letter from the front:

> Upon all our record there is not a single blot, and yet no member of this regiment is considered deserving of a commission, or if so, cannot receive one. I trust you will understand that I speak not of and for myself individually, or that the lack of the pay or honor of a commission induces me to quit the service. Not so by any means, but I see no good that will result to our people by continuing to serve; on the contrary, it seems to me that our continuing to act in a subordinate capacity, with no hope of advancement or promotion, is an absolute injury to our cause. It is a tacit but telling acknowledgment on our part that we are not fit for promotion, and that we are satisfied to remain in a state of marked and acknowledged subservience.

CHAPTER 4

African-American Leaders and President Wilson's Unkept Promises

Among those reasonably impressed with Woodrow Wilson was W. E. B. Du Bois. The forty-four-year-old intellectual, propagandist, and founder of the Pan-African Congress had been the director of publicity and research in the fledgling National Association for the Advancement of Colored People for only a few years before presidential politics intervened. As the editor of the NAACP's house organ, *The Crisis*, Du Bois was initially inclined to support the Socialist Party's presidential nominee, Eugene Debs, but he later came to believe that African-American fortunes rested with the reform governor of New Jersey. Of Woodrow Wilson, he wrote in *The Crisis*, "His personality gives us hope. He will not advance the cause of oligarchy in the South, he will not seek further means of 'Jim Crow' insult, he will not dismiss black men wholesale from office, and he will remember that the Negro in the United States has a right to be heard and considered."[2]

Du Bois was not the only leader who pinned his hopes on the Democratic Party's nominee for president that year. Wilson's promises of a "New Freedom" received a favorable response from Bishop Alexander Walters of the influential African Methodist Episcopal Zion Church. Walters may have had even more reason to entertain raised expectations. During the presidential campaign, he received a letter from the aspiring candidate in which Wilson stated, "The colored people of the United States have made extraordinary progress towards self-support and usefulness, and ought to be encouraged in every possible and proper way. My sympathy with them is of long standing, and I want to assure them through you that should I become President of the United States, they may count on me for absolute fair dealing and everything by which I could assist in advancing the interests of their race in the United States."[3]

But to his dismay, the nation learned that Wilson's "New Freedom" did not include African Americans. Shortly after taking office, Wilson's first administration codified Jim Crow segregation in the nation's capital by signing an executive order requiring photo identification for civil service applicants, and separating federal employees in the Treasury Department and the Post Office, as well as on public conveyances and in eating and restroom facilities. What's more, in 1915, they were personally appalled when the first Democratic president since Grover Cleveland personally approved Hollywood producer D. W. Griffith's racist motion picture, *The Birth of a Nation*, based on Thomas Dixon Jr.'s novel *The Clansman*. Griffith's cinematic representation of Reconstruction celebrated the rise of the Ku Klux Klan and demonized black men and women in the South. After a personal screening of the film in the White House, Wilson gushed, "It is like writing history with lightning, and my only regret is that it is all so terribly true."

African-American Organizations and the Politics of Uplift

Sentiments of racial pride and black consciousness gave rise to a growing number of churches and clubs in cities stretching from Boston to Atlanta to Seattle. Between 1906 and 1911, a number of black fraternities and sororities were formed, including Cornell University's Alpha Phi Alpha, Indiana University's Kappa Alpha Psi, and Howard

University's Omega Psi Phi, Alpha Kappa Alpha, and Delta Sigma Theta. And through-out the country, a growing number of black newspapers emerged to publicize the needs and concerns of ever-expanding black communities in New York, Chicago, Baltimore, Cleveland, Pittsburgh, Atlanta, Norfolk, Savannah, and Los Angeles.[4]

Black insistence on political rights and protections intersected with their sense of self, their demands for citizenship, and the need for a "better class of leadership." As historian Kevin K. Gaines reminds us, a new generation of African Americans came of age at the turn of the twentieth century, and they advocated "racial uplift" as a means of refuting white claims of racial supremacy and black inferiority. According to Gaines, "Believing that the improvement of African Americans' material and moral condition through self-help would diminish white racism, educated African Americans sought to rehabilitate the race's image by embodying respectability, enacted through an ethos of service to the masses."[5]

Uninvited Neighbors: Hostilities between the United States and Mexico

A series of events occurred during the summer of 1917 that caused feelings of consterna-tion among segments of the black community. Between 1914 and 1917, hostilities between the United States and Mexico had simmered to a boiling point as US Marines marched into Vera Cruz in response to a Mexican attack on American sailors in the area. Less than two years later, American troops marched to Mexico when Francisco "Pancho" Villa carried out raids on American civilians and soldiers who resided along its border. Vying to over-throw Mexico's provisional president, Villa hoped to lure the United States into a military skirmish. In response, Woodrow Wilson ordered fifteen thousand army troops to conduct a "Punitive Expedition" against the Villistas. Among the units that reported to duty was the famed 10th Cavalry, with West Point graduate Maj. Charles Young. Led by Brig. Gen. John J. Pershing, troops spent nearly a year in pursuit of Villa, to no avail. Foiled in their attempt to capture the Mexican revolutionary, and becoming increasingly drawn into a possible war with Germany, Pershing's troops were withdrawn from the Mexican border.

During the army's stint of duty in the Southwest, an incident occurred involving the 24th Infantry. In late August of 1917, Camp Logan in Houston, Texas, became the site of racial violence when local whites and members of the 24th's 3rd Battalion squared off against each other in the city streets. For the troops with the 24th Infantry, the racial climate was as stifling as the Texas heat. Since arriving from California that summer, the men of the unit had faced harassment from policemen, often targeted and arrested for violating the Jim Crow ordinances of the city. When local police beat, fired at, and arrested Cpl. Charles Baltimore as he tried to investigate an altercation between a black soldier and a local black woman, black GIs decided to take matters into their own hands. More than 160 soldiers from the battalion armed themselves and stormed the city to confront armed white civilians and policemen. The incident ended with the death of fifteen whites, with twelve white civilians wounded.

The controversy surrounding the actions taken by the soldiers followed an all-too-familiar pattern. The War Department promptly disarmed the battalion and transferred the unit to Columbus, New Mexico. There they remained until they received orders reassigning them to the Philippine Islands, where they would stay for the rest of the world war. Meanwhile, army prosecutors swiftly convened a court-martial during which fifty-four men were tried; thirteen were found guilty and summarily hanged without a review. What's more, after further trials, the army ordered the hanging of twelve additional men and issued lifetime prison sentences for ten others.[6]

When the War Department handed down its decision regarding the actions taken by black troops of the 24th Infantry, sectors of the black community responded with outrage. Stunned by the sequence of events surrounding black troops in Texas that fall, Howard University professor Kelly Miller sarcastically addressed the president: "The Negro, Mr. President, in this emergency, will stand by you and the Nation. Will you and the Nation stand by the Negro?"

CHAPTER 5

Dreams of Double Victory

James G. Thompson, a cafeteria worker at the Wichita, Kansas, Cessna aircraft plant, may have expressed what was on the minds of many young black males in a January 1941 letter to the *Pittsburgh Courier*:

> Being an American of dark complexion and some 26 years, these questions flash through my mind: "Should I sacrifice my life to live half American? Will things be better for the next generation in the peace to follow? Would it be demanding too much to demand full citizenship for the sacrificing of my life? Is the kind of America I know worth defending? Will America be a true and pure democracy after the war? Will Colored Americans suffer still the indignities that have been heaped upon them in the past?"
>
> These and other questions need answering: I want to know, and I believe every colored American, who is thinking, wants to know . . . The V for victory sign is being displayed prominently in all so-called democratic countries which are fighting for victory over aggression, slavery, and tyranny. If this V sign means that to those now engaged in this great conflict, then let we colored Americans adopt the double V for a double victory. The first V for victory over our enemies from without, the second V for victory over our enemies from within. For surely those who perpetrate these ugly prejudices here are seeking to destroy our democratic form of government just as surely as the Axis forces.[7]

Less than two months after his self-styled declaration of war, James Thompson enlisted in the army. By being willing to serve—and die for—his country, he and thousands of other young black men throughout the country had established their own terms for participating in the armed conflict. Their ideas of honorable service and conduct in the heat of battle were focused not only on securing their rights and dignity as American citizens, but also on their hopes of claiming democracy's promise, long after the guns of war had ceased to fire abroad.

CHAPTER 6

Footsteps to Korea: Black Military Service in the Middle 1940s

Charles Bussey fought in Germany during World War II, where he served as an aviator with the 332nd Fighter Group before reassignment stateside as a flight instructor at Tuskegee Army Airfield. After returning to Los Angeles, Bussey attended San Francisco State University and graduated from the Los Angeles Police Academy. However, he felt that the job market offered very few opportunities for ex–fighter pilots like himself. Frustrated by how little postwar America had changed since his wartime service, Bussey elected to return to active duty and reported to Fort Campbell, Kentucky, where he was promptly assigned as a platoon leader with the 74th Engineering Battalion. Shortly afterward, Bussey was reassigned to the US Army of Occupation in Gifu, Japan, where he remained until he reported to the 24th Infantry Regiment.

Such was the case with fellow World War II veteran, Julius Becton Jr. In 1945, young Becton was a second lieutenant, serving in the army with the all-black 93rd Infantry Division, and later, the 542nd Heavy Construction Company in the Philippines. At the end of the war, he was shipped home and reported to Fort Dix, New Jersey, where he was separated from active duty. Fiercely intent on becoming a medical doctor, Becton attended Muhlenberg College in Allentown, Pennsylvania, and got married and started a family. But the allure of military service never really relinquished its hold on the veteran soldier. After he and his wife discovered that his meager income was scarcely enough to support his growing household, he promptly applied to be recalled to active duty in August of 1948. Shortly thereafter he reported to Fort Monmouth, New Jersey, where he was assigned to a signal operations company.[8]

Like Bussey and Becton, the two GIs who received the Medal of Honor for their courageous acts during the Korean War also entered World War II at a relatively young age. Each elected to stay in the military for different reasons.

The Employment of Negro Troops Revisited

Judge William Hastie argued, "The discussion of the basic difficulties involved in the efficient utilization of Negro soldiers is summarized by the statement 'Environment and lack of administrative and educational advantages in prewar days greatly handicap the Negro in performance of his wartime duties.'"

Marcus Ray, a former artillery battalion commander in the 92nd Infantry Division, and the newly appointed civilian aide to the Secretary of War, echoed these sentiments, claiming, "The final answer to the problem of fullest utilization of the Nation's manpower by the Army is not given in the Gillem Board Report." Black weekly newspapers like New York's *Age*, Pittsburgh's *Courier*, and Chicago's *Defender* also heavily criticized the study.[9]

Some believed the board's report was symbolic for other reasons. Lawrence D. Reddick, a noted historian and curator of New York Public Library's Schomburg Center for Research in Black Culture, wrote, "It's possible to interpret the published recommendations as pointing in opposite directions."[10] And still other African-American leaders decided to take a different approach altogether. In September of 1947, Asa Philip Randolph renewed the March on Washington Movement and created the Committee against Jim Crow in Military Service and Training. Chaired by World War II veteran Grant Reynolds, the committee called for civil disobedience demonstrations in Chicago and New York, demanding the end of segregation in the nation's military.[11]

Executive Order 9981

While Executive Order 9981 reflected Missouri-born President Truman's ongoing efforts to promote civil rights as a major agenda of his administration, his decision also may have been firmly grounded in moral and pragmatic reasoning. Clark Clifford, special counsel to the president, made the claim that "Truman felt that it was outrageous that men could be asked to die for their country but not be allowed to fight in same units because of their color." On the other hand, as Philleo Nash, special assistant to the president on minority problems, pointed out at the time, "What means something to the voter is something he can see and handle, such as an Executive Order and is presidential, it gets it out where he can see it."[12]

As Truman's executive order worked its way down to his senior commanders, it fell on deaf ears. While the president had intended to have his edict go into "effect as rapidly as possible, having due regard to the time required to effectuate any necessary changes without impairing efficiency or morale," army commanders simply delayed the implementation of the order and instead accepted the Gillem Board's recommendations, calling for modified segregation. Secretary of the Army Kenneth C. Royall may have said it best when he stated, "The policies of the Gillem Board were sound in the light of actual experience, and the Army was already in accord with the president's order."

African-American GIs and the Beginning of the Korean War

The morale of the 24th Infantry remained high. For Bradley Biggs, a company commander with the regiment, Korea offered him a chance to share an experience that a previous generation had encountered: "I was not in the invasion force that crossed the English Channel during World War II in ships with stopped-up toilets and on seas so rough that soldiers threw up on each other, the deck, their equipment and into the ocean. But, as a twenty-nine-year-old US Army captain, I had a similar experience in a commandeered fishing trawler when my company and I crossed the Sea of Japan from Sasebo, Japan, to Pusan, Korea, in 1950."

Charles Bussey saw Korea in a somewhat similar fashion: "We didn't know what to expect as we landed. It seemed as though we were blundering into a war which had no reason for us as outsiders. But in 1950 the time was right for satisfying the emotional needs I had not sated in World War II. Wars produced promotions, medals, adrenaline, wounds, cowardice, hatred, heroism, valor, and above all, death."[13]

Despite being underequipped and undertrained, elements of the 24th faced the initial test of battle and performed admirably. The 3rd Battalion, commanded by Lt. Col. Samuel

Pierce, arrived at Yechon on July 14 and took positions on the high ground while leading patrols along the roads leading into the town. A day later, one of its platoons, led by Lt. William Ware and a talented platoon sergeant, held its position in the face of fierce enemy fire. For his gallantry, the capable platoon leader earned the army's Distinguished Service Cross.

Ware was not the only black serviceman who distinguished himself at the front. As the days wore on, the performance of other black men during the fighting at Yechon also attracted the attention of headquarters. After discovering that several companies of the 3rd Battalion were drawing fierce enemy mortar and machine-gun fire while trying to enter the town, 77th Engineer Combat Company commander Lt. Charles Bussey decided to take matters into his own hands. After maneuvering several squads into position, Bussey directed a steady stream of machine-gun fire at the enemy, killing several North Korean soldiers and providing valuable relief to the battalion's forces in the process. For his brave action, Bussey received the Silver Star. By the time the attack on Yechon had ended, the regiment had reestablished Allied control over the town. Their efforts were significant, for Yechon represented the first victory won by the US Army in the war. It was also the first South Korean city liberated by American forces.

Not long afterward, sectors of the American public sang the praises of the all-black unit. The *Chicago Tribune* published a story with the headline "Oldest Negro Regiment Adds to War Laurels; 24th Once Beat Indians, Now Smashes Reds." "Negroes Gain First Korean Victory" read a *New York Daily News* headline, and CBS Radio news commentator H. V. Kaltenborn gushed, "Hooray for the colored troops of the 24th Infantry Regiment!" Not to be outdone, members of the black press seized the story of the 24th Infantry Regiment and its bravery at Yechon with great enthusiasm. The *Chicago Defender* exulted, "24th Victory at Yechon Adds New Laurels to Long List of Honors in late July." Around the same time, the *New York Age*, in a story headlined "24th Regiment Refuses to Quit; Repulse Reds," extolled the acts of bravery performed by black GIs who served with the unit. The US Congress immortalized the victory secured by the 24th Infantry in the *Congressional Record*, issuing a commendation to the celebrated all-black unit on August 23.

Endnotes

INTRODUCTION

1 Joanne Braxton, "Paul Laurence Dunbar," in *The Concise Oxford Companion to African American Literature*, eds. William L. Andrews, Frances Smith-Foster, and Trudier Harris (New York: Oxford University Press, 2001), 119–20.

2 Paul Laurence Dunbar, *The Complete Poems of Paul Laurence Dunbar* (New York: Dodd, Mead and Company, 1922), 50–51.

3 William Edward Burghardt Du Bois, *Black Reconstruction in America: An Essay toward a History of the Part Which Black Folk Played in the Attempt to Reconstruct Democracy in America, 1860–1880* (New York: Atheneum, 1935), 104, 111.

4 Most of what we know about war and the politics of memory in the nineteenth century is based on the study of the Civil War and its immediate aftermath. See, for example, the insightful work of David Blight, *Race and Reunion: The Civil War and American Memory* (Cambridge, MA: Harvard University Press, 2003) and Michael Kammen, *Mystic Chords of Memory: The Transformation of Tradition in American Culture* (New York: Alfred A. Knopf, Inc., 1991).

5 US Congress, Senate, Committee on Veterans' Affairs, *Medal of Honor Recipients, 1863–1978: "In the Name of the Congress of the United States"* (Washington, DC: US Government Printing Office, 1979), 1–5; Brevet Major-General St. Clair A. Mulholland, *Military Order Congress Medal of Honor Legion of the United States* (Philadelphia: Town Printing Company, 1905), 51–52.

6 Department of the Army, The Medal of Honor of the United States (1948), 8; Mark C. Mollan, "The Army Medal of Honor: The First Fifty-Five Years," Prologue: *Quarterly of the National Archives and Records Administration* 33:2 (Summer 2001), www.archives.gov/publications/prologue/2001/summer/medal-of-honor-1.html (accessed March 8, 2018).

7 "The Obituary of Milton Lee Olive," undated; Letter, Milton Olive Jr. to Pauline Redmond Coggs, May 1968, all in the Pauline Redmond Coggs Clipping File (in the possession of the author).

8 Lyndon B. Johnson, "Remarks Upon Presenting the Medal of Honor (Posthumous) to the Father of Milton L. Olive III, April 21, 1966, Online, by Gerhard Peters and John T. Woolley, *The American Presidency Project*, www.presidency.ucsb.edu/ws/?pid=27552 (accessed January 9, 2017).

9 Frank N. Schubert, "Reflection Essay: Sesquicentennial Reflection on the Black Regulars," *Journal of Military History* 80:4 (October 2016), 1011–16.

10 Colin L. Powell, with Joseph E. Persico, *My American Journey* (New York: Random House, 1995), 591.

CHAPTER 1: "FOR HONOR, DUTY, AND LIBERTY"

1 Benjamin Quarles, *The Negro in the Civil War* (1953, rep. New York: Russell & Russell, 1968); Dudley Taylor Cornish, *The Sable Arm: Negro Troops in the Union Army, 1861–1865* (1956, rep. New York: W. W. Norton & Company, 1966); James M. McPherson, *The Negro's Civil War: How American Negroes Felt and Acted during the War for the Union* (New York: Pantheon Books, 1965); Ira Berlin, et al., *Freedom: A Documentary History of Emancipation, 1861–1867, Series II: The Black Military Experience* (New York: Cambridge University Press, 1982); Bernard Nalty, *Strength for the Fight* (New York: Free Press, 1986); Joseph T. Glatthaar, *Forged in Battle* (New York: Free Press, 1990); Noah A. Trudeau, *Like Men of War: Black Troops in the Civil War, 1862–1865* (Boston: Little, Brown, 1998); Keith Wilson, *Camp Fires of Freedom: The Camp Life of Black Soldiers during the Civil War* (Kent, OH: Kent State University Press, 2002); John David Smith, ed., *Black Solders in Blue: African American Troops in the Civil War Era* (Chapel Hill: The University of North Carolina Press, 2002); Stephen V. Ash, *Firebrand of Liberty: The Story of Two Black Regiments that Changed the Course of the Civil War* (New York: W. W. Norton & Company, 2008).

2 William Dobak, *Freedom by the Sword: The US Colored Troops, 1862–1867* (Washington, DC: The Center of Military History, 2011), 9–10. For more on Sherman's disparaging views on black units, see Joseph T. Glatthaar, *Forged in Battle*, 197.

3 William W. Freehling, "Sure, Black Troops Helped the Union Win the Civil War, But How?" (Presentation at the Southern Historical Association Meeting, November 2000), courtesy of Frank N. Schubert (in the possession of the author).

4 William A. Dobak, *Freedom by the Sword*, 8; James McPherson, *The Negro's Civil War: How American Negroes Felt and Acted during the War for the Union* (New York: Pantheon Books, 1965), 48–49; Dudley Taylor Cornish, *The Sable Arm*, 130.

5 Milton M. Holland, *Athens* (OH) *Messenger* (February 4, 1864), reprinted in Edwin S. Redkey, ed., *A Grand Army of Black Men: Letters from African American Soldiers in the Union Army, 1861–1865* (New York: Cambridge University Press, 1992), 93.

6 "Interesting Correspondence," *Liberator* (November 6, 1863), 45.

7 "The Flag Never Touched the Ground," in W. F. Beyer and O. F. Keydel, eds., *Deeds of Valor from the Records in the Archives of the United States Government: How American Heroes Won*

the Medal of Honor (Detroit, MI: The Perrien-Keydel Company, 1907), 258–59; Brevet Major-General St. Clair A. Mulholland, *Military Order Congress Medal of Honor Legion of the United States* (Philadelphia: Town Printing Company, 1905), 309–10; Report of Col. Edward N. Hallowell, Fifty-Fourth Massachusetts (Colored) Infantry, November 7, 1863, OR, Ser. I, Vol. 28, Part 1, 362; Letter, Cpl. James G. Gooding to the Editors of the *New Bedford Mercury*, July 20, 1863, in Virginia M. Adams, ed., *On the Altar of Freedom: A Black Soldier's Civil War Letters from the Front / James Henry Gooding* (Amherst: University of Massachusetts Press, 1991), 36–39. For observations made by other noncommissioned officers with the 54th Massachusetts who were present at the front at the time, see Donald Yacovone, ed., *A Voice of Thunder: The Civil War Letters of George E. Stephens* (Urbana: University of Illinois Press, 1997).

8 Matt Helm, "William H. Carney, 1840–1908," BlackPast.Org, www.blackpast.org/aah/carney -william-h-1840-1908 (accessed February 27, 2017); Letter, Gooding to the *New Bedford Mercury*, May 20, 1863, in Adams, ed., *On the Altar of Freedom*, 22.

9 Melvin Claxton and Mark Puls, *Uncommon Valor: A Story of Race, Patriotism, and Glory in the Final Battles of the Civil War* (Hoboken, NJ: John Wiley & Sons, Inc., 2006), 18.

10 Charles Johnson Jr., "Christian Abraham Fleetwood," in *Dictionary of American Negro Biography*, eds. Rayford W. Logan and Michael R. Winston (New York: W. W. Norton & Company, 1982), 123–24.

11 Letter, Christian A. Fleetwood to Dr. James Hall, June 8, 1865, Christian A. Fleetwood Papers, Manuscript Division, Library of Congress, Washington, DC.

12 "The Negro as a Soldier," written by Christian A. Fleetwood, Late Sergeant-Major 4th US Colored Troops, for the Negro Congress at the Cotton States and International Exposition, Atlanta, Georgia, November 11 to November 28, 1895 (Washington, DC: Howard University Print, 1895), 6.

13 Benjamin Butler, *Butler's Book: Autobiography and Personal Reminiscences of Major General Benjamin Butler* (Boston: AM Thayer & Co., 1892), 721–22; Letter, Asst. Adj. Gen. Edward W. Smith to Headquarters Department of Virginia and North Carolina, Army of the James, October 11, 1864, *OR*, Ser. I, Vol. 42, Part 3, 168–69; Chaplain (Col.) John Brinsfield, "The Battle of New Market Heights," *Soldiers* 51:2 (February 1996), 50; Barry Popcock, "A Shower of Stars at New Market Heights; Butler's 'Contrabands' Prove Their Mettle," *Civil War Magazine* 46 (August 1994), 34; Richard J. Sommers, *Richmond Redeemed: The Siege at Petersburg* (Garden City, NY: Doubleday & Company, 1981), 75–76; Letter, Milton Holland to the *Athens* (OH) *Messenger*, July 24, 1864, in *A Grand Army of Black Men*, 106; John E. Aliyetti, "Gallantry Under Fire," *Civil War Times Illustrated* 35:5 (October 1996), 53–54; www.history.army.mil/moh/civilwar_gl.html (accessed February 27, 2017); Letter, MG EOC, HQ, Department of VA, April 17, 1865, to AAG, Brevet Brig. Gen. E. D. Townsend, Record Group 94, Enlisted Branch, LR, 1862–1889, National

Archives and Records Administration II, College Park, MD (hereafter cited as NARA II); Maj. Augustus S. Boernstein, 4th USCT, Headquarters in the Field, VA, to AAG 3rd Division, 18th Army Corps, October 4, 1864, RG 94, NARA II.

14 Christian A. Fleetwood, "Thought Only of Saving the Flag," in *Deeds of Valor: From Records in the Archives of the United States Government; How American Heroes Won the Medal of Honor; History of Our Recent Wars and Explorations, From Personal Reminiscences and Records of Officers and Enlisted Men Who were Rewarded by Congress for Most Conspicuous Acts of Bravery on the Battlefield on the High Seas and in Arctic Explorations*, eds. W. F. Beyer and O. F. Keydel (Detroit, MI: The Perrien-Keydel Co., 1906), 434–35.

15 "Interview with Dorothy Franks," Archie P. McDonald, "Milton M. Holland," by Loblolly Staff, all in Jennifer Johnson, ed., *Milton M. Holland: Panola County Recipient of the Medal of Honor* (Gary, TX: Loblolly, Inc., 1992).

16 "Biographical Sketch: Andrew Jackson Smith," Frank N. Schubert Clipping File (in the possession of the author).

17 "The Battle of Honey Hill," *The Liberator* (December 16, 1864), 3; Charles B. Fox, *Record of the Service of the Fifty-Fifth Regiment of Massachusetts Volunteer Infantry* (Cambridge: Press of J. Wilson and Son, 1868), 41–43; Noah Andre Trudeau, ed., *Voices of the 55th: Letters from the 55th Massachusetts Volunteers, 1861–1865*, 25–27.

18 Andrew Smith, "Adventures of a Colored Boy in War," *National Tribune* (March 21, 1929); Letter, George S. Walker to Burt G. Wilder, October 1914; and Letter, Jordan M. Bobson to Burt Wilder, March 14, 1917, in *Voices of the 55th: Letters from the 55th Massachusetts Volunteers, 1861–1865*, 191, 130–35, 169–70; "Clinton Honors Ex-President, Ex-Slave," *Washington Post* (January 17, 2001), 10.

19 *Records of Medals of Honor Issued to the Officers, and Enlisted Men of the United States Navy, Marine Corps, and Coast Guard, 1862–1917* (Washington, 1917), 7, 79; Herbert Aptheker, "The Negro in the Union Navy," *Journal of Negro History* 32:2 (April 1947), 79; *Deeds of Valor*, vol. II, 61–62; David L. Valuska, "The Negro in the Union Navy: 1861–1865" (PhD dissertation, Lehigh University, 1973), 148–49.

20 Luis F. Emilio, *A Brave Black Regiment: The History of the Fifty-Fourth Regiment of Massachusetts Volunteer Infantry, 1863–1865* (New York: Da Capo Press, 1995), 324–25.

21 "Reception of the Toussaint Guards," *The Liberator* (September 15, 1865); "Reception of the 55th Massachusetts Regiment," *The Liberator* (September 29, 1865).

22 Andrew Smith, "Adventures of a Colored Boy in War," in Noah Andre Trudeau, ed., *Voices of the 55th: Letters from the 55th Massachusetts Volunteers, 1861–1865* (Dayton, OH: Morningside House, Inc., 1996), 191.

23 Claxton and Puls, *Uncommon Valor*, 156; Letter, Fleetwood to Hall, June 8, 1865; "The Negro as a Soldier," written by Christian A. Fleetwood, 18.

24 Butler, *Butler's Book*; George Sherman, "The Negro as a Soldier," in *Personal Narratives of Events in the War of the Rebellion, Being Papers Read Before the Rhode Island Soldiers and Sailors Historical Society* 7 ser. no. 7 (Providence, RI: The Society, 1913); Luis F. Emilio, *A Brave Black Regiment: The History of the Fifty-Fourth Regiment of Massachusetts Volunteer Infantry, 1863–1865* (Boston: Boston Book Company, 1894); Charles Fox, *Record of the Service of the Fifty-Fifth Regiment of Massachusetts Infantry*; Burt G. Wilder, *Fifty-Fifth Regiment of the Massachusetts Volunteer Infantry, Colored: June 1863–September 1865* (1914); "The Grand Army; News from the Departments-New Posts," *National Tribune* (July 24, 1890), 6.

25 "G.A.R. Committees; Colored Men Named to Assist in Welcoming Civil War Veterans to Washington, D.C.," *Washington Colored American* (August 30, 1902), 6; "Died Suddenly," *Washington Bee* (May 21, 1910), 1; "Washington Under the Calcium," *Washington Colored American* (September 27, 1902), 7; *Washington Bee* (June 4, 1892), 1; Johnson Jr., "Christian Abraham Fleetwood," in *Dictionary of American Negro Biography*, 224; "Medal of Honor Men," *Washington Evening Star* (August 20, 1905), 12.

CHAPTER 2: FRONTIER HONOR

1 George W. Ford, First Sergeant, 10th US Cavalry, "Winning the West," *Winners of the West* (April 1924).

2 W. E. B. Du Bois, *Medal of Honor Men Have Received Medals of Honor in United States Army and Navy*, reproduced from the Prints and Photographs Division, Library of Congress, Washington, DC; W. E. B. Du Bois, Official Records, United States Army and Navy Medal of Honor Men, reproduced from the Prints and Photographs Division, Library of Congress, Washington, DC; W. E. B. Du Bois, "The American Negro at Paris," *American Monthly Review of Reviews* 22:5 (November 1900), 575–77; for more on Du Bois's photographs and the commissioning of the American Negro Exhibit for the Paris Exhibition in 1900, please see David Levering Lewis, *W. E. B. Du Bois: Biography of a Race, 1868–1919* (New York: Henry Holt & Company, 1993); Shawn Michelle Smith, *American Archives: Gender, Race, and Class in Visual Culture* (Princeton, NJ: Princeton University Press, 1999); Shawn Michelle Smith, " 'Looking at One's Self through the Eyes of Others': W. E. B. Du Bois's Photographs for the 1900 Paris Exposition," *African American Review* 34:4 (Winter 2000), 581–99.

3 Russell Weigley, *History of the United States Army* (Bloomington: Indiana University Press, 1967, rep. 1984), 267; *Annual Report of the Secretary of War, 1866*, 3–4; Philip H. Sheridan, *Personal Memoirs of P. H. Sheridan, General United States Army*, vol. 2 (New York: Da Capo Press, 1992), 445–46; for more on Philip H. Sheridan, please see Paul A. Hutton, *Phil Sheridan and His Army* (Norman: University of Oklahoma Press, 1999).

4 Regimental Returns, 9th Cavalry, October 1866–February 1867, NARA RG 391 (M-744, Roll 87); Registers of Enlistments in the United States Army, 1798–1914, NARA, RG 94 (MIUSA1798_102891) (Fold3.com, accessed May 10, 2017); Grote Hutcheson, "The Ninth Regiment of Cavalry," 283–84; Patrick A. Bowmaster, "Buffalo Soldier Emanuel Stance Received Medal of Honor," *Wild West* 9:5 (February 1997).

5 Sergeant Emanuel Stance to Lieutenant B. M. Custer, Post Adjutant, Fort McKavett, May 26, 1870, LR, AGO, 1805–1889, NARA, RG 94 (M-929, Roll 2); Endorsement, Captain Henry Carroll, June 1, 1870, NARA, RG 94 (M-929, Roll 2); United States, Department of the Army, Public Information Division, *The Medal of Honor of the United States Army* (Washington, DC: USGPO, 1948), 214; Emanuel Stance to the Adjutant General, United States Army, July 24, 1870, LR, AGO, 1805 1889, NARA, RG 94 (M-929, Roll 2).

6 "General News Items," *Las Vegas Gazette* (May 5, 1877), 4 (downloaded from Newspapers.com on May 18, 2017); Monroe Lee Billington, *New Mexico's Buffalo Soldiers* (Boulder: University Press of Colorado, 1991), 51; General Orders No. 5, Post Adjutant, February, 5, 1877, Fort Bayard, New Mexico, Enlisted Branch, Letters Received, 1862–1889, NARA, RG 94 (M-929, Roll 2); Letter, Adjutant General to Chief Clerk, War Department, March 13, 1879, NARA, RG 94 (M-929, Roll 2).

7 "Clinton Greaves," in Irene Schubert and Frank N. Schubert, eds., *On the Trail of the Buffalo Soldier: New and Revised Biographies of African Americans in the U.S. Army, 1866–1917* (Lanham, MD: Rowman & Littlefield, 1995, rep. 2004), 117; Preston E. Amos, *Above and Beyond in the West: Black Medal of Honor Winners, 1870–1890* (Potomac Corral, The Westerners: Washington, DC, 1974), 8; for more on the efforts made by Wright and others to gain official recognition of Greaves's act of courage, see Frank N. Schubert's very insightful study titled *Black Valor: Buffalo Soldiers and the Medal of Honor, 1870–1898* (Wilmington, DE: Scholarly Resources, Inc., 1997), 46–48.

8 Frost Woodhull, "The Seminole Indian Scouts on the Border," *Frontier Times* 15 (December 1937), 119; Kenneth W. Porter, "The Seminole in Mexico, 1850–1861," *Hispanic American Historical Review* 31:1 (February 1951), 1–36; Kenneth W. Porter, "The Seminole Negro-Indian Scouts, 1870–1881," *Southwestern Historical Quarterly* 55:3 (January 1952), 361; William H. Brown, Wilson Brown, William Loren Katz, and Adam Paine, "Six 'New' Medal of Honor Men," *Journal of Negro History* 53:1 (January 1968), 79–80.

9 Report, 1st Lt. John L. Bullis, 24th Infantry, to Lt. G. W. Smith, 9th Cavalry, Post Adjutant, General Order 10, Headquarters Department of Texas, Fort Clark, Texas, April 27, 1875, NARA, RG 94 (M929, Roll 2).

10 John Allen Johnson, "The Medal of Honor and Sergeant John Ward and Private Pompey Factor," *Arkansas Historical Quarterly* 29:4 (Winter 1970), 372; Special Orders No. 113, Thomas Vincent, Assistant Adjutant General, Headquarters Department of Texas, San Antonio, Texas, May 31, 1879,

RG 94, Orders and Circulars, 1797–1910 (M929, Roll 2); Pompey Factor, Organization Index to Pension Files of Veterans Who Served Between 1861 and 1900, NARA T289, Pension Applications for Service in the US Army between 1861 and 1900, Grouped According to the Unit in Which the Veterans Served, Roll 754, Fold3.com (accessed May 31, 2017); Michael Bowlin, "Honoring Brave Deeds of Long Ago: Descendants Keep Scouts' Memory Alive at Gathering," *Kerrville Times* (May 3, 1992), 1.

11 Arlen L. Fowler, *The Black Infantry in the West, 1869–1891* (Westport, CT: Greenwood Publishing, 1971; rep. Norman: University of Oklahoma Press, 1996), 75, 82–86; Howard Roberts Lamar, *The Far Southwest, 1846–1912: A Territorial History* (New York: W. W. Norton & Company, 1970), 458–86; Larry T. Upton and Larry D. Ball, "Who Robbed Major Wham? Facts and Folklore behind Arizona's Great Paymaster Robbery," *Journal of Arizona History* 38 (Summer 1997).

12 "The Robbery Case: The Trial Now in Progress in the US Court; Major Wham, Lieutenant George S. Cartwright, Sergeant Brown on the Witness Stand," *Arizona Daily Star* (November 16, 1889), 4.

13 "The Wham Robbery; Witnesses Short, Young, Arrington, and Mays," *Arizona Daily Star* (November 17, 1889), 4. For an extended examination of the events surrounding the Wham Robbery of 1889, see Larry D. Ball, *Ambush at Bloody Run: The Wham Paymaster Robbery of 1889: A Story of Politics, Religion, Race, and Banditry in Arizona Territory* (Tucson: Arizona Historical Society, 2000). (I am grateful to Durwood Ball for bringing this to my attention.)

14 Letter, Maj. Joseph W. Wham, Paymaster, US Army, to the Secretary of War, September 1, 1889, Endorsement, AGO, General Correspondence File, 1890–1917, RG 94 (M-929, Roll 2).

15 Col. Zenas R. Bliss to Adj. Gen., USA, November 9, 1889; Memorandum, AGO to CO, 24th Infantry, February 27, 1890, all in AGO, General Correspondence File, 1890–1917, NARA, RG 94 (M-929, Roll 2).

16 Second Endorsement, Col. Robert Hall, Acting Inspector General, Department of Arizona, November 13, 1889, General Correspondence File, 1890–1917, NARA, RG 94 (M-929, Roll 2).

17 Memorandum, John C. Kelton, Adjutant General, January 28, 1890, AGO, General Correspondence File, 1890–1917, NARA, RG 94 (M-929, Roll 2).

18 United States, Department of the Army, Public Information Division, *The Medal of Honor of the United States Army* (Washington, DC: USGPO, 1948), 235. For more on the controversy surrounding the army's issuing of medals of honor to Benjamin Brown and Isaiah Mays, see Schubert, *Black Valor*, 97–98.

19 Frank N. Schubert, ed., *Voices of the Buffalo Soldier: Records, Reports, and Recollections of Military Life and Service in the West* (Albuquerque: University of New Mexico Press, 2003), 163–69.

20 General Court-Martial Orders 39, Headquarters Department of the Platte, Omaha, Nebraska, May 19–20, 1891, Exhibit A, Affidavit of John Denny, Fort Duchesne, Utah, May 8, 1881, all in

Records of the Office of the Judge Advocate General (Army), NARA, RG 153, Court-Martial Case Files, 1809–1894, (M-929, Roll 2).

21 *Army and Navy Journal* 25 (December 31, 1887), 442; E. J. Brooks, Acting Commissioner of Indian Affairs, to Secretary of the Interior, July 10, 1880, in AGO, LR, 1805–1889, NARA, RG 94 (M-929, Roll 2).

22 Irene Schubert and Frank N. Schubert, *On the Trail of the Buffalo Soldier: Biographies of African Americans in the U.S. Army, 1866–1917* (Wilmington, DE: Scholarly Resources, Inc., 1995), 117.

23 United States Department of the Army, The Medal of Honor of the United States Army (Washington, DC: USGPO, 1948), 235; NARA M233, Registers of Enlistments in the United States Army, 1798–1914, NARA, RG 94, Heitman's Register and Dictionary of the US Army, US Army Historical Register, Volume 2, Part III, Officers of Volunteer Regiments during the War with Spain and Philippine Insurrection, 1898 to 1903, 50; William McBryar, World War I Draft Registration Cards, Pennsylvania, Allegheny County, 1917–1918, William McBryar, World War II "Old Man's Draft" Registration Cards; www.fold3.com/search/#s_given_name=William&s_surname=McBryar&offset=12&preview=1 (Fold3.com, accessed September 29, 2017); US Civil War Pension Index: General Index to Pension Files, 1861–1934 for William McBryar, Pennsylvania, Death Certificates, 1906–1964 for William McBryar, www.ancestry.com/interactive/4654/32959_032958-04419?pid=5140158&usePUB=true (Ancestry.com, accessed September 29, 2017).

CHAPTER 3: "HONOR TO THE RACE"

1 Charles Young, *Military Morale of Nations and Races* (Kansas City, MO: Franklin Hudson Publishing Co., 1912), foreword.

2 George P. Marks, III, ed., *The Black Press Views American Imperialism, 1898–1900* (New York: Arno Press, 1971), 7–13; Kevin K. Gaines, *Uplifting the Race: Black Leadership, Politics, and Culture in the Twentieth Century* (Chapel Hill: University of North Carolina Press, 1996), 26–27; "Mrs. Ida Wells-Barnett Calls on President McKinley," *Cleveland Gazette* (April 9, 1898), in Herbert Aptheker, ed., *A Documentary History of the Negro People in the United States, Vol. 2: From the Reconstruction to the Founding of the N.A.A.C.P.* (New York: Citadel Press, 1951, rep. 1992), 798.

3 Marks, *The Black Press Views American Imperialism*, 29–30.

4 Edward L. Baker Jr., "The Environments of the Enlisted Man of the United States Army of Today," *Georgia Baptist* (April 13, 1899), 1.

5 Marvin Fletcher, *The Black Soldier and Officer in the United States Army, 1891–1917*, 34; Russell Weigley, *History of the United States Army*, 301–07; T. G. Steward, *Buffalo Soldiers: The Colored*

Regulars in the United States Army (Amherst, NY: Humanity Books, 1904, rep. 2003), 100–02; William G. Muller, *The Twenty-fourth Infantry, Past and Present.*

6 Report, 1st Lt. Carter P. Johnson, Tenth Cavalry, to Post Adj. Gen. W. H. Carter, February 18, 1899, NARA, RG 94 (M-929, Roll 3); United States, The Medal of Honor of the United States Army (Washington, DC: USGPO, 1948), 239; "George Henry Wanton," *Negro History Bulletin* (January 1, 1941), 87.

7 Letter, Johnson to W. H. Carter, February 18, 1899, NARA; Letter, U.S.V. Brig. Gen. Theo Lehman to Capt. George Ahern, February 25, 1899, NARA; Miles V. Lynk, *The Black Troopers; or, The Daring Heroism of the Negro Soldiers in the Spanish-American War* (New York: AMS Press, 1899, rep. 1971), 51–52; Letter, Asst. Adj. Gen. W. A. Simpson to George H. Wanton, June 23, 1899, NARA, RG 94 (M-929, Roll 3); Letter, Asst. Adj. Gen. W. A. Simpson to William H. Thompkins, June 23, 1899, NARA, RG 94 (M-929, Roll 3).

8 David F. Trask, *The War with Spain* (New York: Macmillan, 1981), 231, 238–40; Francis L. Lewis, "Negro Army Regulars in the Spanish-American War: Smoked Yankees at Santiago de Cuba," (MA thesis: University of Texas at Austin, 1969), 18–19; E. L. Glass, *The History of the Tenth Cavalry, 1866–1921* (Tucson, AZ: Acme Printing, 1921), 33; "Diary of Edward L. Baker, Sergeant Major Tenth Cavalry," cited in T. G. Steward, *Buffalo Soldiers: The Colored Regulars in the United States Army* (Philadelphia: A.M.E. Book Concern, 1904, rep. 2003), 258.

9 Frank N. Schubert, "Edward Lee Baker, Jr.," cited in Rayford W. Logan and Michael R. Winston, eds., *Dictionary of American Negro Biography*, 21; Chaplain C. C. Bateman, U.S.A., "Biographical Sketch of Edward L. Baker, Jr., undated, NARA, RG 94 (M-929, Roll 3); "Diary of Edward L. Baker, Sergeant Major Tenth Cavalry," 271–72.

10 Letter, William McBryar to the Secretary of War, February 3, 1905, NARA, RG 94 (M-929, Roll 2); Buffalo Soldier: First Sergeant Augustus Walley, www.fold3.com/page/732_buffalo_soldierfirst_sgt_augustus_walley#description (Fold3.com, accessed August 31, 2017).

11 Theodore Roosevelt, "The Rough Riders," *Scribner's Magazine* (April 1899); Buffalo Soldier: First Sergeant Augustus Walley, www.fold3.com/page/732_buffalo_soldierfirst_sgt_augustus_walley#description (Fold3.com, accessed August 31, 2017); Herschel V. Cashin, *Under Fire with the Tenth Cavalry* (Chicago: American Publishing House, 1902), 202.

12 David F. Trask, "Battle of San Juan Hill," in John Whiteclay Chambers II, et al., eds., *The Oxford Companion to American Military History* (New York: Oxford University Press, 1999), 635; Richard Harding Davis quoted in David F. Trask, *The War with Spain in 1898*, 239; "Diary of Edward L. Baker, Sergeant Major Tenth Cavalry," 262.

13 Walter Millis, *The Martial Spirit* (Cambridge: Riverside Press, 1931), 290–91; Trask, *The War with Spain in 1898*, 243; Horace B. Bivins, Letter to the Editor, *Southern Workman*, July 8, 1989, cited in Willard B. Gatewood Jr., *"Smoked Yankees" and the Struggle for Empire: Letters from*

Negro Soldiers, 1898–1902 (Urbana: University of Illinois Press, 1971), 49–50; W. H. Crogman, "The Negro Soldier in the Cuban Insurrection and Spanish-American War," in J. L. Nichols and William H. Crogman, eds., *Progress of a Race, or the Remarkable Advancement of the Negro* (Naperville, IL: J. L. Nichols, 1925), 131–38; Marcos E. Kinevan, Brigadier General, USAF (Ret.), *Frontier Cavalryman: Lieutenant John Bigelow with the Buffalo Soldiers in Texas* (El Paso, TX: Texas Western Press, 1998); Frank E. Vandiver, *Black Jack: The Life and Times of John J. Pershing*, vol. 1 (College Station: Texas A & M Press, 1977), 47–104, 136–51, 176–312.

14 "Diary of Edward L. Baker, Sergeant Major Tenth Cavalry," 262–66; Letter, 2nd Lt. Jacob C. Smith, 9th USV Infantry, to Theodore Baldwin, March 15, 1899, NARA, RG 94 (M-929, Roll 3).

15 "More Troops for Montauk; Rough Riders from Tampa and Three Cavalry Regiments from Georgia Arrive," *New York Times* (August 11, 1898), 2; "The Black Regiment," *New York World* (July 9, 1898), 1; Stephen Bonsal, "The Negro Soldier in War and Peace," *North American Review* (June 7, 1909), 186, 616; Edward A. Johnson, *History of the Negro Soldiers in the Spanish-American War* (Raleigh, NC: Capital Publishing Company, 1899), 85; "Men's Gift to Roosevelt," *New York Times* (September 14, 1898), 3.

16 "Brave as the Bravest," *Afro-American Sentinel* (July 30, 1898), 2; "Negro Officers for the Regular Army," The Fair Play (July 29, 1898), 1.

17 The term "immunes" refers to the nearly ten thousand black enlisted men and officers who served in the volunteer regiments during the war. At the time, many quarters of American society subscribed to the superstitious notion that African Americans possessed natural immunity to tropical diseases. Accordingly, state and federal units, along with the 24th Infantry, were assigned to work details in hospital quarters located in the United States and at Siboney during the course of the war. For more on these units, see Marvin Fletcher, "The Black Volunteers in the Spanish-American War," *Military Affairs* 38 (April 1974), 48–53; and Trask, *The War with Spain in 1898*, 311, 326.

18 Michael C. Robinson and Frank N. Schubert, "David Fagen: An Afro-American Rebel in the Philippines, 1899–1901," *Pacific Historical Review* 44:1 (February 1975), 71; Letter to the Editor, William Simms, 1901, cited in Gatewood Jr., *"Smoked Yankees" and the Struggle for Empire*, 237; Robinson and Schubert, "David Fagen," 71.

19 Individual Service Report, Special Orders No. 122, June 1, 1908, Proceedings of Examining Board, Case of 1st Lt. Edward L. Baker, July 9, 1908, Appendices A–C; Special Orders, Maj. Gen. J. Franklin Bell, Chief of Staff to the AGO, January 6, 1910, Memorandum, Commanding General to the AGO, August 27, 1913; General Correspondence File, 1890–1917, NARA, RG 94 (M-929, Roll 3); Frank N. Schubert, "Edward Lee Baker, Jr.," Logan and Winston, eds., *Dictionary of American Negro Biography*, 21.

20 Theodore Roosevelt, *The Rough Riders* (Dallas, TX: Taylor Publishing, 1997, rep., originally published as an article in *Scribner's Magazine* [April 1899]; Letter, Presley Holiday, *New York Age* (April 22, 1899), cited in Gatewood Jr., *"Smoked Yankees" and the Struggle for Empire*, 92–97; John D. Weaver, *The Brownsville Raid* (New York: W. W. Norton & Company, 1970); Marvin Fletcher, *The Black Soldier and Officer in the United States Army, 1891–1917* (Columbia, MO: University of Missouri Press, 1974), 160.

21 Irvin H. Lee, *Negro Medal of Honor Men*, 98; Frank Schubert, *Black Valor*, 141–42; War Department, Special Orders No. 260, November 4, 1914, Affidavit, Cpl. William Thompkins to Adj. Gen., June 27, 1902, Memorandum for Colonel Ennis, September 30, 1902, all in Adjutant General's Office, General Correspondence File, 1890–1917, NARA, RG 94 (M-929, Roll 3).

22 US Army Center of Military History, Medal of Honor Recipients, War with Spain, Robert Penn, www.history.army.mil/html/moh/warsspain.html (accessed on September 28, 2017).

23 Letter, Cora Taylor to President Theodore Roosevelt, January 22, 1906; Letter, National Commander of the Regular Army and Navy Union of the United States of America, Henry Shindler to the Adjutant General, October 6, 1899, all in Adjutant General's Office, General Correspondence File, 1890–1917, NARA, RG 94 (M-929, Roll 3); "Watchman Wears Medal of Honor," *Morning Call* (undated), Memorandum, George H. Wanton to Commanding Officer, Tenth Cavalry, August 6, 1915, Subject: Re-Enlistment as a Married Man, all in Orders and Circulars, 1797–1910, RG 94 (M-929, Roll 3); "George Henry Wanton," *Negro History Bulletin* (January 1, 1941), 87.

CHAPTER 4: CARRYING THE BANNER OF HOPE

1 Gregory L. Mixon, "The Atlanta Riot of 1906" (PhD dissertation, University of Cincinnati, 1989); Rayford W. Logan, *The Betrayal of the Negro: From Rutherford B. Hayes to Woodrow Wilson* (New York: Collier Books, 1965), 350; Nalty, *Strength for the Fight*, 90–97; Leon Litwack, *Trouble in Mind: Black Southerners in the Age of Jim Crow* (New York: Vintage Books), 370–73; C. Vann Woodward, *Origins of the New South, 1877–1913* (Baton Rouge: Louisiana State University Press, 1951), 218–21.

2 "William Monroe Trotter's Address to the President," cited in Herbert Aptheker, ed., *A Documentary History of the Negro People in the United States, Vol. 3: From the N.A.A.C.P. to the New Deal* (New York: Carol Publishing Group, 1973), 73–78; David M. Chalmers, *Hooded Americanism: The First Century of the Ku Klux Klan, 1865–1965* (Garden City, NY: Doubleday, 1965), 26–27; Logan, *The Betrayal of the Negro*, 362–63.

3 James Weldon Johnson, *Along This Way: The Autobiography of James Weldon Johnson* (New York: Da Capo Press, 1933, rep. 2000), 154–56; James Weldon Johnson, "Views and Reviews: Between the Devil and the Deep Sea," *New York Age* (September 27, 1917), 4.

4 James W. Johnson, "Views and Reviews: The Duty of the Hour," *New York Age* (April 5, 1917); Kathryn M. Johnson, "The Negro and the World War," *Half-Century* 2 (June 1917), 13; W. E. B. Du Bois, "Close Ranks," *The Crisis* 16 (July 1918), 111.

5 Letter, Maj. Gen. Tasker H. Bliss, Assistant to the Chief of Staff, to General Robert K. Evans, April 4, 1917; Memorandum, Maj. Gen. Tasker H. Bliss for the Secretary of War, September 7, 1917, Subject: Mobilization and Utilization of Colored Drafted Men, all in Morris J. MacGregor and Bernard C. Nalty, eds., *Blacks in the United States Armed Forces: Basic Documents, Vol. 4: Segregation Entrenched, 1917–1940* (Wilmington, DE: Scholarly Resources, Inc., 1977), 3–5.

6 Memorandum, Maj. Gen. Tasker H. Bliss, Acting Chief of Staff, for the Adjutant General, May 17, 1917, Subject: Officers' Training Camp for Colored Citizens, in MacGregor and Nalty, eds., *Blacks in the United States Armed Forces: Basic Documents, Vol. 4*, 101; Chad L. Williams, *Torchbearers of Democracy: African American Soldiers in the World War I Era* (Chapel Hill: University of North Carolina Press, 2010), 46.

7 "The Spingarn Medal Award and N.A.A.C.P. Conference," *Washington Bee* (May 12, 1917), 1; Letter, President Woodrow Wilson to Secretary of War Newton D. Baker, June 25, 1917; Letter, Secretary of War Newton D. Baker to President Wilson, June 26, 1917, Note, Secretary of War Newton Baker to General Tasker Bliss, June 1917; Letter, Secretary of War Newton Baker to President Woodrow Wilson, July 7, 1917, all in MacGregor and Nalty, eds., *Blacks in the United States Armed Forces: Basic Documents, Vol. 4*; "War Department Says Young Is Now Retired," *New York Age* (August 16, 1917), 1.

8 Fred Moore, "Editorial," *New York Age* (June 28, 1917), 4; "Lieutenant Colonel Young Is to Be Retired," *Chicago Defender* (June 30, 1917), 4; Letter, W. E. B. Du Bois to Lt. Col. Charles Young, June 28, 1917; Letter, Robert R. Moton to President Woodrow Wilson, July 7, 1917, Col. Charles Young Collection, Ohio Historical Society (online, accessed September 15, 2017); "What the N.A.A.C.P. Has Done for the Colored Soldier," *The Crisis* (1918), in Aptheker, ed., *A Documentary History of the Negro People in the United States*, Vol. 3, 207–08; "Colonel Young Visits War Department," *Chicago Defender* (July 6, 1917).

9 American Battle Monuments Commission, *92nd Division Summary of Operations in the World War* (Washington, DC: US Government Printing Office, 1944), 1, 34–36; American Battle Monuments Commission, *93rd Division Summary of Operations in the World War* (Washington, DC: US Government Printing Office, 1944), 1–4, 35–36.

10 Jeffrey T. Sammons and John H. Morrow Jr., *Harlem's Rattlers and the Great War: The Undaunted 369th Regiment and the African American Quest for Equality* (Lawrence: University Press of Kansas, 2014), 97–98.

11 J. Victor, "Henry Johnson's Paradox: A Soldier's Story," *Afro-Americans in New York Life and History* 21:2 (July 1997), 7; Henry Johnson, World War I Draft Registration Card, Registration State; Albany, Roll 1711816, Draft Board: 2, Ancestry.com, US, World I Draft Registration Cards, 1917–1918 [database online], Provo, UT, USA (Ancestry.com, accessed September 20, 2017); Arthur E. Barber and Florette Henri, *The Unknown Soldiers: Black American Troops in World War* I (Philadelphia: Temple University Press, 1974); Emmett J. Scott, *Scott's Official History of the American Negro in the World War* (Chicago: Homewood Press, 1919), 256–59.

12 Sammons and Morrow, *Harlem's Rattlers and the Great War*, 98; Chester D. Heywood, *Negro Combat Troops in the World War, The Story of the 371st Infantry* (Worcester, MA: Commonwealth Press, 1928), 3–4; 13; W. Allison Sweeney, *History of the American Negro in the Great World War* (Chicago: Cuneo-Henneberry, 1919), 131.

13 Monroe Mason and Arthur Furr, *The American Negro Soldier with the Red Hand of France* (Boston: Cornhill Company, 1920), 27–28; Arthur W. Little, *From Harlem to the Rhine: The Story of New York's Colored Volunteers* (New York: Civic Press, 1936), 35, 12–13.

14 Little, *From Harlem to the Rhine*, 54–71; Sammons and Morrow, *Harlem's Rattlers and the Great War*, 158–68.

15 Scott, *Scott's Official History of the American Negro in the World War*, 81; for more on this incident, please see Richard Slotkin, *Lost Battalions: The Great War and the Crisis of American Nationality* (New York: Henry Holt and Company, 2005), 123–25.

16 Scott, *Scott's Official History of the American Negro in the World War*, 199; Little, *From Harlem to the Rhine*, 97.

17 Scott, *Scott's Official History of the American Negro in the World War*, 201.

18 Cable History of the Subject Colored Soldiers, compiled by the Cable Section, General Staff, Cable from Pershing, #P. 454, January 5, 28, 1918, in MacGregor and Nalty, eds., *Blacks in the United States Armed Forces: Basic Documents, Vol. 4*, 135; William S. Braddan, *Under Fire with the 370th Infantry (8th I.N.G.) A.E.F.: Memoirs of the World War* (Chicago, n.d.), 44.

19 Michael Howard, *The First World War* (New York: Oxford University Press, 2002), 99–100; Little, *From Harlem to the Rhine*, 99–100; John J. Pershing, *My Experiences in the World War, Vol. 1* (New York: Frederick A. Stokes Company, 1931), 291.

20 American Battle Monuments Commission, *93rd Division, Summary of Operations in the World War*, 5–6; Scipio, *With the Red Hand Division*, 43–45; W. Allison Sweeney, *History of the American Negro in the Great War: His Splendid Record in the Battle Zones of Europe* (New York: Negro Universities Press, 1919, rep. 1969), 138; Needham Roberts, "Brief Adventures of the First American Soldiers Decorated in the World as Told by Needham Roberts," 4; Chester D. Heywood, *Negro Combat Troops in the World War: The Story of the 371st Infantry* (New York: Negro Universities Press, 1928, 1969), 50.

21 American Battle Monuments Commission, *93rd Division, Summary of Operations in the World War*, 4-8; Little, *From Harlem to the Rhine*, 176–79; Slotkin, *Lost Battalions*, 138

22 Freddie Stowers in the US Army Transport Service, Passenger Lists, 1910–1939, NARA, NAI Number: 6234477, RG 92: Records of the Office of the Quartermaster General, 1774–1985, Roll 534 (Ancestry.com, accessed September 11, 2017); "The Weather," *Newport News Daily Press* (April 7, 1918), 1; Scott, *Scott's Official History of the American Negro in the World War*, 231–32; Braddan, *Under Fire with the 370th Infantry*, 51.

23 Year: 1910; Census Place: Pendleton, Anderson, South Carolina; Roll: T624_1449; Page 14A; Enumeration District: 0058; FHL microfilm: 1375462; Ancestry.com. 1910 Federal Census [database online]. Provo, UT, USA (Ancestry.com, accessed September 11, 2017); Freddie Stowers in the US Army Transport Service, Passenger Lists, 1910–1939, NARA, NAI Number: 6234477, RG 92.

24 American Battle Monuments Commission, *93rd Division, Summary of Operations in the World War*, 5–9.

25 Heywood, *Negro Combat Troops in the World War*, 55.

26 Scipio, *With the Red Hand Division*, 75–79.

27 Heywood, *Negro Combat Troops in the World War*, 162–68; Taylor V. Beattie, "Seventy-Three Years After His Bayonet Assault on Hill 188, Freddie Stowers Got His Medal of Honor," *Military History* (August 2004), 74–76.

28 Slotkin, *Lost Battalions*, 482–84.

29 Victor, "Henry Johnson's Paradox: A Soldier's Story," 7; "Taps Sounded for William H. Johnson, Greatest of World War Heroes; Famous Infantryman Died Recently in Poverty—His and Needham Roberts's Exploits Recalled," *New York Amsterdam News* (July 10, 1929), 1; Michael D. Shear, "Two World War I Soldiers Posthumously Receive Medal of Honor," *New York Times* (June 2, 2015), A11.

30 Shear, "Two World War I Soldiers," A11.

CHAPTER 5: SEIZING THE HERO'S MANTLE

1 "Welcome War Hero at Wyoming Chapel," *Chicago Defender* (March 22, 1947), 19A.

2 Ulysses G. Lee, *The Employment of Negro Troops* (CreateSpace, 2014), 15–50.

3 Jean Byers, "A Study of the Negro in Military Service (June 1947), 7.

4 Phillip McGuire, "Desegregation of the Armed Forces: Black Leadership, Protest, and World War II," *Journal of Negro History* 68:2 (Spring 1983), 147–58.

5 Helen K. Black and William H. Thompson, "A War within a War: A World War II Buffalo Soldier's Story," *Journal of Men's Studies* 20:1 (Winter 2012), 37.

6 Lee, *The Employment of Negro Troops*, 499.

7 Ronald H. Spector, *Eagle Against the Sun: The American War with Japan* (New York: Vintage Books, 1985), 143–44; Lee, *The Employment of Negro Troops*, 497; Nalty, *Strength for the Fight*, 166–67.

8 Spector, *Eagle Against the Sun*, 143; Hildrus A. Poindexter, *My World of Reality* (Detroit: Balamp Publishing, 1973), 127.

9 George Watson, Selective Service Registration Cards, World War II: Multiple Registration, NARA, www.fold3.com/image/605284691 (accessed November 7, 2017); George Watson, Medal of Honor Recipients, 1863–2013 (Washington, DC: US Government Printing Office, 2013), www.fold3.com/image/310761175?terms=George%20Watson (accessed November 7, 2017).

10 Lee, *The Employment of Negro Troops*, 660–61; Gina M. DiNicolo, *The Black Panthers: A Story of Race, War, and Courage: The 761st Tank Battalion in World War II* (Yardley, PA: Westholme Publishing, 2014), 138–41; Trezzvant Anderson, *Come Out Fighting: The Epic Tale of the 761st Tank Battalion, 1942–1945* (Germany: Salzburg, Druckerei and Verlag, 1945), 15, 21.

11 Joe W. Wilson, *The 761st "Black Panther" Tank Battalion in World War II* (Jefferson, NC: McFarland & Company, 1999), 53.

12 George Watson, Selective Service Registration Cards, NARA; Pvt. George Watson, Internet Archive WayBack Machine, https:msc.navy.mil/inventory/citations/watson.html; PFC Willy James, US World War II Draft Cards Young Men, 1940–1947, Ancestry.com (accessed October 16, 2017), Willy James, Find-A-Grave.com, Ruben Rivers, Find-A-Grave.com (accessed October 16, 2017).

13 Lee, *The Employment of Negro Troops*, 664; Ruben Rivers, Medal of Honor Recipients, 1979–2013 (Washington, DC: US Government Printing Office, 2013), www.fold3.com/image/310761170 (accessed November 8, 2017).

14 "He Bled for It: Captain Gets DSC in France," *Pittsburgh Courier* (March 24, 1945), 1, 4; Charles L. Thomas, Medal of Honor Recipients, 1979–2013 (Washington, DC: US Government Printing Office, 2013), www.fold3.com/image/310761173 (accessed November 8, 2017).

15 Lee, *The Employment of Negro Troops*, 536–37.

16 Lee, *The Employment of Negro Troops*, 536–37; Jehu C. Hunter, "Triumph and Tribulation: Reflections on the Combat Experience of the 92nd Infantry," *Proceedings of the First Conference on Black Americans in World War II* (Carlisle Barracks, PA: US Military History Institute, September 9, 1992), 4–5.

17 Hunter, "Triumph and Tribulation," 5–6.

18 Hondon B. Hargrove, *Buffalo Soldiers in Italy: Black Americans in World War II* (Jefferson, NC: McFarland & Company, Inc., 1985), 53–65.

19 John R. Fox, Medal of Honor Recipients, 1979–2013 (Washington, DC: US Government Printing Office, 2013), www.fold3.com/image/310761158 (accessed November 8, 2017); Elliott V. Converse III, Daniel K. Gibran, John A. Cash, Robert K. Griffith Jr., and Richard H. Kohn, *The Exclusion of Black Soldiers from the Medal of Honor in World War II* (Jefferson, NC: McFarland & Company, Inc., 1997), 124; Dennette A. Harrod, "The 336th Infantry and Lieutenant John R. Fox," *Proceedings of the First Conference on Black Americans in World War II* (Carlisle Barracks, PA: US Military History Institute, September 9, 1992), 21.

20 Charles Thomas, Year: 1940; Census Place: Detroit, Wayne, Michigan, Roll: T627_1868; Page: 1B; Enumeration District: 84-954; Ancestry.com. 1940 United States Federal Census [database online], Provo, UT, USA.; Baker, *Lasting Valor*, 123–25.

21 Hargrove, *Buffalo Soldiers in Italy*, 149–52; Lee, *The Employment of Negro Troops*, 580–82.

22 Memorandum, 1st Lt. Vernon Baker to the Commanding General, 92nd Infantry Division (Through Channels), Subject: Narrative of Action, April 5, 195), June 12, 1945, File: Top Secret: 92nd Infantry Division Combat Efficiency Analysis and Supplementary Report, Military Field Branch, NARA II, Suitland, Maryland; "92nd Officer is Awarded DSC; 9 Others Cited," *Chicago Defender* (July 14, 1945), 1; Vernon J. Baker, Medal of Honor Recipients: 1979–2013 (Washington, DC: US Government Printing Office, 2013), www.fold3.com/image/310761154 (accessed November 7, 2017); Baker, *Lasting Valor*, 1.

23 Lee, *The Employment of Negro Troops*; Nalty, *Strength for the Fight*, 176–77.

24 "Edward A. Carter II," Arlington National Cemetery Website, Fold3.com, https:www.fold3.com/image/310761155 (accessed October 30, 2017); Allene G. Carter and Robert L. Allen, *Honoring Sergeant Carter: Redeeming a Black World War II Hero's Legacy* (New York: HarperCollins, 2003), 79–91.

25 Carter and Allen, *Honoring Sergeant Carter*, 98–101.

26 Edward A. Carter Jr., Sergeant, US Army, Courtesy of the Pentagram, January 17, 1997 (accessed November 7, 2017).

27 Edward A. Carter, Medal of Honor Recipients: 1979–2013, www.fold3.com/image/310761155 (accessed November 7, 2017); "Kills Six . . . Gets DSC," *Pittsburgh Courier* (December 8, 1945), 21.

28 Willy F. James Jr., Medal of Honor Recipients: 1979–2013 (Washington, DC: US Government Printing Office, 2013), www.fold3.com/image/310761161 (accessed November 7, 2017); "President Honors and Commemorates Veterans in Margraten, The Netherlands," Press Release, Office of the Press Secretary, The White House, President George W. Bush, March 8, 2005.

29 Letter, Maj. Gen. Edward M. Almond to Maj. Gen. A. V. Arnold, Army Ground Forces Headquarters, January 21, 1948, File: Top Secret: 92nd Infantry Division Combat Efficiency Analysis and Supplementary Report, Military Field Branch, NARA II, Suitland, Maryland.

30 Carter and Allen, *Honoring Sergeant Carter: Redeeming a Black World War II Hero's Legacy*, 117–33.

31 Baker, *Lasting Valor*, 241.

32 "92nd Officer Is Awarded DSC; 9 Others Cited," *Chicago Defender* (July 14, 1945), 1; Baker, *Lasting Valor*, 3, 23–24, 39–41, 85–91.

CHAPTER 6: COLD WAR CIVIL RIGHTS WARRIORS

1 "U.S. Names Ship for Bronxite; Posthumous Honor for Korea Hero," *New York Amsterdam News* (July 12, 1952), 2; "Honoring Memory of Korean War Hero," *New York Times* (July 9, 1952), 3.

2 For example, see Richard J. Stillman, *Integration of the Negro in the U.S. Army Forces* (New York: Praeger, 1968); Lee Bogart, ed., *Project Clear: Social Research and the Desegregation of the United States Army* (New York: Markham, 1969; rep., New Brunswick, NJ: Transaction, 1991); Richard Dalfiume, *Desegregation of the U.S. Armed Forces: Fighting on Two Fronts, 1939–1953* (Columbia: University of Missouri Press, 1969); Morris J. MacGregor, *Defense Studies: Integration of the Armed Forces* (Washington, DC: Center of Military History, 1981); Nalty, *Strength for the Fight*; and, more recently, John Sibley Butler, "African Americans in the Military," in John Whiteclay Chambers II, ed., *The Oxford Companion to American Military History* (New York: Oxford University Press, 1999), 7–9.

3 Roy E. Appleman, *South to the Naktong, North to the Yalu: U.S. Army in the Korean War, June–November 1950* (Washington, DC: Office of the Chief of Military History, Department of the Army, 1961). For important correctives to this interpretation, please see Clair Blair, *The Forgotten War: America in Korea, 1950–1953* (New York: Times Books, 1987); Selika M. Ducksworth, "What Hour of the Night: Black Enlisted Men's Experiences and the Desegregation of the Army During the Korean War, 1950–1951" (PhD dissertation, Ohio State University, 1993); Charles M. Bussey, *Firefight at Yechon: Courage and Racism in the Korean War* (Lincoln: University of Nebraska Press, 2002); William T. Bowers, William M. Hammond, and George L. MacGarrigle, *Black Soldier, White Army: The 24th Infantry Regiment in Korea* (Washington, DC: Center of Military History, 1996); Kimberley L. Phillips, *War! What Is It Good For? Black Freedom Struggles and the U.S. Military from World War II to Iraq* (Chapel Hill: University of North Carolina Press, 2012); and Christine Knauer, *Let Us Fight as Free Men: Black Soldiers and Civil Rights* (Philadelphia: University of Pennsylvania Press, 2014).

4 Phillips, *War! What is It Good For?*, 116; Herbert Shapiro, *White Violence and Black Response: From Reconstruction to Montgomery* (Amherst: University of Massachusetts Press, 1988), 355–77.

5 Morris J. MacGregor Jr., *Integration of the Armed Forces, 1940–1965* (Washington, DC: Center of Military History, 1981), 152–63; Bowers, Hammond, and MacGarrigle, *Black Soldier, White Army,* 31–32.

6 MacGregor, *Integration of the Armed Forces, 1940–1965,* 153–55.

7 MacGregor, *Integration of the Armed Forces, 1940–1965,* 153–55; Executive Order 9981, July 26, 1948, and the President's News Conference of July 26, 1948, cited in Morris J. MacGregor and Bernard C. Nalty, eds., *Blacks in the United States Armed Forces,* Vol. 8, items 164–65 (Wilmington, DE: Scholarly Resources, 1977).

8 Bowers, Hammond, and MacGarrigle, *Black Soldier, White Army,* 37; Memorandum, President's Committee on Equality of Treatment and Opportunity in the Armed Services for Secretary of the Army, September 8, 1949, Subject: Substitution of a General Classification Test Quota for a Racial Quota, in MacGregor and Nalty, eds., *Blacks in the United States Armed Forces,* Vol. 11, item 22; Bussey, *Firefight at Yechon,* 42–44.

9 "24th Regiment Lands in Korea," *Atlanta Daily World* (July 20, 1950), 1; Appleman, *South to the Naktong, North to the Yalu,* 7–18; Roy Flint, "Korean War," in John Whiteclay Chambers II, ed., *The Oxford Companion to American Military History* (New York: Oxford University Press, 1999), 369–73; L. Albert Scipio, *Last of the Black Regulars: A History of the 24th Infantry Regiment (1869–1951),* 85–87.

10 Bowers, Hammond, and MacGarrigle, *Black Soldier, White Army,* 84–85.

11 Appleman, *South to the Naktong, North to the Yalu,* 270.

12 Bowers, Hammond, and MacGarrigle, *Black Soldier, White Army,* 130.

13 Bowers, Hammond, and MacGarrigle, *Black Soldier, White Army,* 130; "Negro Soldier Wins Medal of Honor in Korea," *Chicago Daily Tribune* (June 14 1951), 2.

14 "Negro Soldier Wins Medal of Honor in Korea," 2.

15 Appleman, *South to the Naktong, North to the Yalu,* 270; Bowers, Hammond, and MacGarrigle, *Black Soldier, White Army,* 131; "Negro Soldier Wins Medal of Honor in Korea," 2.

16 Edward F. Murphy, *Korean War Heroes* (Novato, CA: Presidio Press, 1997), 21–22; Joan Potter, *African American Firsts: Famous Little-Known and Unsung Triumphs of Blacks in America* (New York: Kensington Books, 2009), 243; William Thompson in the U.S. World War II Army Enlistment Records, 1983–1946, Ancestry.com. *U.S. World War II Army Enlistment Records, 1938–1946* [database online], Provo, UT, USA: Ancestry.com, 2005; Catherine Reef, *African Americans in the Military* (New York: Facts on File, Inc. 2010); Venice T. Spraggs, "Second Hero of Korea Gets Medal of Honor," *Chicago Defender* (February 23, 1952), 1–2; West Virginia Veterans Memorial, Remember . . . Cornelius H. Charlton, 1929–1951, West Virginia Division of Culture and History.

17 Bowers, Hammond, and MacGarrigle, *Black Soldier, White Army*, 253–56; Cornelius H. Charlton in the World War I, World War II, and Korean War Casualty Listings, Ancestry.com [database online], Provo, UT, USA.

18 "Sergeant Wins Honor Medal: Bravery in Korea Awarded," *Los Angeles Sentinel* (February 14, 1952), A1; "*Redbook* Magazine Features Negro Hero," *Atlanta Daily World* (May 15, 1953), 5; "Progress of Anti-Bias Told at Medal of Honor Presentation," *Atlanta Daily World* (March 18, 1952), 1; Venice T. Spraggs, "Second Hero of Korea Gets Medal of Honor," *Chicago Defender* (February 23, 1952),1; "Receives His Son's Medal for Heroism," *New York Times* (March 13, 1952), 6.

19 Shawn Pogatchnik, "After 39 Years, a Town Honors Its Black Hero," *Los Angeles Times* (May 28, 1990), 3.

20 For more on this, please see Bowers, Hammond, and MacGarrigle, *Black Soldier, White Army*.

CHAPTER 7: SOLDIERS IN THE SECOND INDOCHINA WAR

1 Gerald Faris, "Remembering a Medal of Honor Marine," *Los Angeles Times* (May 6, 1984), SB1.

2 Faris, "Remembering a Medal of Honor Marine"; "James Anderson Jr.," George Lang, Raymond L. Collins, and Gerard F. White, comp., *Medal of Honor Recipients: 1863–1994, Vol. II: World War II to Somalia* (New York: Facts on File, Inc., 1995), 657; Gary L. Telfer, Lane Rogers, and V. Keith Fleming Jr., *U.S. Marines in Vietnam: Fighting the North Vietnamese, 1967* (Washington, DC: History and Museums Division Headquarters, 1984), 9–12.

3 "Vietnam War Medal of Honor Recipients (A–L) Medal of Honor Citations, US Army Center of Military History (accessed November 28, 2017); "James Anderson Jr."

4 "U.S. Gives First Medal of Honor to a Negro Marine," *New York Times* (August 22, 1968), 3; "Marines Honor Former Harbor College Student Who Gave Life," *Los Angeles Sentinel* (June 20, 1985), A4.

5 Charles C. Moskos Jr., "The American Dilemma in Uniform: Race in the Military," *The Annals of the American Academy of Political and Social Science, Vol. 406: The Military and American Society* (March 1973), 94–106; James Westheider, *African Americans and the Vietnam War: Fighting on Two Fronts* (New York: New York University Press, 1997).

6 Nalty, *Strength for the Fight*, 276–81; MacGregor, *Integration of the Armed Forces*, 504.

7 MacGregor, *Integration of the Armed Forces*, 501–22.

8 MacGregor, *Integration of the Armed Forces*, 522; Eric Pace, "Percentage of Negroes Drafted Is Higher than that for Whites," *New York Times* (January 3, 1966), 6.

9 MacGregor, *Integration of the Armed Forces*, 568; President's Task Force on Manpower Commission, *One-Third of a Nation: A Report on Young Men Found Unqualified for Military Service* (Washington, DC: US Government Printing Office, 1964).

10 President's Task Force on Manpower Commission, *One-Third of a Nation*; Office Secretary of Defense, *Project One Hundred Thousand: Characteristics and Performance of "New Standards" Men, September 1968* (Washington, DC: US Government Printing Office, 1968); Benjamin Welles, "Negroes Expected to Make Up 30% of Draft 'Salvage,'" *New York Times* (August 25, 1966), 1.

11 Thomas Meehan, "Moynihan of the Moynihan Report," *New York Times* (July 31, 1966), 54.

12 "The Negro Soldier," *Chicago Defender* (March 18, 1967), 12; "Draft System Seen [as] Unfair to Negroes," *Los Angeles Times* (May 5, 1967), G5.

13 "Powell Rips Draft," *New York Amsterdam News* (May 14, 1966), 1; "Dr. King Calls Draft Unfair to U.S. Negro," *New York Times* (November 3, 1966), 29; Whitney M. Young Jr., "The Negro and the Armed Forces," *New York Amsterdam News* (April 1, 1967), 12.

14 "Nation's Newest War Hero Is Product of N.C. Slums," *Danville Register* (March 10, 1967), 1; "Lawrence Joel," in George Lang, Raymond L. Collins, and Gerard F. White, comp., *Medal of Honor Recipients: 1863–1994, Vol. II: World War II to Somalia* (New York: Facts on File, Inc., 1995), 700.

15 Graham A. Cosmas, *United States Army in Vietnam, MACV: The Joint Command in the Years of Escalation, 1962–1967* (Washington, DC: Center of Military History, 2006), 217–18.

16 "Vietnam War Medal of Honor Recipients (A–L) Medal of Honor Citations, US Army Center of Military History (accessed November 28, 2017); "Lawrence Joel," in Lang, Collins, and White, comp., *Medal of Honor Recipients: 1863–1994, Vol. II*, 700; "Nation's Newest War Hero Is Product of N.C. Slums," 1; "Although Wounded, He Heard Their Pleas, Saving 13," *Danville Register* (November 18, 1966), 1.

17 "President Gives Medal of Honor to Medic," *New York Times* (March 10, 1967), 20; Walter Rugaber, "Winston-Salem Hails Negro Hero," *New York Times* (April 9, 1967), 8.

18 Cosmas, *MACV: The Joint Command in the Years of Escalation*, 234–35.

19 Ward Just, "30,000 Dead Caused Little Notice, Comment," *Anniston Star* (December 18, 1968), 1D.

20 Vietnam War Medal of Honor Recipients (M–Z), Medal of Honor Citations, US Army Center of Military History (accessed November 28, 2017); "Riley Leroy Pitts," in Lang, Collins, and White, comp., *Medal of Honor Recipients: 1863–1994, Vol. II*, 731–32; "The Newsmakers: Reason for Pride–Heroism in Vietnam," *Los Angeles Times* (December 11, 1968), M2; "Coca-Cola Underwrites OU Scholarship; Honors First Black Congressional Medal of Honor Recipient," *New Pittsburgh Courier* (April 29, 1995), 1.

21 USA (Ret). Ira A. Hunt Jr., *The 9th Infantry Division in Vietnam: Unparalleled and Unequaled* (Lexington: University Press of Kentucky, 2010).

22 Hunt, *The 9th Infantry Division in Vietnam*. "Oral History Interview with Clarence Sasser," US Army Medical Department, http://ameddregiment.amedd.army.mil/moh/bios/sasserInt.html (accessed November 28, 2017).

23 "Oral History Interview with Clarence Sasser."

24 Vietnam War Medal of Honor Recipients (M–Z) Medal of Honor Citations; "Clarence Eugene Sasser" in Lang, Collins, and White, comp., *Medal of Honor Recipients: 1863–1994, Vol. II*, 739–40; "Oral History Interview with Clarence Sasser."

25 Clarence Sasser, Medal of Honor Recipient, "Stories of Valor," Public Broadcasting System, www.pbs.org/weta/americanvalor/stories/sasser.html (accessed November 28, 2017); "Nixon Presents Medals of Honor to 3 Soldiers Who Fought in Vietnam," *New York Times* (March 8, 1969), 10; "Oral History Interview with Clarence Sasser."

26 Graham A. Cosmas, *MACV: The Joint Command in the Years of Withdrawal, 1968–1973* (Washington, DC: Center of Military History, 2007), 13–14.

27 Jeff Edwards, "Charles Rogers: Medal of Honor Recipient," https://m.warhistoryonline.com/?s=Charles+Rogers%3A+Medal+of+Honor+ (accessed November 28, 2017).

28 Vietnam War Medal of Honor Recipients (M–Z) Medal of Honor Citations.

29 Richard Nixon, "Remarks on Awarding the Congressional Medal of Honor to Twelve Members of the Armed Services, May 14, 1970, online, by Gerhard Peters and John T. Woolley, *The American Presidency Project*, www.presidency.ucsb.edu/ws/?pid=27552 (accessed November 28, 2017).

30 Vietnam War Medal of Honor Recipients (A-L) Medal of Honor Citations.

31 Lea Sitton Stanley, *Philadelphia Inquirer* (April 8, 1997), B1.

32 James E. Westheider, "African Americans, Civil Rights, and the Armed Forces during the Vietnam War," in Douglas Walter Bristol Jr. and Heather Marie Stur, eds., *Integrating the U.S. Military: Race, Gender, and Sexual Orientation Since World War II* (Baltimore: Johns Hopkins University Press, 2017), 96–121; David Parks, *GI Diary* (Washington, DC: Howard University Press, 1968, rep. 1984), 105–06; "Honor Winners Back War Effort," *Florence Morning News* (April 16, 1967), 8A.

33 Edward J. Boyer, "Vietnam's Heartbreak Played Out in a Hero's Tragedy," *Los Angeles Times* (November 11, 2000), B1.

34 Vietnam War Medal of Honor Recipients (A-L) Medal of Honor Citations.

35 Jon Nordheimer, "From Dakto to Detroit: Death of a Troubled Hero," *New York Times* (May 26, 1971), 1.

EPILOGUE: KEEPING THE FAITH

1 President George H. W. Bush Public Papers, Remarks at a Ceremony for the Posthumous Presentation of the Medal of Honor to Corporal Freddie Stowers, April 24, 1991, George Bush Presidential Library and Museum, https://bush41library.tamu.edu/archives/public-papers/2916 (accessed November 30, 2017); Jim DuPlessis, "Bush Pays Tribute to Black Soldier Who Led Charge," *Greenville News* (April 25, 1991), 1; Donnie Radcliffe, "At Last, a Black Badge of Courage," *Washington Post* (April 25, 1991), C3.

2 Elliott V. Converse III, Daniel K. Gibran, John A. Cash, Robert K. Griffith Jr., and Richard H. Kohn, *The Exclusion of Black Soldiers from the Medal of Honor in World War II*, 3–5; Baker, *Lasting Valor*, 286.

3 "Veteran Receives Medal of Honor Decades Later," Tell Me More, Washington, DC: NPR (February 26, 2014); "Florida Man Shocked to Learn of Medal of Honor," *Gainesville Sun* (February 22, 2014), 1.

4 Ibid.

5 Jada Smith, "Medals of Honor Go to 24 Veterans Who Had Been Denied," *New York Times* (March 19, 2014), A15.

APPENDIX

1 *Cleveland Daily Leader* (October 3, 1864); *The Liberator* (October 14, 1864); *Columbus Daily Ohio Statesman* (October 19, 1864); Thomas Morris Chester, "Chapin's Bluff, 5 1/2 Miles from Richmond," October 5, 1864, in R. J. M. Blackett, ed., *Thomas Morris Chester, Black Civil War Correspondent: His Dispatches from the Virginia Front* (Baton Rouge: Louisiana State University Press, 1989), 140, 151; Proceedings of the National Convention of Colored Men, held in the City of Syracuse, New York, October 4–8, 1864, with the Bill of Wrongs and Rights and the Address to the American People, in Howard H. Bell, ed., *Minutes of the Proceedings of the National Negro Conventions, 1830–1864* (New York: Arno Press, 1969), 1–62.

2 W. E. B. Du Bois, "Politics," *The Crisis* 4 (August 1912), 180–81. For more on Du Bois's thinking about Wilson, please see David Levering Lewis's masterful biography, titled *W. E. B. Du Bois: Biography of a Race, 1868–1919* (New York: Henry Holt and Company, 1993).

3 Woodrow Wilson to Bishop Alexander Bishop, nd., cited in Aptheker, ed., *A Documentary History of the Negro People in the United States*, Vol. 3.

4 Clark Flint Kellogg, *NAACP: A History of The National Association for the Advancement of Colored People, Vol. 1: 1909–1920* (Baltimore: Johns Hopkins University Press, 1967); Deborah Gray White, *Too Heavy a Load: Black Women in Defense of Themselves* (New York: Norton,

1999); Stephen R. Fox, *The Guardian of Boston: William Monroe Trotter* (New York: Atheneum, 1970); Alfreda M. Duster, ed., *Crusade for Justice: The Autobiography of Ida B. Wells* (Chicago: University of Chicago Press, 1970), 375–77.

5 Kevin K. Gaines, *Uplifting the Race: Black Leadership, Politics, and Culture in the Twentieth Century* (Chapel Hill: University of North Carolina Press, 1996), 14.

6 Garna L. Christian, *Black Soldiers in Jim Crow Texas, 1899–1917* (College Station: Texas A & M University Press, 1995) and Robert V. Haynes, *A Night of Violence: The Houston Riot of 1917* (Baton Rouge: Louisiana State University Press, 1976).

7 Robert F. Jefferson, *Fighting for Hope: African American Troops of the 93rd Infantry Division in World War II and Postwar America* (Baltimore: Johns Hopkins University Press, 2008), 33–34; "Should I Sacrifice to Live 'Half American'?: Suggest Double V V for Double Victory Against Axis Forces and Ugly Prejudices on the Home Front," *Pittsburgh Courier* (January 31, 1942), 3.

8 Bussey, *Firefight at Yechon*, 13–69; Lt. Gen. Julius Becton Jr., *Autobiography of Becton: A Soldier and Public Servant* (Annapolis, MD: Naval Institute Press), 23–31.

9 "Gillem Report Called Failure by Roy Wilkins," *Chicago Defender* (April 20, 1946), 13; Phillips, *War! What is It Good For?*, 85; "Gillem Report Doesn't Solve Manpower Problem," *Pittsburgh Courier* (April 5, 1947), 4; "Capital Spotlight," *Pittsburgh Courier* (October 19, 1946), 10.

10 MacGregor, *Integration of the Armed Forces, 1940–1965*, 163.

11 For more on this, see Christine Knauer, *Let Us Fight as Free Men*, 63–111.

12 Knauer, *Let Us Fight as Free Men*, 112–13. For more discussion on Truman's thinking, see Nalty, *Strength for the Fight*.

13 Lt. Col. Bradley Biggs, "The 24th Infantry Regiment: The 'Deuce-Four' in Korea," *Military Review* (September–October 2003), 56; Bussey, *Firefight at Yechon*, 82–83.

Index

Photo Credits

Page iii: © iStock.com/Herianus; pages vi, 51, 66: National Archives; page xvi: Private Collection/Bridgeman Images; page 4: courtesy of Moorland-Spingarn Research Center, Howard University; pages 7, 9, 15, 23, 34 (right), 48 (left), 90, 155 (left): courtesy of the Library of Congress; page 12: courtesy of the Congressional Medal of Honor Society; pages 30, 76, 97, 99 (right), 103 (left and right), 108 (left), 143: courtesy of the US Army Archives; page 42: Private Collection/Peter Newark Military Pictures/Bridgeman Images; page 116: Omniphoto/UIG/Bridgeman Images; page 127: courtesy of the US Navy Archives; page 131: courtesy of the US Army Archives/Truman Presidential Library; page 134: Pictures from History/Bridgeman Images; page 154 (right): courtesy of the White House Photograph Office; page 155 (right): courtesy of the US Marines; page 160: courtesy of US Army Archives/photo by Sgt. Mikki L. Sprenkle

PANTHEON OF HEROES PHOTOS

Photo of William H. Carney courtesy of Moorland-Spingarn Research Center, Howard University; photos of Robert Blake, Joachim Pease, James Mifflin, Aaron Anderson, Pompey Factor, George Watson, and Cornelius Charlton courtesy of the US Navy Archives; photos of John Lawson, James Mifflin, Milton Holland, Christian Fleetwood, Powhatan Beaty, Alexander Kelly, James Gardiner, James Harris, Aaron Anderson, John Denny, Thomas Shaw, Isaiah Mays, Dennis Bell, and John Warren Jr. courtesy of the Library of Congress; photos of Thomas Hawkins and Robert Pinn, public domain; photo of Andrew Jackson Smith courtesy of the Congressional Medal of Honor Society; photos of Brent Woods, William McBryar, John Fox, Charles Thomas, Edward Carter, Vernon Baker, Milton Olive III, Lawrence Joel, and Oscar Austin courtesy of the US Army Archives; photo of Edward Baker: National Archives; photo of James Anderson Jr. courtesy of the US Marines; photo of Dwight Johnson courtesy of the White House Photograph Office; photo of Melvin Morris courtesy of US Army Archives/photo by Sgt. Mikki L. Sprenkle

About the Author

Robert F. Jefferson, Jr. is an associate professor of history at the University of New Mexico. Dr. Jefferson holds a PhD in American history from the University of Michigan. Originally from South Carolina, he currently resides in Albuquerque, New Mexico.